For Joan,
Feb. 18, 1970
Joe

Corporations and the Cold War

Corporations and the Cold War is the second volume in the series entitled *Studies in Imperialism and the Cold War* edited by David Horowitz for the Bertrand Russell Peace Foundation.

Corporations
and the Cold War

edited by David Horowitz

New York and London

Notes on the Contributors

G. William Domhoff teaches courses on the American power structure, on dreams, and on psychoanalytic theory at the University of California at Santa Cruz, where he is an associate professor of psychology. He is the author of *Who Rules America?* (1967), co-editor of and contributor to *C. Wright Mills and the Power Elite* (1968), and author of a set of essays on the American power structure to be published in 1970. He has also published research articles on dreams and essays on psychoanalytic theory in scholarly journals.

William Appleman Williams was born and grew up in Atlantic, Iowa. He was graduated and commissioned from the United States Naval Academy in 1944, and was retired from the Navy in 1947 for reasons of physical disability. He then attended Leeds University and obtained his M.A. and Ph.D. degrees from the University of Wisconsin. He has recently resigned from there to devote full time to undergraduate teaching at Oregon State University. He has published many books, including *The Shaping of American Diplomacy* (1956), *The Tragedy of American Diplomacy* (1962), *Contours of American History* (1966), and, most recently, *The Roots of the Modern American Empire* (1969).

Lloyd C. Gardner is Professor of History at Rutgers University. He received his B.A. from Ohio Wesleyan University in 1956, and his Ph.D. from the University of Wisconsin in 1960. He is the author of *Economic Aspects of New Deal Diplomacy* (1964), and *Architects of Illusion: Men and Ideas in American Foreign Policy, 1941-1949*, to be published in 1970. He has edited *A Different Frontier: Selected Readings in the Foundations of American Expansion* (1966), and has contributed to many volumes.

He is presently at work on a long study of American foreign policy, 1920-1921.

David W. Eakins received his Ph.D. from the University of Wisconsin in 1966 and has been an assistant professor of history at San Jose State College since 1962. He is a former editor of *Studies on the Left,* and was co-editor (with James Weinstein) of *Towards a New America,* a collection of essays from *Studies on the Left.* He is presently working on a book on the history of corporate liberal policy research in the United States.

Joseph D. Phillips was born in California and received his B.A. from the University of California at Berkeley in 1937. Before entering the service in World War II, he worked as an economist for several government agencies. After graduate work at Berkeley, he received his Ph.D. from Columbia in 1951. He taught economics at Wesleyan University, the University of California at Santa Barbara, Champlain College, and Idaho State before going to the University of Illinois in 1956, where he is a research professor in the Bureau of Economic and Business Research. His publications include *Little Business in the American Economy* (1958) and *The Self-Employed in the United States* (1962).

Charles E. Nathanson graduated from Harvard in 1963. Until the fall of 1965 he worked and wrote full time for *I. F. Stone's Weekly.* He is currently writing a doctoral dissertation in sociology at Brandeis University and teaching at the New England Conservatory of Music.

Contents

Introduction
by David Horowitz

Who makes United States foreign policy? The question is by no means academic, for the historical record shows that over the last fifty years and more, United States policy has consistently run in channels which are antagonistic to the most cherished ideals of the American Republic, issuing finally in the conflicts which we associate with the "Cold War." Those ideals—enshrined in the Declaration of Independence—are democratic in character, and recognize above all the right of nations to self-determination, the freedom to carve out their own paths of historical development. Included in this freedom is the equally sacred privilege of any oppressed people to overthrow by force the institutions of their oppressors and to secure for themselves, after the example of the American revolutionaries, the rights to "life, liberty, and the pursuit of happiness."

Yet the record shows that as the United States has assumed the role of a great and then dominant world power, it has more and more consistently opposed the major social revolutions of our time. Moreover, in violation of the principle of self-determination, it has intervened militarily, diplomatically, and economically to crush or to cause grave setbacks to these revolutions, whether in Russia or Mexico, China or Cuba, Greece or Vietnam.*

Nowhere has this pattern of policy been more evident, certainly, than in the American intervention in Vietnam. In 1945, the Democratic Republic of Vietnam was proclaimed in a document modeled on the American Declaration of Independence and at first was recognized by the former colonial power France. Yet when that power sought to reassert control of its former

---

* The cases of Russia, China, Greece, and Vietnam are considered in volume one of this series, *Containment and Revolution.*

9

colonial territory, establishing a puppet regime in Saigon for this purpose, it found support in United States policy. Not only did Washington back France's illegitimate war of conquest with economic and military aid, but when the French failed, Washington itself took over the struggle to defeat the Vietnamese Republic through the quisling government in Saigon. Indeed, more than twenty years after the proclamation of Vietnam's Declaration of Independence, the Vietnamese peasants are still being assaulted by the United States armed forces in what has undoubtedly become the most savage and ruthless intervention on historical record.

Nor was this counter-revolutionary expedition exceptional as United States Cold War policy, despite the unprecedented ferocity and outright depravity of its execution. As already noted, it formed rather a consistent pattern with other U.S. interventions in Santo Domingo, Cuba, Guatemala, the Congo, the Middle East, China, Greece, and elsewhere during the Cold War years, and in Russia, Mexico, Cuba, China, and other countries earlier in the century. Indeed, counter-revolutionary intervention, which is at the heart of the Cold War and its conflicts, has been a characteristic of U.S. foreign policy ever since the United States embarked on a course of overseas economic expansion following the closing of the geographical frontier more than seventy years ago.

How is this counter-revolutionary policy, which runs directly counter to the high ideals of the American Republic, to be explained? How is it to be explained that the largest "defense" program of any nation in history (and of the United States in particular, which, prior to the postwar decades never in peacetime maintained a conscription army) is organized around the unprecedented, "un-American," and patently interventionary concept of *counter-insurgency*?

These paradoxes can only be explained if it can be shown that there is a group wielding predominant power in the American polity, one whose interests run counter to what have been America's most basic ideals, and which can impose its own interpretation of the American tradition onto the framework of policy-making in the state. If it can be shown that there is a *class* among the plurality of competing interest groups which enjoys a predominance of power and can establish its own outlook as a prevailing ideology, and if it can be shown that these interests are expansionist, anti-revolutionary, and tending to be militarist by nature, then an explanation of the paradoxical character of American policy will have been found, and beyond that, the sources of the Cold War conflicts and their permanence.

Such a "ruling class" can, in fact, be readily shown to exist. Its locus of power and interest is the giant corporations and financial institutions which dominate the American economy, and, moreover, the economy of the entire Western world. "In terms of power," writes one authority on the corporations (himself a corporation executive and former United States policymaker), "without regard to asset positions, not only do 500 corporations control two-thirds of the non-farm economy, but within each of that 500 a still smaller group has the ultimate decision-making power. This is, I think, the highest concentration of economic power in recorded history." In addition, "since the United States carries on not quite half of the manufacturing production of the entire world today, these 500 groupings—each with its own little dominating pyramid within it—represents a concentration of power over economies which makes the medieval feudal system look like a Sunday school party."[1]

As this observer points out many of these corporations have budgets, and some of them have payrolls which, with their customers, affect a greater number of people than most of the hundred-odd sovereign countries of the world. Indeed, the fifty largest corporations employ almost three times as many people as the five largest U.S. states, while their combined sales are over five times greater than the taxes the states collect. As one American political scientist summarized it:

Our ideology permits us to rest happy in the thought that the Anti-Trust Division of the Justice Department could, if it so desired, "break up" General Dynamics or International Business Machines into congeries of separate companies. The fact of power, however, is that this has not, cannot, and will not be done because government is weaker than the corporate institutions purportedly subordinate to it. This is the politics of capitalism. It is not at all expressive of a conspiracy but rather a harmony of political forms and economic interests on a plane determined by the on-going needs of corporate institutions.[2]

It is, in the last analysis, the dependence of men individually and collectively on the corporately organized and controlled economy that provides the basis of the corporate domination of United States policy, especially United States foreign policy. The basic fulcrum of this corporate power is the investment decision, which is effectively made by a minute group of men relative to the economy as a whole. This decision includes how much the corporations spend, what they produce, where the products are to be manufactured, and who is to participate in the processes of production.

> A single corporation can draw up an investment program calling for the expenditure of several billions of dollars on new plants and products. A decision such as this may well determine the quality of life for a substantial segment of society: Men and materials will move across continents; old communities will decay and new ones will prosper; tastes and habits will alter; new skills will be demanded, and the education of a nation will adjust itself accordingly; even government will fall into line, providing public services that corporate developments make necessary.[3]

But this is not the whole extent of the power of the corporate investment decision. In the national economy, the small oligarchy of corporate and financial rulers, who are responsible to no one,[4] determine through their investment outlays the level of output and employment for the economy as a whole. As Keynes observed, the national prosperity is excessively dependent on the confidence of the business community. This confidence can be irreparably injured by a government which pursues a course of policy inimical to business interests. In other words, basic to the political success at the polls for any government, as to the success of its specific programs, will be the way the government's policies affect the system of incentives on which the economy runs—a system of incentives which is also the basis of the privileges of the social upper classes.

This does not mean of course that the business community as

such must prefer a particular candidate or party for that candidate or party to be victorious. It means, much more fundamentally, that short of committing political suicide, no party or government can step outside the framework of the corporate system and its politics and embark on a course which consistently threatens the power and privileges of the giant corporations. Either a government must seize the commanding heights of the economy at once, i.e., initiate a course of social revolution, or run things more or less in the normal way, that is, according to the priorities and channels determined by the system of incentive payments to the corporate controllers of the means of production. This is an unspoken but well understood fact conditioning politics in capitalist countries, which explains among other things why the pattern of resource allocation—the priority of guns over butter, of highway construction over schools and hospitals—is so similar in all of them. It also explains why, despite the congressional and parliamentary enactment of progressive tax laws in all these countries, the spirit of the law has everywhere been thwarted, and nowhere has the significant redistribution of income promised by these democratically ratified statutes taken place.

The sheer economic pressure which the corporations can exert over the policies of democratically elected governments is lucidly manifest in the experience of the Wilson Labour government in England. For while owing its office to labor votes and labor money, this government was forced by "the economic situation," i.e., by domestic and international capital, to pursue precisely the policies which it had condemned as *anti*-labor while in opposition.

Of course under normal conditions, and particularly in the United States where no labor party exists, the corporations have less subtle means at their disposal for ensuring policies conducive to their continued vigor and growth. For

all the political activities and functions which may be said to constitute the essential characteristics of the [democratic] system—indoctrinating and propagandizing the voting public, organizing and maintaining political parties, running electoral campaigns—can be carried out only by means of money, lots of money. And since . . .

the big corporations are the source of big money, they are also the main sources of political power.[5]

The means by which the upper classes maintain their privileged position and vested interests in countries where universal suffrage prevails vary with the differing traditions, social institutions, and class structures of the countries involved. They vary also with their historical roles. Thus, in the twentieth century, as the United States has replaced Britain as the guardian power and policeman of the international system of property and privilege, the corporate ruling class, with its equally expanding overseas interests, has less and less been able to entrust policy to indirectly controlled representatives and has more and more had to enter directly the seats of government itself.

In the postwar period, the strategic agencies of foreign policy —the State Department, the CIA, the Pentagon, and the Treasury, as well as the key Ambassadorial posts—have all been dominated by representatives and rulers of America's principal corporate-financial empires. In addition, all the special committees and task forces on foreign policy guidelines have been presided over by the men of this business elite, so that on all important levels of foreign policy-making, "business serves as the fount of critical assumptions or goals and strategically placed personnel."[6]

While the corporate-based upper class in general occupies a prodigious number of positions in the highest reaches of the "democratic" state, it need not strive to occupy all the top places to impose its own interpretation of the national interest on American policy. For precisely because the prevailing ideology of United States politics in general, and of the federal government in particular, is corporate ideology, reflecting the corporate outlook and interests, and because, therefore, the framework of articulated policy choices lies well within the horizon of this outlook, political outsiders may be tolerated and even highly effective in serving the corporate system and its programs.

There are two principal ways (in addition to those already discussed) by which corporate ideology comes to prevail in the larger political realm. In the first place, it does so through the corporate (and upper class) control of the means of communication and the means of production of ideas and ideology (the mass media, the foundations,[7] universities, etc.). However, even this control, which is vast but not ubiquitous in ensuring the general predominance of the ideas of the dominant class, is not left to work at random. Thus, in Professor Domhoff's investigation of the American ruling class, he found that "in most instances" non-upper class political leaders "were selected, trained, and employed in [special] institutions which function to the benefit of members of the upper class and which are controlled by members of the upper class." Such leaders, Professor Domhoff concluded, "are selected for advancement in terms of the interests of members of the upper class."

The second basic way in which corporate ideology comes to prevail, particularly at the foreign policy level, is by the very fact that the dominant reality of society is corporate, and therefore political "realism" dictates for any statesman or politician that he work in its framework and accept its assumptions. If the horizon of political choice is limited to an area in which the corporate interest is not directly challenged, because it would be both imprudent and impractical (utopian) to do so, if the framework of private property in the means of production is accepted as not realistically subject to change, then the "national" interest, which is the concept under which politicians and statesmen tend to operate (particularly in foreign policy), necessarily coincides with the interests of the corporations, the repositories of the nation's wealth, the organizers of its productive power, and hence the guardians of the material basis of its strength. In a class-divided society under normal (i.e., non-revolutionary) conditions, the national interest vis-à-vis external interests inevitably is interpreted as the interest of the dominant or ruling class. Thus, in a corporate capitalist society, the corporate outlook as a matter of course becomes the dominant outlook of the state in foreign affairs.

This is not to say that there is never a conflict over foreign policy between the corporations as such and the state. Just as inevitably there are differences between the corporate interests themselves, within a general framework of interests, so there are differences between the corporate community outside the state and the corporate representatives and their agents in the state, resulting from the difference in vantage and the wider and narrower interests that each group must take into account.* But here, too, the horizon of choice, the framework of decisive interests, is defined by the necessity of preserving and strengthening the status quo order of corporate capitalism and consequently the interests of the social classes most benefited by it.

What then is the nature of corporate ideology as it dominates U.S. foreign policy, and what is its role in the development of the Cold War? As a result of the pioneering work of Professor William Appleman Williams and his students,[8] these questions can be answered precisely and succinctly. The chief function of corporate ideology is, of course, to make an explicit identification of the national tradition and interest—the American Way of Life—with its own particular interest. This identification is accomplished by means of an economic determinism which takes as its cardinal principle the proposition that political freedom is inseparably bound up with corporate property, that a "free enterprise" economy is the indispensable foundation of a free polity (where "free enterprise" is defined so as to coincide with the status quo order of corporate capitalism, not an outdated system of independent farmers and traders).

Starting from this root premise, the ideology, as articulated by American policy-makers since the nineteenth century, maintains that an expanding "frontier" of ever new and accessible markets is absolutely essential for capitalist America's domestic prosperity,[9] and hence that the extension of the American system and its institutions abroad is a primary necessity for the preservation of the American democratic–free enterprise order at home. Originally formulated as an "Open Door" foreign policy to prevent the closing of the external frontier by European colonialism, and to ensure American access to and eventual domination of global markets, this policy has become in the postwar period a policy of preserving and extending American hegemony and the free enterprise system throughout the external frontier, or,

---

* We are dealing here with the United States. In countries where a labor party assumes government office, the relationship is more complex, but for the reasons outlined above the policy results are basically the same.

as it is now called, the "free world." From Woodrow Wilson's World War I cry that the world must be made safe for democracy, it was but a logical historical step to Secretary of State Byrnes' remark at the close of World War II that the world must be made safe for the United States. This is the core of America's messianic crusade: that the world must be made over in the American image (read: subjected to the American corporate system) if the American Way of Life (read: the corporate economy) is to survive at home.

If expansion (and militarism) had held the key not only to American prosperity,[10] but to American security as well, the postwar period would undoubtedly have realized Secretary of State Byrnes' ambitious goal. In the last stages of the war and the first of the peace, the United States successfully penetrated the old European empires (mainly those of France, Great Britain, and the Netherlands), assumed control of Japan and its former dependencies, and extended its own power, globally, to an unprecedented degree. By 1949, the United States had liens on some 400 military bases, while the expansion of direct overseas investments was taking place at a phenomenal rate. Thus, while between 1929 and 1946 U.S. foreign investments had actually declined from $7.9 to $7.2 billion, between 1946 and 1967 they increased an incredible eight-fold to more than $60 billion. It is this global stake in the wealth and resources of the external frontier that forms the basis of the U.S. commitment to the worldwide status quo (though it may not always provide the whole explanation for particular commitments and/or engagements). It is this commitment to the internal status quo in other countries (the State Department actually runs a course for foreign service officers and ambassadors called "Overseas Internal Defense") that renders Washington's expansionist program not the key to security but the very source of Cold War conflict, with its permanent menace to mankind's survival.

For the expansion of corporate overseas investment has to an overwhelming degree not produced beneficial results, and the status quo, of which the corporations inevitably constitute a dominating part, is almost everywhere a status quo of mass human misery and incalculable suffering. As one corporation observer writes:

> No one acquainted with the behavior of Western corporations on their pilgrimages for profit during the last fifty years can really be surprised that the . . . explosions now taking place [in the underdeveloped world] are doing so in an anti-American, anti-capitalist, anti-Western context. For many years these continents have been happy hunting grounds for corporate adventurers, who have taken out great resources and great profits and left behind great poverty, great expectations and great resentment. Gunnar Myrdal points out that capitalist intervention in underdeveloped countries thus far has almost uniformly had the result of making the rich richer and the poor poorer . . .[11]

This has indeed been the undeniable historical consequence of capitalist corporate expansion, although this is not what one is led to believe by the orthodox theorists and academic model builders who function so frequently as the sophisticated apologists of the American empire and the policy of counter-revolutionary intervention necessary to maintain it.

In the writings of such theorists, the expansion of America's monopolistic giants and their control of the markets and resources of the poverty-stricken regions is presented as entailing the *net* export of capital to these capital-starved areas, the transfer of industrial technologies and skills, and the flow of wealth generally from the rich world to the poor. From this point of view, revolutions in the underdeveloped world which challenge the presence and domination of foreign corporations and their states are either misguided or sinister in intent, and contrary to the real needs and interests of the countries involved. Indeed, for those who maintain this view, revolutions are regarded as alien-inspired efforts aimed at subverting and seizing control of the countries in question during the period of great difficulty and instability prior to the so-called take-off into self-sustaining growth. This is the argument advanced by Walt W. Rostow, former director of the State Department's Policy Planning Staff and the chief rationalizer of America's expansionist counter-revolutionary crusade.

In fact, this view rests neither on historical experience, which shows the presence of foreign capital and power to have had a profoundly adverse effect on the development potential of the penetrated regions, nor on a sound empirical basis. Far from resulting in a transfer of wealth from richer to poorer regions, the penetration of the underdeveloped world by the imperialist and neo-imperialist systems of the developed states has had the opposite effect. As a result of direct U.S. overseas investments between 1950 and 1965, for example, there was a *net capital* flow of $16 billion *to the United States,* and this was just a part of the negative transfer. Similarly, when looked at in their political and economic settings, the much heralded benefits of the advanced technologies transplanted into these areas, but remaining under the control of international corporations, also tend to be circumscribed and even adverse in their effects. Indeed, regarded in terms of its impact on total societies, rather than on particular economic sectors, the operation of opening the backward and weak areas to the competitive penetration of the advanced and powerful capitalist states has been nothing short of a catastrophe. For as Paul Baran showed in his pioneering work, *The Political Economy of Growth,* it is precisely the penetration of the underdeveloped world by advanced capitalism that has in the past obstructed its development and continues in the present to prevent it. Conversely, it has been primarily their ability to escape from the net of foreign investment and domination that has made a chosen few of these countries, like Japan, an exception to the rule. Professor Gunder Frank and others have continued the work that Baran initiated, showing how foreign capitalist investment produces the pattern of underdevelopment (or "growth without development" as it is sometimes called) which is the permanent nightmare of these regions.

The view expounded by these writers, which is based on a thoroughgoing and concrete historical and social analysis, makes fully intelligible the fact of anti-imperialist revolution in the underdeveloped world and its inevitable conflict with the Western powers. Only this view can show revolution as the real full-blooded historical phenomenon that it is, rather than the implausibly contrived product of foreign-generated conspiratorial intrigue.* It also explains why communist and socialist revolutions have been so intimately and integrally bound up in the contemporary era with struggles for national liberation and self-determination. For the gateway to national political independence and economic development in the penetrated and dependent regions leads inevitably through the *class* revolution—i.e., the expropriation of the corporations' foreign and domestic agents who dominate the politics and economies of these countries, siphon off the national wealth, and prevent its utilization for overall national industrial development.

However, while the recent history of the Cold War can be seen to fall easily into this structural pattern of corporate expansion and national resistance, of social revolutionary upsurge and counter-revolutionary intervention, the international conflicts of the entire postwar period present a somewhat more complicated problem for analysis. For in the early postwar years, the conflict between Russia and the United States over the peace settlement in Europe dominated relations between all states to an exceptional degree. Moreover, while this conflict was certainly related to the Open Door expansion of the corporate system[12] and the rising nationalist and anti-capitalist revolutions in the underdeveloped world (from southeastern Europe to Asia), its domination by great-power politics and by the abrupt power shifts resulting from the war, gave to it a different appearance and a somewhat different character than the conflicts of the later period.

This exception notwithstanding, the fanatical anti-Communism which took root in this period and which has been such a central and consistent feature of America's messianic Cold War crusade, fulfills a clearly discernible and indispensable function in corporate ideology and the success of the corporate program. For as a system which is by nature expansionist (from the sheer pressure of the world market and the competitive struggle to

---

* Perhaps the acme of absurdity in promoting the conspiracy theory was reached when President Johnson justified the intervention of 30,000 Marines in the Dominican Republic by the presence of 53 alleged Communists supposed to be behind the Dominican Revolution.

control it) and which generates nationalist resistance and revolt that must be countered and contained, the American corporate empire is beset by a real and basically insoluble problem: how can it justify the counter-revolutionary intervention necessary to extend and to preserve itself in terms of an American ideology of democratic pluralism and revolutionary self-determination. The corporate answer to this dilemma, arrived at early in American history, and in which anti-Communism now plays the central role, is to present the intervention as a program of "containment" against a third threatening imperial force or party. Thus just as the United States thrust into the markets of China at the turn of the century was carried out under the cover of containing European colonialism, so the takeovers in Cuba and the Philippines were presented as efforts to save those countries from the clutches of imperial Spain. The pre-Communist origins of what has become a crucial ideological gambit in U.S. foreign relations are symbolized in the fact that when Bolshevism first triumphed in Russia, and there was no external Communist power on which to blame the revolution, Lenin and Trotsky were presented as *German* agents, and U.S. counter-revolutionary intervention as an attempt to contain German imperialist expansion.[13] When the second major Communist revolution was occurring in China, it could of course be presented by the State Department as a takeover by Russia, despite the substantial evidence available to document the rift between Stalin and Mao, about which the State Department was well aware. From then on, any Communist revolution, no matter how nationalist in character or content, became in State Department White Papers the illegitimate offspring of "Communist imperialism" centered in some conveniently located Communist capital.

Historically, of course, there has never been a legitimate resistance or revolt from the point of view of the ruling power. American revolutionaries themselves were portrayed by their opponents as agents of the French. So it is as but part of this old historical pattern that U.S. counter-revolutionary intervention in defense of the social status quo in Vietnam should be officially justified by portraying the Vietnamese guerillas in the south as mere agents of their brothers in the north, and then by insinuating that the north is a puppet of Moscow or Peking. In this way, Washington, like all previous ruling powers, seeks to present its own role as that of the would-be protector of its intended victim, and in this case also as defending self-determination and therefore acting in accord with America's traditional ideals.

The increasingly violent contradiction between the American policies of expansion and counter-revolutionary intervention, and American ideals has its roots in a past that long pre-dates the Cold War, although it is undoubtedly the Cold War ascendance of U.S. power that has made the contradiction so acute. This contradiction between American program and American creed reflects an equally important conflict between the structures of American social and political life, and the American democratic framework. For in a profound sense, foreign policy is but an extension of domestic policy: the inequality of privilege and power in American society mirrors (and serves) an even more insidious global inequality. Similarly, the gathering revolt against the corporate system at home is but one of the outward ripples of the post-1917 global revolutionary upsurge against the imperialist world system that America in part inherited and in part has taken over from the old European colonial powers. It should be clear from this that neither world history nor American policy, neither the Cold War nor the U.S. role in it, can be understood without a previous understanding of the class character of American society and the nature of the corporate system that underpins and structures it. All too few works of historiography and social analysis have been cognizant of this primary relationship and even fewer have oriented their inquiries accordingly. This small volume is offered as a modest attempt to rectify the deficiency and to initiate an inquiry (which it is hoped others will continue) into the forces that dominate the contemporary historical stage, those which are moving the action through permanent crisis toward a series of violent and increasingly destructive denouements.

—*New York, December 1967*

Notes

1. A. A. Berle, Jr., "Economic Power and the Free Society" in Andrew Hacker, ed., *The Corporation Take-Over* (New York: Doubleday, 1965), p. 97. This is a collection of papers originally prepared for the Center for the Study of Democratic Institutions, Santa Barbara.

2. Hacker, *The Corporation Take-over,* Introduction, pp. 10-11.

3. Hacker, *The Corporation Take-Over,* p. 9.

4. Berle, in Hacker, p. 91 Cf. C. Wright Mills, *The Power Elite* (New York: Oxford University Press, 1956), p. 126n: "As political organizations [the corporations] are of course totalitarian and dictatorial, although externally, they display much public relations and liberal rhetoric of defense."

5. Paul Baran and Paul M. Sweezy, *Monopoly Capital* (New York: Monthly Review Press, 1966), p. 155.

6. Gabriel Kolko, *The Roots of American Foreign Policy* (Boston: The Beacon Press, 1969), p. 26.

7. See Horowitz, "Charity Begins at Home," *Ramparts,* April 1969; "The Billion Dollar Brains," *Ramparts,* May 1969; and "The Sinews of Empire," *Ramparts,* October 1969.

8. William Appleman Williams, *The Tragedy of American Diplomacy* (New York: Delta Books, 1962); Walter LaFeber, *The New Empire, An Interpretation of American Expansion 1860-1898* (Ithaca: Cornell University Press, 1963); Lloyd C. Gardner, *Economic Aspects of New Deal Diplomacy* (Madison: University of Wisconsin Press, 1964). On the immediate Cold War origins, see also Gar Alperovitz (another Williams student), *Atomic Diplomacy: Hiroshima and Potsdam* (New York: Simon & Schuster, 1965).

9. See the essays by Professors Gardner, Eakins, and Williams in this volume.

10. On the ultimate connection between corporate capitalist prosperity and militarism, see Rosa Luxemburg, *The Accumulation of Capital* (New York Monthly Review Press, 1968); Joan Robinson, "Marx, Marshall and Keynes," in *Collected Economic Papers II* (New York: Oxford University Press, 1960); and Baran and Sweezy, *Monopoly Capital.* Cf. also the essays by Professor Phillips and C. Nathanson in the present volume.

11. W. H. Ferry, "Irresponsibilities in Metrocorporate America," in Hacker, *The Corporation Take-Over.*

12. See the essay by Professor Gardner in this volume.

13. Cf. William Appleman Williams, "American Intervention in the Russian Revolution, 1917-1920," in *Containment and Revolution.*

Who Made American Foreign Policy 1945-1963?

By G. William Domhoff

Introduction

In this essay we will attempt to demonstrate that American foreign policy during the postwar era was initiated, planned, and carried out by the richest, most powerful, and most international-minded owners and managers of major corporations and financial institutions. None of the factors that are often of importance on domestic issues—Congress, labor, public opinion—had anything but an occasional and minor effect on foreign policy. If there is one "issue-area" that is truly and solely the domain of a power elite grounded in an American upper class of corporate rich, it is foreign policy.

In preparation for an empirical demonstration of these assertions, it is necessary to provide a general framework. In *Who Rules America?* I presented the evidence for the existence in the United States of a social upper class of rich businessmen and their descendants.[1] This social class of business aristocrats, which is nationwide in its scope, gradually came into existence in the last part of the nineteenth century. Based upon fabulous corporate wealth, it is knit together by exclusive private schools, Ivy League colleges, expensive summer resorts, sedate gentlemen's clubs, and a variety of other social institutions too numerous to mention here. From the point of view of research on the control of foreign policy, the most important outcome of this investigation of the social upper class was a set of criteria for identifying its members. The most useful of these were a listing in any edition of the *Social Register* except for that of Washington, D.C. (which automatically lists important government figures regard-

I wish to thank my undergraduate research assistant, Mark Goldowitz, for his help in gathering and organizing much of the material for this paper.

less of social background); attendance at the most prestigious of the private schools (e.g., St. Paul's, Choate, Groton, Middlesex); and membership in the most elite of the city clubs for men (e.g., the California Club of Los Angeles, the Pacific Union of San Francisco, the Knickerbocker of New York, the Somerset of Boston, the Rittenhouse of Philadelphia). Using these criteria, along with four minor ones that were less useful, it was possible to show that members of this privileged class control major businesses, large charitable foundations, and leading opinion-forming associations. For example, to present one small part of the evidence, 62 percent of all directors of the largest fifteen banks were members of the upper class, as were 54 percent of the outside directors of the top twenty industrial corporations and 53 percent of all directors of the leading fifteen transportation companies.[2] In the case of charitable foundations, twelve of the thirteen with assets over $100 million in the early 1960's were controlled by this same small group.[3] It is not possible to repeat all of the evidence, but suffice it to say that there were several thousand men, a great many of whom were members of the social upper class, who interlocked and overlapped in most of the major non-governmental institutions of American society.

This group of interlocking overlappers make up what C. Wright Mills called the "power elite."[4] We have borrowed this term from Mills, but redefined it in such a way as to make it more suitable for an analysis based upon socioeconomic classes. Whereas Mills defined the power elite as those who hold command posts in the major institutions of American society, we define the power elite as active, working members of the upper class and high-level employees in institutions controlled by members of the upper class. Thus, for example, the presidents of U.S. Steel and the Rockefeller Foundation are members of the power elite whether they are members of the upper class or not because both of those institutions are controlled by members of that small social group. While this conception of the power elite is formally different from Mills' definition, it leads empirically to identifying the same persons he did as a power elite. Again to take only a quick example, the military, which is one arm of Mills' power elite, is controlled by the corporate rich through their control of the Department of Defense and through non-governmental army, navy, and air force associations which are financed and directed by corporate executives and their companies.*[5]

Building on the aforementioned criteria of upper-class membership and redefinition of the power elite, *Who Rules America?* presented evidence which suggests that the power elite control the most important agencies and departments of the federal government. In particular, the departments most concerned with foreign policy—State, Defense Treasury—were outposts of the power elite, invariably run by representatives of the biggest and most internationally oriented corporations.[7] However, the book did not go into detail on foreign policy or any other issue-area because the primary goal of that book was to show which institutions, as opposed to issues, are dominated by the power elite. While the issue-area of foreign policy is basically controlled by State, Defense, Treasury, and certain private associations noted in *Who Rules America?*, it is possible and worthwhile to go into greater detail on it. There are two reasons for such an undertaking.

First, if it is true, as many would now argue, that foreign policy issues determine the framework within which all types of policy-making take place, and if the power elite tend to dominate this issue-area, then it follows that the power elite rule America, even if they do not involve themselves or fight for their optimum outcome on every domestic, state, and local issue. Mills put the case very well: "If it is too much to say that, for many of the elite, domestic politics have become important mainly as ways of retaining power at home in order to exert abroad the power of the national establishment, surely it is true that domestic decisions

---

* "Corporate rich," "corporate elite," and "power elite" are roughly synonymous terms. The corporate rich or corporate elite are the core of the power elite which is the operating arm of the social upper class. In turn, this social upper class can be called a "governing class" or "ruling class." It also should be added that the oft-heard phrase "establishment" has about the same meaning as "power elite."[6]

in virtually all areas of life are increasingly justified by, if not made with, close reference to the dangers and opportunities abroad."[8] Second, such a study is able to answer in considerable detail the charge that those claiming control by the corporate rich do not show the specific mechanisms by which this supposed control is accomplished. In the case of foreign policy, at least, we have found such a determination very straightforward.

To begin at the beginning, foreign-policy-making takes place within an "environment" or setting: the international community of nations, American public opinion, the mass media, political interest groups, agencies of the Executive branch, and committees of the Congress. However, as we hope to show, the effect of some of these is rarely felt and is often used as an excuse or rationalization (e.g., public opinion), while others are usually by-passed (e.g., Congress). Furthermore, it is possible to be much more concrete in spelling out the immediate context within which decision-makers function. In general, the most important institutions in foreign policy decision-making are large corporations, closely related charitable foundations, two or three discussion and research associations financed by these corporations and foundations, the National Security Council of the federal government, and special committees appointed by the President. To be sure, this is only the most important core, for there are several other private and university-affiliated research and opinion-molding organizations, not to mention several other agencies of the federal government.

The Council on Foreign Relations

To give empirical flesh to all these generalizations, there is no better starting point than the Council on Foreign Relations (CFR). It is the key "middle term," so to speak, between the large corporations on the one hand and the federal government on the other. By studying its connections in both directions, we will be able to establish the first link in the specific mechanisms by which the corporate rich formulate and transfer their wishes into government policy. While it would be hard to underestimate the importance of this organization in understanding the overall framework for American foreign policy, we do not want to over-emphasize it, and we will see that there are other links between big business and big government.

The Council on Foreign Relations is a non-partisan research and discussion group dedicated to informing citizens about world affairs and creating an interest in international relations. Despite its reputed prominence and the fact that it was founded in 1921, most information on it comes from its own publications: a fifteen-year history, a twenty-five-year history, and annual reports. One of the few who has written on it, Washington journalist Joseph Kraft, noted in 1958 that it was mentioned only five times in *Time* magazine in the period 1953-1958.[9] We can go one step further and say that there has never been any research paper on it in any scholarly journal indexed in the *Social Science and Humanities Index*. While this is surprising, there are several ways to establish CFR's importance. They include testimony by journalists and scholars, the acknowledged pre-eminence of its journal (*Foreign Affairs*), the nature of its financial backing, the composition of its leadership and membership, and the presence of its members in federal government positions.

To begin with expert testimony, Kraft called CFR a "school for statesmen" which "comes close to being an organ of what C. Wright Mills has called the Power Elite—a group of men, similar in interest and outlook, shaping events from invulnerable positions behind the scenes."[10] Douglass Cater, a journalist who served on the staff of President Lyndon B. Johnson, has noted that 'a diligent scholar would do well to delve into the role of the purely unofficial Council on Foreign Relations in the care and breeding of an incipient American Establishment."[11] The *New York Times* called it "a testing ground for new ideas, with enough political and financial power to bring the ideas to the attention of the policy-makers in Washington."[12] Political scientist Lester Milbrath noted that "the Council on Foreign Relations, while not financed by government, works so closely with it that it is difficult to distinguish Council actions stimulated by government from autonomous actions."[13]

Empirically speaking, such "reputational" evidence is the least important of our ammunition. Far more important is CFR's financing and leadership. Aside from membership dues, dividends from invested gifts and bequests, and profits from the sale of *Foreign Affairs,* the most important sources of income are leading corporations and major foundations. In 1957-1958, for example, Chase Manhattan, Continental Can, Ford Motor, Bankers Trust, Cities Service, Gulf, Otis Elevator, General Motors Overseas Operations, Brown Brothers, Harriman, and International General Electric were paying from $1,000 to $10,000 per year for the "corporation service," depending upon the size of the company and its interest in international affairs.* More generally, in 1960-1961, eighty-four large corporations and financial institutions contributed 12 percent ($112,200) of CFR's total income. As to the foundations, the major contributors over the years have been the Rockefeller Foundation and the Carnegie Corporation, with the Ford Foundation joining in with a large grant in the 1950's. According to Kraft, a $2.5 million grant in the early 1950's from the Ford, Rockefeller, and Carnegie foundations made the council "the most important single private agency conducting research in foreign affairs."[15] In 1960-1961, foundation money accounted for 25 percent of CFR income.

The foundations which support CFR are in turn directed by men from Bechtel Construction, Chase Manhattan, Cummins Engine, Corning Glass, Kimberly-Clark, Monsanto Chemical, and dozens of other corporations. And, to complete the circle, most foundation directors are members of CFR. In the early 1960's, Dan Smoot found that 12 of 20 Rockefeller Foundation trustees, 10 of 15 Ford Foundation trustees, and 10 of 14 Carnegie Corporation trustees were members of CFR.[16] Nor is this interlocking recent: in 1922, for example, CFR honorary president

---

* The benefits of subscribing to this corporation service are as follows: free consultation with all members of the CFR staff, subscriptions to *Foreign Affairs* for leading officers of the corporation, the use of the council's excellent library (which is second to none in its field), and the right to nominate one "promising young executive" to participate in seminars whch the council conducts each fall and spring for the benefit of the corporations.[14]

Elihu Root was president of the Carnegie Corporation, while John W. Davis, the corporation lawyer who ran for President on the Democratic ticket in 1924, was a trustee of both the Carnegie Corporation and CFR.

A consideration of the leadership and membership of CFR are equally conclusive in establishing its relationship to the power elite. Its founders included two lawyers and two Wall Street bankers.[17] The single permanent official at its outset, Hamilton Fish Armstrong, and the first editor of *Foreign Affairs,* Archibald Coolidge, were both from well-known upper-class families. Nor has anything changed since the early 1920's, with 14 of the 22 recent or current directors as of the early 1960's being listed in the *Social Register.* Among the most prominent of the recent directors highly visible in the corporate elite are Frank Altschul, Elliott V. Bell, Thomas K. Finletter (one-time Secretary of the Air Force), Devereux C. Josephs, John J. McCloy, David Rockefeller, and Adlai E. Stevenson.

The CFR limits itself to 700 New York area residents and 700 non-New York residents (no women or foreigners are allowed to join). As of the mid-sixties, 46 percent of the resident members and 49 percent of the non-resident members were listed in the *Social Register.*[18] The council's only other formal associates are the Committees on Foreign Relations that have been formed in about thirty cities across the country. These committees come together at dinners and other occasions to hear speakers (mostly supplied by CFR) and exchange ideas. The committee program has been financed since 1938 by the Carnegie Corporation.[19] We were able to locate information on 509 committee members from 29 cities ranging in size and importance from Philadelphia, Detroit, and Atlanta to Albuquerque, Boise, and Little Rock. A significant minority (41 percent) were corporate executives and bankers. Twenty-one percent were lawyers, almost half of whom (44 percent) were also corporate directors. Thus, a small majority (51 percent) were directly involved in business enterprises. Another significant group consisted of educators (22 percent), most of whom were college presidents, political scientists, economists, and deans. Seven percent of those studied were editors or publishers, while the remainder were small numbers of government officials, politicians, church leaders, physicians, accountants, and museum directors.*

Turning to the all-important question of government involvement, the presence of CFR members in government has been attested to by Kraft, Cater, Smoot, CFR histories, and the *New York Times,* but the point is made most authoritatively by John J. McCloy—Wall Street lawyer, former chairman of Chase Manhattan, trustee of the Ford Foundation, director of CFR, and a government appointee in a variety of roles since the early 1940's: "Whenever we needed a man," said McCloy in explaining the presence of CFR members in the modern defense establishment that fought World War II, "we thumbed through the roll of Council members and put through a call to New York."[20] According to Kraft, "When John McCloy went to Bonn as U.S. High Commissioner, he took with him a staff composed almost exclusively of men who had interested themselves in German affairs at the Council."[21] CFR members were also prominent in the U.S. delegation to the founding of the United Nations, and several dozen have held high posts in postwar administrations. One *Annual Report* noted the following in an obituary notice:

> Mr. Dulles was a member of the Council almost from the start. He wrote an article on "The Allied Debts" for the first issue of *Foreign Affairs* and six more articles thereafter, including two while Secretary of State. He participated in numerous study and discussion groups over the years and spoke often at Council afternoon meetings and dinners, twice as Secretary of State.[22]

Now that we have located CFR in sociological space as an institution of the corporate rich, we are in a position to see what it does and how effective it is in shaping foreign policy. As to what CFR does, in addition to serving as a talent pool and training ground for government service, it is a tax-exempt, nonpartisan organization which sponsors education, discussion, and research on all aspects of foreign affairs. As part of its educational effort, it brings before its exclusive membership leading

---

* My thanks to Sue Brenn, an undergraduate research assistant, for gathering the information on CFR committee members for the early 1960's.

scholars and government officials from all nations to make off-the-record speeches and to answer questions from members. And, as Kraft notes, this not only "educates" the members, but it gives them a chance to "size up" important leaders with whom they will have to deal.*[23] Also under the heading of education, CFR publishes *Foreign Affairs*, by far the most important journal in its field, and three annual surveys—*Political Handbook of the World, The United States in World Affairs,* and *Documents on American Foreign Relations.*

Despite the importance of speeches and publications, we think the most important aspect of the CFR program is its special discussion and study groups, which bring together about twenty-five businessmen, government officials, military men, and scholars for detailed discussions of specific topics in the area of foreign affairs. Discussion groups explore problems in a general way, trying to define issues and alternatives, and often lead to a study group. Study groups revolve around the work of a council research fellow (financed by Carnegie, Ford, and Rockefeller) or a staff member. This group leader usually presents monthly papers which are discussed and criticized by the rest of the group. The goal of such study groups is a detailed statement of the problem by the scholar leading the discussion. In 1957-1958, for example, the council published six books which grew out of study groups. Perhaps the most famous of these was written by Henry Kissinger, then a bright young Harvard product who was asked by CFR to head a study group. His *Nuclear Weapons and Foreign Policy* was "a best-seller which has been closely read in the highest Administration circles and foreign offices abroad."[24] As for his study group, it included "two former chairmen of the Atomic Energy Commission, a Nobel Prize winner in physics, two former civilian secretaries in the Defense Department, and representatives just below the highest level from the State Department, the Central Intelligence Agency, and the three armed services."[25] When economist Percy Bidwell of the CFR staff led a discussion of foreign tariffs, an issue which will be discussed later in this

---

* A perusal of any CFR annual report will show that a foreign official visiting in New York who is anyone at all will be speaking or meeting with the council.

paper, the study group included ten corporate representatives, ten economists, two communications experts from MIT's Center for International Studies, a minor Defense Department official, and a foreign service officer.[26]

It is within these discussion and study groups, where privacy is the rule so that members are encouraged to speak freely, that members of the power elite study and plan how best to attain American objectives in world affairs. It is here that they discuss alternatives and hash out differences, far from the limelight of official government and mass media. As the *New York Times* says of these "unpublicized luncheons" and "closed seminars": "Except for its annual public Elihu Root Lectures, the Council's talks and seminars are strictly off the record. An indiscretion can be grounds for termination or suspension of membership. . . ."*[27] Such discussions also help to reduce the effect of political changes. In Kraft's words: ". . . the Council plays a special part in helping to bridge the gap between the two parties, affording unofficially a measure of continuity when the guard changes in Washington."[28]

Given the privacy of its discussions (it is quite open about everything else), can we know the relationship between CFR and government policy? Can we go beyond the fact that CFR conducts research and discussions and that its members hold responsible positions in the federal government? It is not only secrecy which makes this question hard to answer; there is also the problem that CFR as an organization does not take a partisan stand. To answer such a question satisfactorily would require a large number of studies of various decisions and their outcomes,

---

* Critics of a power elite theory often call it "conspiratorial," which is the academic equivalent of ending a discussion by yelling Communist. It is difficult to lay this charge to rest once and for all because these critics really mean something much broader than the dictionary definition of conspiracy. All right, then, if "conspiracy" means that these men are aware of their interests, know each other personally, meet together privately and off the record, and try to hammer out a consensus on how to anticipate or react to events and issues, then there is some conspiring that goes on in CFR, not to mention in the Committee for Economic Development, the Business Council, the National Security Council, and the Central Intelligence Agency.

including an understanding of who initiated, supported, and opposed various proposals.[29] In lieu of such studies, which are almost impossible under even the best of circumstances, several suggestive examples will have to suffice, along with the general testimony of Kraft ("It has been the seat of some basic government decisions, has set the context for many more") and the *New York Times* ("Discussion groups, scholarly papers, and studies sponsored by the Council laid the groundwork for the Marshall Plan for European recovery, set American policy guidelines for the North Atlantic Treaty Organization, and currently are evolving a long-range analysis of American attitudes toward China").[30] More concretely, Kraft claims that CFR action was responsible for putting Greenland out of bounds for the Nazis, for shaping the United Nations charter, and for softening the American position on German postwar reparations, among others. One of the most impressive pieces of evidence is that four CFR planning groups set up in 1939 with aid from the Rockefeller Foundation, were taken (along with most of their personnel) into the State Department in 1942 "as the nub of its Advisory Committee on Postwar Planning Problems."[31] And it was supposedly a special CFR briefing session in early 1947 that convinced Undersecretary of State Robert Lovett of Brown Brothers, Harriman that "it would be our principal task at State to awaken the nation to the dangers of Communist aggression."[32]

In summarizing CFR and its role, despite the fact that it is an organization "most Americans have never heard of,"[33] we think we have clearly established by a variety of means that it is a key connection between the federal government and the owners and managers of the country's largest corporations. If it is not all-embracing in its importance, it is certainly a considerable understatement to speak of CFR members and members of similar power elite associations, as one scholar does, as "external bureaucrats" who supply the government with information, perspectives, and manpower.[34] In our view, what knowledge we have of CFR suggests that through it the corporate rich formulate general guidelines for American foreign policy and provide the personnel to carry out this policy. But we also know that the evidence we have presented is not enough for those scholars who prefer to analyze actual decisions. Then too, skeptics can point out that CFR has no "policy" (other than the all-important policy of international involvement, as opposed to isolationism, for which it is called "Communist" and "un-American" by older-fashioned, nationalistic critics). Furthermore, skeptics can say that CFR's members have other institution and association affiliations that may be more important in determining their outlook. For all of these reasons, we will let the case for CFR rest at this point, noting the presence of its directors and members only in passing, and instead emphasizing the direct corporate connections of important decision-makers.*

Other Links

The Council on Foreign Relations is by no means the only middle term between the corporations and the federal government in the issue-area of foreign policy. There are many others, perhaps the most important of which are the Committee for Economic Development, the RAND Corporation, and a handful of research institutes affiliated with elite universities. Turning to the first of these, the Committee for Economic Development (CED) is a tax-exempt research organization which is in many ways the counterpart on economic policy to the Council on Foreign Relations. While its concentration on monetary and economic problems makes it more prominent on issues involving Treasury and Commerce, it has on several occasions played a major role in shaping foreign policy.[36] Organized in the early

---

* It should be noted that Kraft is among the skeptics. Despite all the comments we have quoted from him on the power of CFR, he concludes that "even that cock will not fight" as far as calling CFR part of any power elite. This is because CFR has assumed "semi-official duties only in emergencies," because it "has never accepted government financial support," and because its recommendations "have subsequently all stood test at the polls or in Congress." Furthermore, there are "divergent views" within the council, and such an organization is necessary because issues are too complicated for the ordinary citizen, who is all wrapped up in his private life. Kraft's concluding sentence seems to be a challenge to those who might criticize—he quotes Voltaire asking, "What have you got that's better?"[35]

1940's to prepare for postwar reconversion to a civilian economy, CED's original leaders were financier Jesse Jones, then Secretary of Commerce, and millionaires Paul Hoffman and William Benton. These three men brought together corporation executives and bankers with outstanding economists for weekend study sessions which were intensified versions of the CFR study groups. Out of these sessions have come the guidelines for American economic policy in the postwar era, including some of the provisions of the Employment Act of 1946, the stabilized budget concept, long-range fiscal and monetary policy, and certain aspects of the Marshall Plan. Perhaps the most impressive evidence for CED prominence in foreign policy is that its corporate elite members and hired economists were the men who moved into the government to administer the Marshall Plan. That CED head Paul Hoffman of Studebaker and the Ford Foundation became administrator of the Marshall Plan is only the surface of the iceberg.

The relationship of CED to the corporations really does not need to be established, for membership is expressly limited to businessmen and implicitly to representatives of the biggest and most important corporations in the country. Among its original and most active members have been Ralph Flanders, the Vermont toolmaker and Boston banker; Thomas B. McCabe, head of Scott Paper Company; Clarence Francis of General Foods; Marion B. Folsom of Eastman Kodak; William L. Clayton of Clayton, Anderson; William L. Batt of SKF Industries; Charles E. Wilson of General Electric; Eric A. Johnston of the Brown-Johnston Company; Chester C. Davis of the Federal Reserve Bank of St. Louis; and S. Bayard Colgate of Colgate-Palmolive-Peet. As with CFR, many CED members have become officials in the federal government: 38 of the trustees during CED's first fifteen years held elected or appointed positions.[37] Flanders and Benton became senators, McCabe became head of the Federal Reserve Bank under President Truman, and Folsom, Clayton, William C. Foster, and Wayne C. Taylor held important posts in major departments. As of the early 1960's, 48 of 190 CED trustees were at the same time members of CFR.

Perhaps the best-known of the power elite's large research

organizations is the RAND Corporation, a name which is an abbreviation of "Research ANd Development." It has been credited with many technical innovations and operational suggestions.[38] Started after the war with government research contracts and Ford Foundation money to "think" for the air force, RAND has since expanded its staff and facilities to provide this service for the entire federal government. Its 500-man professional staff is well paid and well educated (150 have Ph.D.'s) because RAND was purposely set up as a non-governmental agency so that civil service rules and salary scales could be avoided in order to attract the finest talent money could buy. It is governed by a board of trustees which is dominated by representatives of the corporate rich. In 1963, when RAND published a report on its first fifteen years, the board included executives from CBS, Hewlett-Packard, Owens-Corning Fiberglass International, Monsanto Chemical, and New England Electric System, as well as the president of one of the Carnegie foundations, a leading official in the Council on Foreign Relations, the former vice-president of the Carnegie Corporation (then president of Cornell), and the presidents of MIT and Rice universities.*[39] Seven of the seventeen trustees were members of CFR and of fifteen former trustees, seven were leading figures in the corporate world (the rest were university administrators or physicists). The most important of these former trustees was H. Rowan Gaither, a West Coast attorney and Ford Foundation trustee who was one of RAND's key organizers. His legacy is seen in two of the 1963 trustees who are not with one of the companies listed above: Frederick Anderson is a partner in the investment firm of Draper, Gaither, and Anderson; Edwin E. Huddleson, Jr., is a partner in the law firm of Cooley, Crowley, Gaither, Godward, Castro, and Huddleson.

In addition to CFR, CED, and RAND there are many other associations and research organizations controlled by members of the power elite. About 300 study centers consult for the Defense

---

* The president of RAND since its inception, F. R. Collbohm, is a former vice-president of Douglas Aircraft.

Department alone.*[40] But instead of trying to outline any more specific links, we want to turn to a more general, less direct link between the corporate rich and the federal government, the world of academic scholarship. As we have seen in the case of CFR, CED, and RAND, corporate leaders are not adverse to seeking advice from professional researchers, a fact which has led to claims that "experts" control the country. Without emphasizing the direct power of these scholars, for they are often ignored and seldom have decision-making roles, we can add that the power elite pay for their training and encourage them by monetary inducements to study certain questions rather than others. This is accomplished, first, by the general framework created at major universities through financing and through service on boards of trustees.[42] Second, it is accomplished by foundation grants which encourage research on specific questions. Thus, Rockefeller, Carnegie, and Ford money are responsible in one way or another for almost all American research on non-Western areas.[43] While many of these grants are to universities for scholarships and to individuals for specific research projects, the foundations also provide money for institutes affiliated with universities. For example, Ford and Carnegie money finance a Russian Research Center at Harvard, Rockefeller money finances a Russian Research Center at Columbia. Consider the situation on the specific topic of military affairs:

> Between 1950 and 1960, Harvard, Princeton, Columbia, Chicago, Pennsylvania, MIT, and Johns Hopkins all opened special institutes for the study of defense problems. . . . Ford ($214,800 for Harvard's Defense Studies Center) and Carnegie ($141,000 for Chicago's Center for the Study of American Foreign Policy and Military Policy) rained down funds. Books by the dozen (fifteen in nine years from Princeton alone) rolled out.[44]

---

*Many of these organizations are discussed in Arthur Herzog's *The War-Peace Establishment,* although not all the organizations noted in his book are outposts of the power elite. Herzog also testifies to the importance of CFR without discussing it: ". . . a private but highly influential circle that comes close to being the foreign policy establishment of the U.S."[41]

The interrelationship of corporate-controlled foundations, think factories, and university research institutes can be demonstrated by studying the prefaces to leading books in the field of foreign affairs. For example, Gabriel A. Almond of the very prominent Princeton Center of International Studies (publisher of *World Affairs,* which is second only to CFR's *Foreign Affairs* in this field) offers thanks to the Carnegie Corporation for the funds which made possible his study, *The Appeals of Communism.* Carnegie also supplied the funds for *The Civic Culture: Political Attitudes and Democracy in Five Nations,* co-authored by Almond and Sidney Verba. Thomas C. Schelling of the Center for International Affairs at Harvard wrote *The Strategy of Conflict* during a year-long stay at the RAND Corporation, while Herman Kahn did most of the research for *On Thermonuclear War,* published by the Princeton center, while at the RAND Corporation. Lucian Pye's *Aspects of Political Development* was written while at the MIT Center for International Studies, with the help of Carnegie money. Walt W. Rostow of the MIT center, a leading adviser to Democratic Presidents during the 1960's, wrote his "non-communist manifesto," *Stages of Economic Growth,* during a "reflective year" grant provided by the Carnegie Corporation.* Harry Eckstein edited *Internal War* for the Princeton center with the help of Carnegie funds; an earlier version of Eckstein's own contribution to that book, "On the Etiology of Internal Wars," was published in *Social Science and National Security,* a book which had government circulation only.†

---

* It is now known that this center received CIA funds as well as foundation grants during the 1950's. Its director, Max Millikan, who was also head of the World Peace Foundation during the 1950's, had served as an assistant director of the CIA in Washington.[45]

† According to one source, it is "standard procedure at MIT and elsewhere" to publish two versions, "one classified for circulation within the intelligence community, the other 'sanitized' for public consumption."[46] While we do not believe for a minute that the power elite tell these scholars what to say, it should be clear that members of the power elite see no reason to discontinue their support of such efforts. The whole thing has been explained by political scientist David Easton: "A deeper social reason

Up to this point we have approached our question from one direction only. That is, we started with various non-governmental institutions known to be involved in foreign affairs and showed through studies of their financing, membership, and leadership that they are controlled by the corporate rich. We then presented evidence as to the importance of these arms of the power elite in determining government policy. As impressive as the evidence from this approach is, it is not sufficient in and of itself. It is also necessary to start from the other direction, the important institutions and agencies within the government that are concerned with foreign policy, and work back to their ties with the corporate elite. It is to this task that we turn in this section. Our goal is to complete the framework within which specific foreign policy events must be analyzed. As with non-government institutions, there are too many government units to analyze them all in any detail. Fortunately, as on the non-government side, there are some that are more important than others. These include the State Department and the Defense Department, and one that stands above all others, the National Security Council (NSC), which was created in 1947 as the top policy-making unit of the federal government.

The National Security Council

The NSC was developed by the corporate rich, after much debate among the armed services and their various protagonists

---

for the failure of political science to transcend its limitations . . . lies in the proximity of political research to social forces that determine social policy. . . . Entrenched power groups in society, those who have a firm hold on a particular pattern of distribution of social goods, material and spiritual, have a special reason to look askance at this probing into the nature and source of their social positions and activities. They are prone to stimulate research of a kind that does not inquire into the fundamentals of the existing arrangement of things."[47] Or, as noted in a preliminary report of an American Political Science Association committee on professional standards, ". . . problems arise not so much because a scholar is told by his sponsors what to write but rather because a scholar may, wittingly or unwittingly, condition his manuscript to the assumed or divined values of his financial sponsors."[48]

in Congress, on the basis of experience in attempting to coordinate departments and military units during World War II. It is strictly an advisory group, headed by the President and now including as statutory members the Vice-President, the Secretary of State, the Secretary of Defense, and the director of the Office of Civil and Defense Mobilization. However, "the President can also ask other key aides to take part in Council deliberations."[49] As statutory advisers it has the director of the Central Intelligence Agency and the chairman of the Joint Chiefs of Staff. The machinery of the NSC is very flexible and has been used in different ways by different Presidents. President Eisenhower, for example, enlarged and formalized the NSC, giving it many powers traditionally thought of as belonging to departments. President Kennedy dismantled much of this machinery, cut its size to a minimum, met with it less frequently, and gave more responsibility for carrying out NSC decisions to the departments. However different Presidents may use it, the NSC is a key foreign policy organ of the U.S. government.*

Before studying the personnel of the NSC, it is instructive to summarize briefly a detailed case study on how the National Security Act was formulated.[50] Such an account demonstrates the importance of specially appointed "outsiders" in shaping government policy. In this case, the key outsider was investment banker Ferdinand Eberstadt, a former partner in the finance house of Dillon, Read who had gone on to start his own investment house. Eberstadt was asked to come up with a plan to satisfy all sides in the argument over how to reorganize the national defense establishment. The appointment came from the Secretary of the Navy, James Forrestal, a former president of Dillon, Read and a good friend of Eberstadt's. Eberstadt in turn talked informally with other financiers, including Bernard Baruch, developing the report which was the basis for the agreement which finally led to the National Security Act.[51] The final form of the act was determined by a compromise between the differences of

---

* For details on the NSC and its use by various Presidents, see the testimony by members of the power elite and scholars in *The National Security Council: Jackson Subcommittee Papers on Policy-Making at the Presidential Level* (New York: Frederick Praeger, 1965).

Forrestal and Secretary of War Robert Patterson, a Wall Street lawyer who had gone into government service early in the 1940's as a special assistant to Secretary of War Henry L. Stimson. Along with military leaders Lauris Norstad, Forrest Sherman, and Arthur Radford, the important figures in bringing about the compromise between Forrestal and Patterson were three very prominent members of the corporate elite, Robert Lovett, John J. McCloy, and Stuart Symington.*52

Who are the men who sit on the National Security Council? We partially answered this question in *Who Rules America?* by showing that the heads of State, Defense, and Treasury during the postwar years have almost without exception been members of the power elite. (Although not a statutory member, the Secretary of the Treasury has been asked by all three administrations under consideration to sit on the NSC.) For example, Robert Lovett of Brown Brothers, Harriman served as Secretary of Defense, as did Charles Erwin Wilson of General Motors, Neil McElroy of Proctor and Gamble, Artemus Gates of Morgan Guaranty Trust, and Robert McNamara of Ford Motor. Treasurers have included John Snyder of the First National Bank of St. Louis, George Humphrey of Hanna Mining, Robert Anderson of the W. T. Waggoner oil estate and the Federal Reserve Bank of Dallas, and Douglas Dillon of Dillon, Read; heads of State included John Foster Dulles of Sullivan and Cromwell, Dean Rusk of the Rockefeller Foundation, Dean Acheson of Covington and Burling, General George C. Marshall, and Boston aristocrat Christian Herter. We can now be more specific by looking at the composi-

---

* The National Security Act provided for the coordination of the entire defense establishment. In addition to the National Security Council, it also established the Secretary of Defense, the Central Intelligence Agency, and the National Security Resources Board (now reorganized as the Office of Civil and Defense Mobilization). It was a weak act which left the Secretary of Defense in a very tenuous position. Later amendments strengthened his control over the three services (and removed their heads from the NSC) and gave him a larger staff. The amendments also strengthened the control of the Joint Chiefs of Staff over operational military units. With these and other slight modifications, the National Security Act and the National Security Council remain at the heart of the U.S. system for foreign and defense policy.

tion of the NSC when it was studied by journalists during the Truman, Eisenhower, and Kennedy administrations.

When John Fischer of *Harper's Magazine* wrote of "Mr. Truman's Politburo" as "the most powerful and least publicized of all government agencies," it included, in addition to Acheson, Marshall, and Snyder, the following corporate rich: Averell Harriman of Brown Brothers, Harriman, Charles Edward Wilson of General Electric, and Stuart Symington of Emerson Electric.[53] The secretary of the NSC was a big businessman from St. Louis, Sidney Souers. His assistant was James Lay, a former employee of utilities companies whom Souers had met during World War II. Others present for NSC meetings were Alben Barkley, Vice-President, General Walter Bedell Smith, director of the CIA, and General Omar Bradley, chairman of the Joint Chiefs of Staff.*

When *U.S. News and World Report* ran a story in 1956 on "How Ike Makes the Big Decisions,"[55] the following were regularly a part of the NSC, in addition to Dulles, Humphrey, and Charles Erwin Wilson:

Richard Nixon, Vice-President, who was selected and financed for a political career by top corporate executives in Southern California.[56]

Arthur S. Flemming, a lawyer who was formerly president of Ohio Wesleyan University.

Percival Brundage, a partner in Price, Waterhouse & Company.

Allan Dulles, a former partner in the large corporate law firm of Sullivan and Cromwell.

Lewis Strauss, investment banker and personal financial adviser to the Rockefellers.

William H. Jackson, a lawyer who managed the investment firm of John Hay Whitney, as well as sitting on the board of Great Northern Paper and Bankers Trust.

---

* If Fischer is right, the NSC was especially important under Truman: "Mr. Truman has delegated his authority in foreign affairs to the uttermost limit that the Constitution permits. From the day he took office, he apparently recognized his own shortcomings in this field, and he has leaned heavily—sometimes almost pathetically—on the judgment of his 'experts.' "[54]

Dillon Anderson, a Houston corporation lawyer who was the President's Special Assistant for National Security Affairs.[57]

Harold Stassen, former governor of Minnesota and former president of the University of Pennsylvania.

Admiral Arthur W. Radford, chairman of the Joint Chiefs of Staff.

Managing the NSC for President Kennedy was aristocrat McGeorge Bundy, who played a leading role in foreign affairs throughout the 1960's until he left government service to become president of the Ford Foundation. His staff included Walt Rostow of the MIT Center for International Studies, Harvard economist Carl Kaysen, Michael Forrestal (son of the former president of Dillon, Read), and Robert Komer (a government official). The following were members of the NSC Executive Committee which met regularly over a period of two weeks to determine American reaction during the Cuban missile crisis of 1962:[58]

Lyndon Johnson, Vice-President, representative of Texas oil interests.[59]

Dean Rusk, formerly president of the Rockefeller Foundation.

Robert McNamara, formerly president of Ford Motors.

Robert F. Kennedy, a multimillionaire from Boston.

Douglas Dillon, a former president of Dillon, Read.

Roswell Gilpatric, a corporation lawyer from New York.

McGeorge Bundy, a Boston aristocrat who was formerly a dean at Harvard.

Adlai Stevenson, a corporation lawyer from Chicago.

John McCone, a multimillionaire industrialist from Los Angeles.

Dean Acheson, a corporation lawyer and former Secretary of State.

Robert Lovett, an investment banker with Brown Brothers, Harriman.

General Maxwell Taylor, a Presidential adviser at the time, and former chairman of the Mexican Light and Power Company, Ltd.

Major General Marshall S. Carter, Deputy Director of the CIA.

George Ball, a Washington corporation lawyer, later to become a partner in Lehman Brothers.

Edwin M. Martin, a State Department official specializing in Latin America.

Llewellyn Thompson, a foreign service officer.

Theodore C. Sorensen, Presidential speechwriter and adviser.

Special Government Committees

It is important to look at one other "institution" of the federal government which is essential in understanding how the corporate rich are involved in foreign policy. These are the special commissions, "blue ribbon" citizen committees, and "task forces" appointed by the President to make recommendations on specific problems:

> Despite the extensive government apparatus for policy-making on problems of national security, the American President in the postwar period has, from time to time, appointed groups of private citizens to investigate particular problems and report to the National Security Council. Some of these groups have performed their task without the public's ever becoming aware of their existence; others have in one way or another come to public attention. Among the latter are those which have become known under the names of their chairman: Finletter, Gray, Paley, Sarnoff, Gaither, Draper, Boechenstein, and Killian.[60]

These committees are almost without exception headed by members of the corporate rich and staffed by the employees and scholars of the foundations, associations, and institutes outlined in previous sections. For example, among the eight committee heads mentioned in the previous quotation, seven are corporate executives and the eighth is the chairman of MIT. All are affiliated with the Council on Foreign Relations, three with the Committee for Economic Development. We believe it is by means of these committees that the policy recommendations of the power elite's non-government groups are given official sanction: they become the "reports" of the specially appointed committees.

The circuit between corporations (and their foundations and associations) and the government is thus completed.

Two such committees, the Gaither Committee and the Clay Committee, have been studied in detail by social scientists. The Gaither Committee was appointed in the late 1950's by President Eisenhower to reconsider American military preparedness. H. Rowan Gaither, its head, is the aforementioned attorney and Ford Foundation official who was instrumental in organizing the RAND Corporation. Other members of the corporate elite on the eleven-man committee were Robert C. Sprague, William C. Foster, and William Webster (also a trustee of RAND). Two other prominent members were James A. Perkins, a vice-president of the Carnegie Corporation at the time, and scientist Jerome Weisner, who became a 'wealthy man" as one of the owners of the Rockefeller-financed ITEK Corporation.[61] Other members were James Baxter, a college president; Robert Calkins, an economist who had been a CED consultant before becoming head of The Brookings Institution (yet another research organization founded, financed, and directed by the corporate rich); John Corson, research director for the Cooperative League of America; Robert C. Prim, a mathematician who directed research for Bell Telephone; and Hector Skifter, a radio engineer who was a consultant for the Department of Defense. Six of the eleven are members of CFR.

Much of the detail work of the Gaither Committee was assigned to a technical staff drawn from the military and from various non-government institutes, including RAND and the Institute for Defense Analysis. The committee also had an advisory panel of corporate and military leaders. The final report, highly critical of the emphasis on nuclear weapons and the de-emphasis of conventional ground forces, was discussed at a special meeting of the NSC on November 7, 1957. Over forty people attended, including financiers Robert Lovett and John J. McCloy, who predicted that the business community would support the President if he requested increased spending for defense.[62] President Eisenhower was hesitant, but it is interesting that the Kennedy Administration adopted an approach much like that advocated by the Gaither Report. Among President Kennedy's appointees who had been on the Gaither Committee or its advisory panel were arms control chief Foster, disarmament negotiator McCloy, and science adviser Weisner.*

Equally impressive was the composition and effect of the Clay Committee, selected by President Kennedy to reconsider U.S. foreign aid policy. In addition to Lucius Clay, a retired army general who sat on the boards of a half-dozen major corporations, the committee consisted of financier Robert Anderson, financier Robert Lovett, banker Eugene Black, corporation lawyer Herman Phleger, corporate leader L. F. McCollum, college president Clifford Hardin, economist Edward S. Mason (a member of CFR, a consultant to CED), physician Howard A. Rusk (no relation to Dean Rusk), and labor leader George Meany. All but Lovett, Rusk, and Meany are in CFR. With Meany dissenting, the committee suggested large cuts and other changes in foreign aid. Although the cuts were apparently more than President Kennedy expected, "In an aid message to the Congress President Kennedy deferentially referred to the Clay Report seven times, setting forth in detail how the new aid program was based on the application of standards 'affirmed by the Clay Committee.' "66

The Military and Foreign Policy

Up to this point, we have presented what could be termed "positive" evidence for control of foreign policy by the power elite, first from the direction of prestigious non-government institutions, then from the direction of the government institutions most involved in foreign policy. We now want to approach the problem from another angle, by considering the possible power of other groups. This gives us a chance to use the detailed

---

* The military stance of the 1960's may also derive from the report of a special Rockefeller-financed panel on international security of the late 1950's, said to be very similar to the still-secret Gaither Report.63 In any case, there were four people who participated in the Gaither Committee work who also helped with the Rockefeller report.64 More generally, the first three of six Rockefeller-financed panels (*Prospect for America*) were directly concerned with foreign affairs. Members of those three panels who became part of the Kennedy Administration were A. A. Berle, Jr., Chester Bowles, Harlan Cleveland, Roswell Gilpatric, and Dean Rusk.65

research of a great many social scientists, the upshot of which is that there is really no other candidate that can be claimed to have any great effect on the making of foreign policy.

The military is often put forth as a key determiner of policy, particularly when it involves military spending or military action. David Riesman, for example, wrote that military men "control defense and, in part, foreign policy."[67] If this view has not been laid to rest by the sociological study of the *Professional Soldier* by Morris Janowitz, which concluded that the military does not have any significant effect on foreign policy, then it has been by the case studies coming out of the Institute of War and Peace at Columbia University, particularly a study entitled *The Common Defense* by Samuel P. Huntington. Summarizing his own work and that of his colleagues on several postwar defense decisions they analyzed in detail, Huntington concludes that:

> Perhaps more striking is the relatively unimportant role which they played in proposing changes in policy. In no case did they effectively prevent major new policies and in no case did they effectively prevent changes in old ones . . . more than anything else, one is struck by the tendency of the military to embrace the broad policy *status quo*. . . . General Landon was much more ready to accept existing policy than the State Department members of the NSC-68 drafting group . . . even in the New Look the initiative for a new strategy and its principal ideas came as much from the President, Humphrey, and Dulles as from Radford. . . . A year later it was the civilian Gaither Committee, not the Joint Chiefs, which challenged existing policy and succeeded in producing minor change in it. The initiative in military policy rested with the civilian executives, the decision on military policy with the President.[38]

It is difficult to go beyond Huntington's emphatic and unequivocal conclusion, but we might say that the key civilians in each case were members of the corporate rich. We have already seen this in the Gaither Report; here we will only add brief comments on the all-important National Security Council document NSC-68, formulated shortly before the Korean War. This position paper, calling for a general rearmament, was, according to Huntington, the U.S. reaction to the first Soviet nuclear test and the Communist takeover in China.[69] The initiative for the study came from corporation executive Sidney Souers, NSC secretary at the time, and corporation lawyer Dean Acheson, Secretary of State. The chairman of the study was Paul Nitze, head of the State Department's Policy Planning Staff. Nitze, who was later to play an important role in the Kennedy Administration, was a partner in Dillon, Read, which had already contributed Forrestal, Eberstadt, and William H. Draper to the postwar effort, and was later to contribute Douglas Dillon, first as Ambassador to France, then as Undersecretary of State and Secretary of Treasury.*

In short, if the United States in the postwar era has adopted what Mills called a military definition of reality, it is because this was chosen by leading members of the corporate rich on the basis of their understanding of national goals and international events, not because it was somehow foisted on them by the military men they interact with at high-level military "colleges," promote and retire within the Department of Defense, and hire into large corporations upon retirement.

Congress and Foreign Policy

Although Congress is involved in foreign affairs through certain Constitutional powers and through its final authority for financial appropriations, it is seldom offered as a significant factor in making foreign policy. Nevertheless, the possibility must be considered. One political scientist concerned with Congress, James A. Robinson, concludes that "Congress's influence in foreign policy is primarily (and increasingly) one of legitimating and amending policies initiated by the executive to deal with problems usually identified by the executive."[70] Lewis A. Dexter summarizes a great many interviews on Capitol Hill by reporting that no one he talked to ever claimed that Congress had any role in formulating defense policy, while Roger Hilsman and H. Field Haviland, Jr. both conclude that superior information and other resources give the Executive the initiative over the

---

* Only Brown Brothers, Harriman among finance houses comes close to this performance, contributing Lovett, Harriman, and Senator Prescott Bush of Connecticut.

legislators.[71] Further, it seems that Congress has given up some of its determinative powers on foreign matters: with the enactment of the Reciprocal Trade Act in the 1930's, it turned over much of its power on tariffs; in the postwar era it has by and large lost its right to declare war.

In a summary of the role of Congress in sixteen postwar foreign policy issues that have been the object of case studies, Robinson is able to find only one initiated by Congress and three where Congress had "major influence." The one clear case where a member of Congress was both an initiator and the major influence was the Monroney Resolution; but this was merely "a simple Senate resolution suggesting that the Administration study the possibility of proposing to other governments the establishment of an international development association as an affiliate of the World Bank."[72]

The interpretation of the other two cases of "major influence" is open to question. As to the less important of the two, Congress is said to have had major influence on the Vandenberg Resolution of 1948, which "provided the legitimation for the origins of United States participation in the development of the North Atlantic Treaty."[73] However, the idea was initiated by Secretary of State Marshall and Undersecretary of State Lovett, and it was written by Lovett and Vandenberg in close collaboration. Robinson considers Vandenberg to be the "predominant influence" because he suggested that several Senate-initiated concerns about the United Nations be included in the resolution.

The most important issue on which Congress supposedly had a major influence was the problem of whether or not to aid the French at Dien Bien Phu in 1954. According to the conventional account, Secretary of State Dulles was urging President Eisenhower to provide the French with air support, as was the chairman of the Joint Chiefs of Staff, Admiral Arthur W. Radford. To prepare for this possibility, Eisenhower asked Dulles and Radford to call together eight key Congressional leaders for the purpose of discussing a joint resolution on the part of Congress which would express support for the action. When the Congressmen learned that the British were reluctant to join such a venture and that other military advisers were opposed, they conditioned their support on British acceptance of the plan and certain concessions by the French. Dulles then tried to bring the British and French into the agreement, but in the end had to acquiesce in their plan to negotiate a truce and divide the country. This conventional summary of the decision-making process is then interpreted as an example of Congressional veto power, often with a reference to Chalmers Roberts' account in *The Reporter*.[74]

Surprisingly enough, a close reading of Roberts' article leads to quite a different conclusion, for he states unequivocally that the pivotal role was played by the National Security Council. His account, based upon confidential talks with insiders and never questioned as to its reliability, tells how the crucial decision was reached long before Congressional leaders were finally approached:

> It is my understanding, although I cannot produce the top-secret NSC paper to prove it, that some time between Ely's arrival on March 20 [with the news that the French could not hold out much longer] and the Dulles-Radford approach to the Congressional leaders on April 3, the NSC had taken a firm position that the United States could not afford the loss of Indo-China to the Communists, and that if it were necessary to prevent that loss, the United States would intervene in the war—*provided* the intervention was an allied venture and *provided* the French would give Indo-China a real grant of independence so as to eliminate the colonialism issue. The decision may have been taken at the March 25 meeting. It is also my understanding that this NSC paper has on it the approving initials D.D.E.*[75]

Roberts goes on to say that Dulles then made a speech in New York on March 29 calling for a "united action" of the major powers. Roberts implies that it is neither surprising nor particularly obstructive that the legislators should repeat this demand:

> The newspapers were still full of reactions to this speech when the Congressional leaders, at the April 3 secret meeting with Dulles and Radford, insisted that Dulles should line up allies for "united action" before trying to get a joint resolution of Congress that would commit the nation to war.[76]

---

*Even the italics are Roberts's.

As it turned out, Dulles could not get the British and French to go along with the American plan. They already had other plans, and the French continued to be as obstinate as they had been during the previous five years about granting any of the concessions to Vietnam that the U.S. had been demanding as completely necessary. (The French feared an "American take-over" and wanted to keep trade and cultural influence in the area if they lost the war.[77]) The one question that thus remains is whether or not Congress could have shown independent power by refusing to grant the President's request to take part in a "united action." "This point," says Chalmers Roberts, "is worth a final word":

> On returning from Geneva in mid-May, I asked that question of numerous senators and representatives. Their replies made clear that Congress would, in the end, have done what Eisenhower asked, provided he had asked for it forcefully and explained the facts and their relation to the national interest of the United States.[78]

In short, on the basis of Roberts's account there is not the slightest reason to believe that Congress had anything to do with the U.S. decision to refrain from bombing Dien Bien Phu. The important decision was made in the National Security Council and would not have been resisted by Congress. What the outcome actually suggests is the limitations of American power over the British and French, along with the reluctance of a majority of the leading decision-makers within the NSC to risk involvement in a major war in Asia at that time.[79]

If Congress exercises no decision-making power in the area of foreign policy, it does seem to have the power to harass certain initiatives by the Executive branch because of its control of the purse strings. However, even this seeming veto power melts away or is neutralized when the power elite make a concerted effort. Two rather nice examples demonstrate this, the first concerning tariff policy, the second concerning aid policy. In the first case, leading members of the power elite during the 1950's were advocating further reductions in tariffs, as they had been doing for some time. They had gone through the usual procedures: a special commission to study the matter (headed by former Inland Steel executive Clarence Randall) and a special committee of private individuals to influence opinion (the Committee for a National Trade Policy, headed by John Coleman of Burroughs Manufacturing, Charles Taft, Harry Bullis of General Mills, John J. McCloy of Chase Manhattan, and corporation lawyer George Ball).* Congress resisted their plans, and they received much less than they asked throughout the 1950's. Behind this Congressional reluctance, however, were powerful business interests—in short, there was a conflict within the power elite. President Kennedy moved to remedy the situation when he took office. First, he appointed George Ball of the Committee for a National Trade Policy as Undersecretary of State for Economic Affairs, making him "the man who was personally responsible for the conduct of the nation's foreign economic policy."[80] Second, to help with his Trade Expansion Act, Kennedy appointed as his special aide Howard C. Petersen, president of the Fidelity-Philadelphia Trust and the head of a CED committee on tariff policy.[81] As he had done previously as a CED spokesman, Petersen, along with others, met with leaders of the aggrieved industries, primarily chemicals and textiles, and offered them special concessions. These maneuvers and changes "cut the protectionist coalition to shreds."[82] The bill passed Congress: "It was the indirect effect of the administration's approach to and conversion of the textile lobby and to numerous other businessmen that indirectly affected Congress."[83]

The second example is more complex. When fully elaborated, it shows both disagreement within the power elite and the lengths to which members of the power elite must go before having their way with a Congress that has many delaying powers. To put it as briefly as possible, and ignoring members of the power elite within Congress (they are few), many members of Congress in the mid-1950's were increasingly restive about the foreign aid program. Several wished to reassess the entire program, but since they were almost totally lacking in the expertise

---

* At least two staff members of the Randall Commission were at the same time in the CFR study group on tariffs mentioned earlier.

to conduct the necessary inquiry, several reports were undertaken by a variety of "independent" research organizations. According to a scholarly account by H. Field Haviland, Jr. of The Brookings Institution, the most important of these reports was done by Max Milliken and Walt Rostow of the Center for International Studies at MIT.[84] This organization, as we have already pointed out, was supported by both the CIA and by major foundations, and is thus sponsored by the same group of men who are heavily represented in the Executive branch. Haviland also claims that "the other reports were in harmony with the Milliken-Rostow thesis."[85] This is perhaps to be expected. They were done by, among others, The Brookings Institution and the National Planning Association (in 1958 the latter had ten of its forty-three directors in common with CFR, eight with CED*).

Despite the relative unanimity of the reports, there was still resistance within Congress. Once again, however, it is likely that this reflected an ongoing struggle within the power elite, who are by no means unanimous on the amount and conditions for granting foreign aid. As in the case of tariffs, this Congressional veto power (which amounts to reducing aid requests) would, we believe, diminish if the power elite could make up its collective mind. The disagreement in this instance manifested itself in terms of two reports by corporate elite groups. The first, by yet another specially appointed Presidential committee, was known as the Fairless Report after its chairman, Benjamin Fairless of U.S. Steel. The second report was by an official government agency called the International Development Advisory Board, created in 1950 as "the chief public advisory group associated with the economic assistance program."[86] Its head at that time was corporate leader Eric Johnston, one of CED's founders and a former president of the U.S. Chamber of Commerce. The differences in the two reports reflect a long-standing disagreement within the corporate elite that has been sketched out very nicely by political scientists David McLelland and Charles Wood-

---

* Four NPA officers were in both CFR and CED. Of twenty-one of the forty-three NPA directors directly involved in the business world, six were leading labor leaders, and two were farm representatives.

house.[87] Sitting on the more conservative committee along with Fairless and labor leader John L. Lewis were five prominent members of the power elite:

> Colgate W. Darden, Jr., married to the daughter of Irénée duPont, president of the University of Virginia, and a director of DuPont, U.S. Rubber, and the Life Insurance Company of Virginia.

> Richard R. Deupree, chairman of the board of Proctor and Gamble.

> Whitelaw Reid, chairman of the board of the *New York Herald Tribune*.

> Walter Bedell Smith, vice-chairman of the board of American Machine and Foundry Company, former military officer, and former director of the CIA.

> Jesse W. Tapp, chairman of the board of the Bank of America.

The second corporate group was more diversified sociologically. In addition to Johnston and five other corporate leaders, it included two college deans, two labor union leaders, one farm organization representative, a member of the U.S. Committee for UNICEF, and the president of Virginia State College.

After tracing the 1957 aid bill through the conflict over these two reports and the usual nightmarish tangle within Congress, Haviland concludes his case study as follows:

> . . . this case study highlights the conclusion that, despite the powerful "veto" function of the Congress, as well as the stimulating effect of the special legislative studies, the executive branch had the advantage of the initiative, supported by tremendous staff and intelligence resources. Behind the facade of the "administration position," however, were important and continuing differences within and among the principal departments and agencies concerned, usually related to vested institutional interests and closely tied parallel differences within the Congress and the general public.*[88]

---

* The reference to differences within the government concerns, among other things, the fact that Eisenhower appointed a fiscal conservative, George Humphrey of Hanna Mining, to head Treasury, and an isolationist, John Hollister of the Taft law firm in Cincinnati, to head the International Cooperative Administration.[89]

If Congress is not a mere rubber stamp that jumps every time the power elite in and around the Executive branch snaps its fingers, it is for all its complaining, delaying, and threatening a rather impotent body when compared with the Executive branch, which can get its way with Congress on foreign affairs any time it wants with patience,[90] tact,[91] research,[92] and vigorous leadership by the President.[93] And when Congress seems most resistant, a closer look often reveals disagreement within the power elite.

Public Opinion and Foreign Policy

Public opinion used to be considered by some scholars as an important factor in determining foreign policy, but studies over the past decade have by and large failed to support this hypothesis. Today it is usually put forth by journalists caught up in the rush of day-to-day events and by politicians wishing to cater to the voters or disguise their real motives. The most comprehensive overall schema on this problem is provided by James N. Rosenau in his *Public Opinion and Foreign Policy*.[94] On the basis of empirical research by himself and others, he divides the population into three groups: the mass public, the attentive public, and the opinion leaders. The overwhelming majority of the people are in the first group. They are seldom aware of foreign policy issues, read little about them, get what opinions they have from the mass media, and react emotionally to slogans and crises. The second group, making up at best a few percent of the population, are slightly better educated than the mass public, have a little more money, and read more on foreign affairs. They tend to acquire their opinions from the "quality media" such as the *New York Times, Harper's Magazine* and *The Reporter*.[95] On the few occasions they have been studied in any detail, it is found they are businessmen, lawyers, and professional people,[96] and, as we will see, they are the people who join discussion groups and associations concerned with foreign policy. They actually provide the "public" which the opinion-leaders use as their sounding board. The third group, opinion-leaders, are those who shape public opinion. In theory, according to Rosenau, opinion-leaders may or may not be the same persons who are decision-makers. He concludes, however, that on foreign policy the opinion-leaders tend to be the same persons who are the decision-makers within the federal government.[97] In short, at least on the issue of foreign policy, the power elite is also a major factor in shaping public opinion.

Huntington comes to similar conclusions from decision-making analyses of military and defense policies. He finds the public-opinion-poll evidence against any determinative force by public opinion so "overwhelming" that "even a wide margin of error would not invalidate the conclusions drawn from them."[98] Reviewing this evidence, he finds that public opinion was never important, was often in conflict with what the Administration was doing, and often changed after the Administration took its action. By juxtaposing quotes from corporate leaders with opinion poll data, he shows that claims of responding to popular demand can be no more than an illusion or rationalization. In 1953, when Budget Director Joseph Dodge of The Detroit Bank said there would be cuts in military expenditures to "meet public demand," a Gallup poll found only 19 percent of the people thought the U.S. was spending too much for defense.[99] In early 1957, shortly after Defense Chief Charles Wilson of General Motors said that "the people in the country are in no mood to spend more dollars," a Gallup poll showed that only 9 percent thought defense spending should be cut. Sixty percent thought it should stay about the same and 22 percent thought it ought to be increased.[100]

On the basis of the work by Rosenau, Huntington, and others, it is possible to suggest that public opinion is actually shaped by the foreign policy pursued by the power elite rather than the other way around. This may not be the case with domestic policy, where people have their own observations and personal contacts to aid their understanding, but it is the reality in foreign affairs, where people have to rely on what the power elite tells them through the Executive branch, foreign policy discussion associations, and the mass media. By far the most important factor in this is the attitude of the President, who, as we have noted briefly in this chapter and showed in greater detail in *Who*

Rules America?, surrounds himself with members of the power elite as department heads, advisers, diplomats, and special emissaries.[101] As political scientist Aaron Wildavsky notes,[102] most people are willing to follow the President on foreign policy, and Samuel Lubell has documented this in interviews with a great many people at the time the Russian sputnik was launched:

> . . . especially striking was how closely the public's reactions corresponded to the explanatory "line" which was coming from the White House. . . . In talking about sputnik, most people tended to paraphrase what Eisenhower himself had said. . . . In no community did I find any tendency on the part of the public to look for leadership to anyone else—to their newspapers, or radio commentators, to Congressmen, or to men of science. Nor, with some exception, could people be said to be in advance of the President, or to be demanding more action than he was[103]

Another political scientist, Elmer Cornwell, provides further evidence of the President's importance in shaping public opinion.[104]

It used to be thought that public opinion was powerful because the public would seek revenge at the polls, thus making the elected officials responsible to its whims and demands. However, studies show that revenge voting over a single issue is seldom the case[105] and that politicians are aware of this fact.[106] The important thing is the overall relationship of the politician to his constituents. In the case of the Presidency, this is doubly true. Nor does the evidence support the idea that government officials are sometimes so cowed by public opinion that they will fear to take action in the future on unpopular issues that have caused discontent in the past. This theory was popular following the Korean War with those who feared that public wrath over the drawn-out, indecisive nature of that war would inhibit an American President from undertaking similar actions in the future.[107]

The most important foreign policy issue of recent years supposedly affected by public opinion concerned the decision of whether or not to support the French in Vietnam in 1954. According to the argument put forth, for example, by both Herbert

Aptheker and Richard Rovere in criticizing Mills for down-grading the power of the masses, the public prohibited this inter-vention by frightening the Congressmen who had returned to the grass roots between sessions of the Congress.[108] This in turn caused the Congressmen to "veto" the request for permission to give air support to the French. We have discussed this decision in terms of the misinterpretation of the role of Congress. Here it is only necessary to add that polls at this time showed a majority of the public willing to go along with the contem-plated action in Vietnam:

Asked in May and September of 1953 and again in April of 1954 whether the American Air Force should be used if necessary to prevent Communists taking over all of Indochina, from 52 to 60 percent agreed that it should. In all three of the polls, a larger per-centage still, that is from 59 to 65 percent, favored sending American troops, with always about a third of the sample opposed to either alternative.[109]

The Presidency and the Executive branch in general are not the only means by which the power elite influences public opinion on foreign policy. It also does so through certain associations and through the creation of special citizens' committees designed to influence opinion on a single issue. The most important associa-tions are the oft-noted Council on Foreign Relations, the Foreign Policy Association, and the National Advertising Council. As shown in *Who Rules America?*, these three are tightly inter-locked.[110] Most FPA directors are CFR members as well as business leaders, while the corporation-financed NAC has repre-sentatives from CFR, FPA, and CED among its directors. Except for its publications, CFR works primarily with opinion within the elite. It is the FPA which deals with public opinion within the attentive public. This group sponsors World Affairs Coun-cils, discussion groups, and speakers. The FPA is "non-partisan," but the important fact remains, as Rosenau notes, that an organi-zation such as FPA "establishes the width, depth, and direction of the channel" of communication.[111] And, as Bernard C. Cohen concludes in a study of groups such as FPA (which summarizes evidence showing that the members are better educated and have higher incomes than the general population), they seldom seriously discuss political policies at all, let alone alternative policies. They tend to keep discussions apolitical, emphasizing the social, economic, cultural, and historical aspects of foreign affairs. They also provide a great deal of positive information on the nature and role of the United Nations, which has gotten them a bad name in some circles.[112]

The National Advertising Council is probably less important than the CFR and FPA. It merely places corporate-financed advertising in the mass media. These advertisements advocate general propositions such as "support the United Nations" or "give money to Radio Free Europe." These communications may have a "sleeper effect" or create general ideological acceptance of international involvement, but such effects are difficult to measure or prove. Perhaps what we should say in the case of the NAC is that the power elite utilizes all avenues to reach the general public.

As noted, the power elite also tries to influence public opinion through the formation of publicity committees composed of prominent private citizens. The origins of one such committee have been studied in considerable detail by James N. Rosenau in *National Leadership and Foreign Policy*.[113] In early 1958, President Eisenhower asked corporate executive Eric Johnston, founder of CED and a former president of the U.S. Chamber of Commerce, to head a special White House meeting to convey information to the public on foreign policy aspects of national security.[114] Johnston and his staff invited over 1,000 corporate, organization, community, and labor leaders to this one-day conference of meetings and speeches. Out of the meetings came a new citizens' committee, the Committee for International Economic Growth (CIEG), charged with the responsibility of carrying the conference's message to the entire populace. Its original members, in addition to Johnston, were General (and corporate director) Lucius Clay, Milton Eisenhower (president of Johns Hopkins), Barney Balaban (a motion-picture theater owner and president of Paramount Pictures), General Alfred Gruenther,

Mrs. Eleanor Roosevelt, Mrs. Helen R. Reid (her husband was a wealthy businessman, her sons are Whitelaw and Ogden Reid), and George Meany (labor leader).*

There are numerous other such committees, but none have been studied in any detail. One of the most important helped convince the country of the need for the Marshall Plan:

> When the Committee for the Marshall Plan was formed, Stimson [Wall Street lawyer, CFR director, former Secretary of State and Secretary of War] agreed to serve as national chairman. Former Secretary of War Robert P. Patterson became chairman of an executive committee. . . . The executive committee included Dean Acheson (then in private life), Winthrop W. Aldrich, James B. Carey, David Dubinsky, Herbert H. Lehman, Philip Reed, and Herbert Bayard Swope.† Its membership consisted of more than three hundred prominent citizens in different parts of the country. . . . Regional committees were promptly organized, the cooperation of national organizations enlisted, and relevant publications given wide circulation. The Committee promoted broad news and editorial coverage in metropolitan newspapers, set up a speakers' bureau, and employed a news agency which arranged for press releases, a special mat service for small town and country newspapers, and national and local radio broadcasts.[116]

Within certain limits, then, there is every reason to believe that the power elite is relatively successful in shaping public

---

* Rosenau also sent an eight-page, 71-item questionnaire to 1,067 conference participants. He received a return of 61 percent, a much greater return than is usually expected from mailed questionnaires. From all evidence the returns are a representative sample of the participants, although Rosenau takes pains to make no special claims for them. Reluctant to generalize, and immediately emphasizing the diversity of the total group, he does summarize his findings by saying that "the national leader is a middle-aged, white, Protestant, upper-class male from the Eastern seaboard, who has had extensive education and who is likely to be a businessman while at the same time holding a variety of unremunerated posts in outside organizataions."[115]

† Winthrop Aldrich is a banker and an uncle of the Rockefeller brothers; James B. Carey is a labor leader; Herbert Lehman was of the Lehman Brothers investment firm; Philip Reed is an executive with General Electric; Herbert Bayard Swope is a former New York newspaper editor and the brother of a former president of General Electric; and David Dubinsky is a labor leader.

opinion on foreign policy through its control of the Executive branch, through organizations such as CFR and FPA, and through special committees such as CIEG and the Committee for the Marshall Plan. As Gabriel Almond concludes in *The American People and Foreign Policy,* "one might almost say 'who mobilizes elites, mobilizes the public.' "[117]

Conclusion

In this paper we have shown who dominates the all-important issue-area of foreign policy, namely, a power elite which is rooted in the dividends and salaries of large corporations and financial institutions. We have done this in two different ways, one positive, one negative. The positive way was to present criteria for membership in a power elite that is the operating arm of the national upper class and then show that the key persons and institutions in and out of government who determine foreign policy are part of this power elite. The negative way was a process of elimination. We summarized evidence which suggests that other possible candidates for control of foreign policy—the military, Congress, public opinion—are of very minor importance for this issue-area, although they may be important on other issues.

In addition to showing *who* made foreign policy, we have shown *how* they do it—through participation in key government positions, through serving on specially appointed committees and task forces, and through financing and leading major non-government policy-planning, opinion-forming, and opinion-disseminating organizations.

It is also important to note what has not been demonstrated. We have not proved that the power elite act only or primarily in terms of the interests of the corporations which are their ultimate base of power. We have not shown *why* they do what they do. However, it is certainly possible to make the beginnings of a case on this on the basis of the economists' assumption that people tend to act in their self-interest, and the psychologists' and sociologists' finding that people perceive and interpret the world in terms of their individual upbringing, cultural background, and occupational roles. We would consider the following facts significant: The power elite are by and large part of an upper class of corporate rich which owns an overwhelming amount of corporate stock and has a set of educational and social institutions that are distinctive to this small group. Most of the power elite's members also receive non-dividend income and other "higher emoluments" from the corporations and their closely related charitable foundations. When these considerations are put alongside the very great importance of overseas operations to the health of many large American businesses, it is really hard to believe that we don't know why the corporate rich are so concerned with these matters.*

Notes

1. G. William Domhoff, *Who Rules America?* (Englewood Cliffs, N. J.: Prentice Hall, 1967).

2. *Ibid.,* pp. 53-55.

3. *Ibid.,* p. 65.

4. C. Wright Mills, *The Power Elite* (New York: Oxford University Press, 1956); for a discussion of the "interlocking overlappers" see Richard Rovere's review of *The Power Elite* under that title, as reprinted in his *The American Establishment* (New York: Harcourt, Brace & World, 1962).

5. Domhoff, *Who Rules America?,* Chap. 5.

6. *Ibid.,* p. 8, quoting E. Digby Baltzell's *The Protestant Establishment* (New York: Random House, 1964), p. 8.

7. *Ibid.,* Chap. 4, and later in this essay.

8. Mills, *The Power Elite,* p. 186.

---

* "Thus, of the 500 largest corporations, 386 had notable foreign operations. A score or two of the large companies have a third or more of their total assets abroad; some eighty of these firms derived 25 percent or more of their sales and earnings from overseas. Sales of foreign-based U.S. manufacturing firms have increased more than five times since 1950. In 1965, it has been conservatively estimated, earnings on foreign investments amounted to more than 20 percent of after-tax profits of domestic non-financial corporations."[118]

9. Joseph Kraft, "School for Statesmen," *Harper's Magazine,* July 1958, p. 64.

10. *Ibid.,* pp. 64, 68.

11. Douglass Cater, *Power in Washington* (New York: Random House, 1964), p. 247.

12. *New York Times,* May 15, 1966, "Experts on Policy Looking to Youth," section one, p. 34.

13. Lester Milbrath, "Interest Groups and Foreign Policy," in James N. Rosenau, ed., *Domestic Sources of Foreign Policy* (New York: The Free Press, 1967), p. 247.

14. *Annual Report of the Council on Foreign Relations, 1957-1958.*

15. Kraft, "School for Statesmen," p. 68.

16. Dan Smoot, *The Invisible Government* (Dallas, 1962), pp. 168-171.

17. Kraft, "School for Statesmen," p. 65.

18. John F. Whitney, Jr., "The Council on Foreign Relations, Inc.," January 1968, a paper for Professor Hoyt B. Ballard's graduate seminar in government at Texas A & I University.

19. Smoot, *The Invisible Government,* p. 21.

20. Quoted in Kraft, "School for Statesmen," p. 67.

21. *Ibid.,* p. 68.

22. *Annual Report of the Council on Foreign Relations, 1958-1959,* p. 4.

23. Kraft, "School for Statesmen," p. 66.

24. *Ibid.*

25. *Ibid.*

26. Percy W. Bidwell, *What the Tariff Means to American Industries,* published for the Council on Foreign Relations by Harpers Bros. (New York, 1956).

27. *New York Times,* May 15, 1966, p. 34.

28. Kraft, "School for Statesmen," p. 68.

29. Robert A. Dahl, *Who Governs?* (New Haven: Yale University Press, 1961), pp. 66, 331.

30. Kraft, "School for Statesmen," p. 64; *New York Times,* May 15, 1966, section one, p. 34.

31. Kraft, "School for Statesmen," p. 67. Much of Kraft's information on CFR involvement in specific issues is drawn from CFR's self-published twenty-five-year history. It contains further details and information on other issues as well. See *The Council on Foreign Relations, A Record of Twenty-five Years* (New York, 1947).

32. Quoted in Kraft, "School for Statesmen," p. 68.

33. *Ibid.,* p. 64.

34. Chadwick F. Alger, "The External Bureaucracy in United States Foreign Affairs," *Administration Science Quarterly,* June 1962.

35. Kraft, "School for Statesmen," p. 68.

36. Karl Schriftgeisser, *Business Comes of Age* (New York: Harper & Row, 1960); and David Eakins, "The Development of Corporate Liberal Policy Research, 1885-1965," (Ph.D. diss., University of Wisconsin, 1966).

37. Schriftgeisser, *Business Comes of Age,* pp. 25, 62, 162.

38. Joseph Kraft, "RAND: Arsenal for Ideas," *Profiles in Power* (New York: New American Library, 1966); Saul Friedman, "The RAND Corporation and Our Policy Makers," *The Atlantic Monthly,* September 1963.

39. RAND Corporation, *The First Fifteen Years* (Santa Monica, California, 1963).

40. Arthur Herzog, *The War-Peace Establishment* (New York: Harper & Row, 1965), p. 54.

41. *Ibid.,* p. 36.

42. Domhoff, *Who Rules America?,* pp. 77-79.

43. George M. Beckmann, "The Role of the Foundations," *The Annals of the American Academy of Political and Social Science,* November 1964.

44. Joseph Kraft, "The Military Schoolmen," in *Profiles in Power,* p. 52.

45. David Wise and Thomas B. Ross, *The Invisible Government* (New York: Random House, 1964), p. 243.

46. *Ibid.*

47. David Easton, *The Political System* (New York: Alfred A. Knopf, 1953), pp. 50-51.

48. Robert J. Samuelson, "Political Science: CIA, Ethics Stir Otherwise Placid Convention," *Science,* September 22, 1967, p. 1415.

49. Henry M. Jackson, ed., *The National Security Council: Jackson Subcommittee Papers on Policy-Making at the Presidential Level* (New York: Frederick Praeger, 1965), p. 31.

50. Demetrios Caraley, *The Politics of Military Unification* (New York: Columbia University Press, 1966).

51. Margaret Coit, *Mr. Baruch* (Boston: Houghton Mifflin, 1957), p. 623.

52. Caraley, *The Politics of Military Unification,* pp. 149-151.

53. John Fischer, "Mr. Truman's Politburo," *Harper's Magazine,* June 1951, p. 29.

54. *Ibid.,* p. 31.

55. *U.S. News and World Report,* April 20, 1956.

56. Ernest Brashear, "Who Is Richard Nixon?" *The New Republic,* September 1 and September 8, 1952.

57. For details on Dillon Anderson and his role, see "Dillon Anderson of Texas: The Keeper of the Nation's Secrets," *Newsweek,* February 13, 1956.

58. Wise and Ross, *The Invisible Government,* p. 293; Arthur M. Schlesinger, *A Thousand Days* (Boston: Houghton Mifflin, 1965), p. 302.

59. Robert Sherrill, "Johnson and the Oil Men," *Ramparts,* January 1967; David Welsh, "LBJ's Favorite Construction Co.," *Ramparts,* December 1967.

60. Morton H. Halperin, "The Gaither Committee and the Policy Process," *World Politics,* April 1961, p. 360.

61. For details on ITEK and other such ventures, see "Rocky Ride on Route 128," *Forbes,* September 1, 1965; for details on Weisner and his connection with ITEK, see Lester Tanzer, *The Kennedy Circle* (New York: David McKay, 1961).

62. Halperin, "The Gaither Committee and the Policy Process," p. 368.

63. *Ibid.,* p. 382.

64. Samuel P. Huntington, *The Common Defense* (New York Columbia University Press, 1961), p. 456.

65. The Rockefeller Panel Report, *Prospect for America* (New York: Doubleday & Co., 1961), pp. 8, 94, 160.

66. Usha Mahajani, "Kennedy and the Strategy of Aid: The Clay Report and After," *Western Political Quarterly,* 18, 1965, p. 657.

67. David Riesman, *The Lonely Crowd* (New Haven: Yale University Press, 1950), p. 254.

68. Huntington, *The Common Defense,* p. 115.

69. *Ibid.,* pp. 47-50.

70. James A. Robinson, *Congress and Foreign Policy-Making* (Homewood, Illinois: Dorsey Press, 1962), p. v.

71. Dexter's spoken paper is quoted in part by Cater in *Power in Washington,* p. 135; Roger Hilsman, "Congressional-Executive Relations and the Foreign Policy Consensus," *American Political Science Review,* September 1958; H. Field Haviland, Jr., "Foreign Aid and the Policy Process: 1957," *American Political Science Review,* September 1958.

72. Robinson, *Congress and Foreign Policy-Making,* p. 62.

73. *Ibid.,* pp. 45-46.

74. Chalmers Roberts, "The Day We Didn't Go To War," *The Reporter,* September 14, 1954.

75. *Ibid.,* pp. 32, 34.

76. *Ibid.,* p. 34.

77. Melvin Gurtov, *The First Vietnam Crisis* (New York: Columbia University Press, 1967), pp. 23-24, 42, 78, 84, 137-138.

78. Roberts, "The Day We Didn't Go To War," p. 35.

79. See Gurtov, *The First Vietnam Crisis,* for details.

80. Raymond A. Bauer, Ithiel de Sola Pool, and Lewis A. Dexter, *American Business and Public Policy* (New York: Atherton, 1963), p. 74.

81. Schriftgeisser, *Business Comes of Age,* pp. 181-187; Bauer, et al., *American Business and Public Policy,* p. 78.

82. Bauer, et al., *American Business and Public Policy,* p. 79. These authors do not mention Petersen's corporate or CED connections.

83. *Ibid.,* p. 422.

84. Haviland, "Foreign Aid and the Policy Process: 1957," pp. 691-692.

85. *Ibid.,* p. 692.

86. *Ibid.,* p. 694.

87. David S. McLellan and Charles E. Woodhouse, "The Business Elite and Foreign Policy," *Western Political Quarterly,* March 1960; Charles E. Woodhouse and David S. McLellan, "American Business Leaders and Foreign Policy: A Study in Perspectives," *The American Journal of Economics and Sociology,* July 1966.

88. Haviland, "Foreign Aid and the Policy Process: 1957," p. 717.

89. *Ibid.,* p. 718.

90. Quentin L. Quade, "The Truman Administration and the Separation of Powers: The Case of the Marshall Plan," *The Review of Politics,* 27, 1965, p. 74.

91. *Ibid.,* p. 74.

92. Hilsman, "Congressional-Executive Relations and the Foreign Policy Consensus," p. 729; Haviland, "Foreign Aid and the Policy Process: 1957," p. 717.

93. Haviland, "Foreign Aid and the Policy Process: 1957," p. 723.

94. James N. Rosenau, *Public Opinion and Foreign Policy* (New York: Random House, 1961).

95. *Ibid.,* p. 40.

96. Kenneth P. Adler and David Brobrow, "Interest and Influence in Foreign Affairs," *Public Opinion Quarterly,* Spring 1956.

97. Rosenau, *Public Opinion and Foreign Policy,* p. 60.

98. Huntington, *The Common Defense,* p. 235.

99. *Ibid.,* p. 238.

100. *Ibid.,* p. 239.

101. Domhoff, *Who Rules America?,* Chap. 4.

102. Aaron Wildavsky "The Two Presidencies," *Trans-Action,* December 1966, p. 9.

103. Samuel Lubell, "Sputnik and American Public Opinion," *Columbia University Forum,* Winter 1957, p. 18.

104. Elmer Cornwell, *Presidential Leadership of Public Opinion* (Bloomington, Indiana: Indiana University Press, 1965).

105. Kenneth Waltz, "Electoral Punishment and Foreign Policy Crisis," in James N. Rosenau, ed., *Domestic Sources of Foreign Policy* (New York, 1967), pp. 283-234.

106. Bauer, et. al., *American Business and Public Policy,* pp. 415 ff.

107. Waltz, "Electoral Punishment and Foreign Policy Crisis," p. 284.

108. Herbert Aptheker, *The World of C. Wright Mills* (New York: Marzani & Munsell, 1960), pp. 25-27; Rovere, "The Interlocking Overlappers," pp. 261-262.

109. Waltz, "Electoral Punishment and Foreign Policy Crisis," p. 286.

110. Domhoff, *Who Rules America?,* pp. 73-74, 76.

111. Rosenau, *Public Opinion and Foreign Policy,* p. 95.

112. Bernard C. Cohen, *Citizen Education in World Affairs* (Princeton: Princeton University Press, 1953), pp. 117-125.

113. James N. Rosenau, *National Leadership and Foreign Policy* (Princeton: Princeton University Press, 1963).

114. *Ibid.,* p. 55.

115. *Ibid.,* p. 130.

116. Harvey B. Price, *The Marshall Plan and Its Meaning* (Ithaca, New York: Cornell University Press, 1955), p. 56.

117. Gabriel Almond, *The American People and Foreign Policy* (New York: Harcourt, Brace & World, 1950), p. 138.

118. Harry Magdoff, "Rationalizing the Irrational," *The Nation,* September 18, 1967, p. 247. For further reference, see Harry Magdoff, *The Age of Imperialism* (New York: Monthly Review Press, 1969).

The Large Corporation
and American Foreign Policy
by William Appleman Williams

The large corporation is generally acknowledged to have wielded an extensive influence in American domestic affairs since 1890. While it has never dominated American society in the literal sense, clearly it has been and is an *imperium in imperio;* for throughout the century it has proposed and disposed in competition and collaboration with the government. Such power and authority also enabled the large corporation—if it so chose—to play an equally important role in the day-by-day and long term relations between the United States and the rest of the world. It did so choose and, directly and indirectly, at home as well as overseas, it has exercised that potential in foreign affairs. There is considerable evidence to suggest, indeed, that the central features of the large corporation's conception of the world—its definition and explanation of reality—had by 1950 come to delineate crucial aspects of American foreign policy.

The extent to which that correlation exists, and hence the relevance of fundamental questions which it raises, can most effectively be gauged by examining various facets of the relationship between the large corporation and foreign policy. These may be outlined as follows:

1) Though the concept of the large corporation as used herein includes financial as well as industrial institutions, the study is not concerned directly with the long and learned discussion about the precise number of such firms and the decimal percentages of their concentrated power. Those calculations and related investigations make it clear that the large corporation, in its fundamental role as the organizer of a disorganized nineteenth-century capitalism, in its supplementary function as architect of

All but the final section of this essay originally appeared in the September 1958 issue of the *American Socialist*.

71

a vast network of subcontracting, marketing, and servicing connections, and through its influence and participation in local and national government, has exerted a predominant influence in the American political economy since the crisis of the 1890's.

2) The large corporation exercises several kinds of influence on foreign policy: direct and indirect, and economic and intellectual. In each of those ways, moreover, the large corporation's power can be used either to initiate, delay, or veto foreign policy proposals. Some of its most important influence has been of a negative character, as when it postponed, emasculated, or killed other programs.

Viewed collectively as an institution, for example, the large corporation is the dynamic and crucial private element in the American economic system. Its economic decisions and actions affect political and social developments as well as economic affairs. And since it is central to the economy *per se*, government investment and spending are also undertaken to an extensive degree through the large corporation. A specific corporation, on the other hand, can and does function as a special economic interest in the conduct of foreign affairs. A good example of such action, which also illustrates the negative side of corporation influence, is offered by the corporations which resisted President Franklin Delano Roosevelt's efforts to send more aid to the Allies prior to Pearl Harbor.

All of those economic and other influences appear as facts to intellectuals and politicians attempting to formulate a coherent overview of American society or an appropriate foreign policy. Finally, the leaders of the large corporation function as intellectuals (a category which includes some academics but is not defined thereby) in their work of knowing, systematizing, interpreting, and acting upon the reality about them. Their conception of the world takes on dramatic importance when they enter the government.

3) The rise of the large corporation in the 1890's confronted the labor movement with the problem of choosing and implementing a basic response to the new structure of American industry. In theory, at any rate, labor had a number of options. It could have deployed its power to destroy the corporation and substituted a system of cooperative enterprises, to socialize the

corporation and thereby the system, to break it up and re-establish the world of the individual entrepreneur, to regulate it through the government, or to organize labor itself within the new framework established by the corporation. If all of its efforts are considered, it can be argued that at least some segment of labor tried each of those solutions. But labor's basic approach was to organize labor on the terms specified by the large corporation: first in segments paralleling management's division of labor, and finally according to the system itself.

The decision to organize within the existing corporation reinforced the influence of the corporation on foreign policy. Since it did not demand a share in investment decisions, labor's policy served to extend and consolidate the position and power of the corporation in the American political economy. The *net* result was to help business organize business. That basic situation was not seriously altered even when labor turned to the government as a tool for regulating such a corporate economy. Not only was the corporation equally influential in politics, but labor's objectives did not challenge—let alone threaten—the key role of the corporation in the economy. In all essentials, therefore, as well as in most particulars, labor foreign policy was (and is) corporation foreign policy. As with the corporation, labor sometimes divided within itself, but it never proposed or fought militantly for a fundamentally different foreign policy.

4) In terms of the extent and character of its interest and influence, the foreign affairs role of the large corporation has developed as a process. There have been conflicts over foreign policy between industrial and financial corporations, and even within some of them; and the institution itself exercised less influence in 1890 than it did in 1900, 1926, or 1969.

Because they have an important bearing on the problem of analysis and interpretation, it also seems wise to review key aspects of the relationship between overseas economic expansion and foreign policy. An apt illustration of the existing confusion on this issue is provided by the assertion that the United States would have to export and invest, on a *pro rata* basis, as much as Great Britain did at the apex of its empire before such overseas economic expansion could be considered crucial to the American economy. Such an analysis may or may not be useful for purposes of personal or public persuasion, but when examined on its own terms it is neither very relevant nor very helpful to an understanding of the political economy of American foreign policy. To consider only the most obvious aspect, it is extremely difficult to establish a valid basis for comparing the two nations. And if, to make an effort to do so, America's industrial regions are treated as the "mother country," then much of what is usually considered domestic commerce and investment has to be classed as foreign or colonial enterprise.

Even in its more moderate versions, that kind of commentary on overseas economic activity is wide of the mark. There are two broad questions at issue with regard to the statistics of overseas economic expansion, and they cannot be mixed up without confusing the analysis and the interpretation. One concerns the overall importance of such expansion to the national economy. The answer to that depends less upon gross percentages than upon the role in the American economy of the industries which do depend in significant ways (including raw materials as well as markets) on foreign operations. Measured against total national product, for example, the export of American cars and trucks seems a minor matter. But it is not possible at one and the same time to call the automobile business the key industry in the economy and then dismiss the fact that approximately 15 percent of its total sales between 1921 and 1931 were made in foreign markets.

The other major point concerns the role of such foreign enterprises and markets in the making of American foreign policy. That effect can be direct in terms of domestic political and economic pressures, or indirect through the results of overseas American economic activity on the foreign policy of another nation. Even in the early part of the century, from 1897 to 1914, the overseas economic expansion of the United States was more impressive than many people realize. Loans totaled over a billion dollars. Direct investments amounted to $2,652,300,000 by 1914. While it is true that the nation also owed money abroad during that period, that point is not too important to an understanding of American foreign affairs. For the loans and investments had a bearing on American foreign policy even though balance of payment computations reduce the net figure. Businessmen with interests in Mexico or Manchuria, for example, did not stop trying to influence American policy (or cease affecting Mexican or Asian attitudes) just because their investments or loans or sales were theoretically and arithmetically cancelled out by the debts other Americans incurred in France or Germany.

Another misleading approach emphasizes the point that America's overseas economic expansion amounted to no more than 10 or 12 percent of its national production during those years. But 10 percent of any economic operation is a significant proportion; without it the enterprise may stagnate or slide into bankruptcy. In that connection, the most recent studies by economists reveal that exports did indeed spark recovery from the depression of the 1890's. In any event, businessmen, other economic groups, and many intellectuals *thought* the 10 percent made a crucial difference, and most of them concluded that they could get it only by overseas expansion.

All other considerations aside, that reason would make the figure important if it were only 1 percent. Or, to make the point even clearer (and historically relevant), it would still be significant if all an entrepreneur did was to pressure the government to support an effort that failed. In that case the economic indicators would be negative but the relevance to foreign policy might be very high. Such was precisely the case, for example, with the American-China Development Company. It ultimately disappeared from the scene, but before it died it exerted an extensive influence on American policy in Asia.

In another way, overseas economic operations which seem small on paper may mean the difference between survival and failure to a given firm or industry. Faced by the near monopoly control over key raw materials exercised by the United States Steel Corporation after 1903, Charles Schwab had to go to Chile to get the ore supplies that were necessary to sustain the Bethlehem Steel Company. Schwab's investment was only $35 million, but it played a vital role in his affairs and exercised a significant influence on Chilean-American relations. Or, to reverse the example, economic activity which seems incidental judged by American standards is often fundamental to a weaker economy. That aspect of the problem can be illustrated by the situation in Manchuria between 1897 and 1904, where approximately one-tenth of 1 percent of America's national product gave the Americans who were involved a major role in the economic life of that region. And that, in turn, led to crucial decisions in Amercian foreign policy.

It is impossible, in short, to judge the bearing of overseas economic expansion upon American diplomacy in terms of gross statistics. The important factors are the relative significance of the activity and the way it is interpreted and acted upon by people and groups who are at best only symbolized by abstract aggregate figures. And by those criteria there is no question about the great relevance to its foreign policy of America's proposed and actual overseas economic expansion since 1890.

Viewed from those various perspectives, it is possible to discern four overlapping eras, or phases, in the developing role of the large corporation in American foreign affairs: 1) The Consciousness of Maturity and the Specters of Stagnation and Revolution: 1890-1903. 2) The Great Debate over Loans or Exports: 1895-1914. 3) The Triumph of the Corporation and the Internationalization of Business: 1912-1940. 4) The Era of Integration with the State: 1933-1950. And 5) The Crisis of the Corporate Foreign Policy. That framework offers a useful guide for the more detailed examination of the ideas, actions, and influence of the large corporation in connection with American foreign policy since 1890.

1

The crisis of the 1890's was a major turning point in American history. It closed out the Age of Jacksonian Laissez-Faire and unfrocked the individual entrepreneur as the dynamic leader of American economic life. At the same time, it was the cultural coming-out party of a new corporate system based on the large corporation and similar highly organized groups throughout American society. Initiated in the late 1880's by the Standard Oil Company, the massive centralizing and consolidating movement of the 1890's was undertaken to reorganize, rationalize, and supplant the system of individualistic capitalism which had been dying throughout the long-wave depression touched off by the Panic of 1873. In one sense, therefore, the merger mania of the decade was prompted by the drive to lower production costs. But almost immediately the large corporation leaders and the giant bankers became aware of the disturbing fact that they had more efficiency than they could employ at a satisfactory profit rate. Implicitly or explicitly, therefore, they became equally concerned with markets for their respective goods and services. At the same time, they were challenged on the political front by other Americans who sought either to restore the old system or reform and regulate the new one.

For many years, the domestic side of the resulting debate over the condition and prospects of the political economy was usually described as a struggle between the Progressives and the Conservatives; and the foreign policy side of the conflict was analyzed by transposing those categories as Anti-Imperialists and Imperialists. Recent investigations have challenged that historiography by suggesting that many of the Progressives were themselves Imperialists. Though helpful in some respects, the revisionist interpretation does not really clarify the basic issues. It is true that the imperialist and anti-imperialist nomenclature has some relevance to a short period of eighteen months when the question of what to do with Cuba and the Philippines was hotly debated. But that approach offers very little insight into the period prior to the outbreak of the Spanish-American War, and still less into the resolution of the brief fight over imperialism.

One of the main sources of the confusion is the habit of equating colonialism and imperialism, an approach which tends to hide the fact that a nation can follow a policy of anti-colonialism and still remain the head of a large economic empire. Colonialism is defined by the large scale emigration of *people* from the mother country to the foreign region. Imperialism is characterized by the *economic* expansion of the mother country and may or may not involve the establishment of a small colony of administrative and military personnel from the empire country in the weaker area. Furthermore, no more than a soapbox full of Americans advocated colonialism in the true and historic meaning of the institution. The debate about Cuba and the Philippines was an argument over whether or not to adopt the pattern of imperialism developed by Britain after the Indian Mutiny of 1857; and if that system were not followed, what kind of an American program of expansion was to be substituted.

Perhaps another consideration is even more important to a fuller understanding of the debate between the Imperialists and the Anti-Imperialists. Only a tiny and insignificant handful of Americans were against any and all kinds of expansion. The fact is that such men as Grover Cleveland and William Jennings Bryan, who are usually thought of as Anti-Imperialists, actually advocated the expansion of America's economic system and political influence. Bryan favored the kind of imperial anti-colonialism that the British practiced throughout the nineteenth century in such countries as Argentina, and which English historians have recently characterized by the phrases "informal empire" and "the imperialism of free trade."

In essence, therefore, Bryan deserves as much credit as Theodore Roosevelt for launching America's empire. Roosevelt at first favored the traditional imperial policy of establishing formal administrative and military colonies within the subject society, but he ultimately adopted Bryan's approach which was based on extending the Monroe Doctrine to cover the foreign country. That policy, which served as the basis of the Open Door Notes, was in turn founded on the assumption that America's economic and moral power would control the development of the weaker region. Direct military intervention might be necessary to establish American authority (in the case of the Philippines, Bryan called it "restoring order"), and to sustain it in an emergency, but preponderant economic power was the key to such imperial anti-colonialism.

For several reasons, the large corporation played a crucial role in resolving the original conflict between the Imperialists and the Anti-Imperialists. First, it was the source of the overwhelming economic power which made it possible to bypass traditional imperialism. Second, it advocated and took the lead (through such organizations as the National Association of Manufacturers, the National Civic Federation, and the American Asiatic Association) in popularizing the idea that foreign markets provided the solution to the domestic economic crisis and the dangers of political and social upheaval. Shared or adopted by every other special economic group in the country, including the Bryan agrarians, the Gompers labor movement, and the small business-men, that proposal had mushroomed into a widely accepted panacea by 1897.

Jerry Simpson, a sometimes radical farmer from Kansas, exemplified agrarian agreement in his anguished cry of 1894: "We are driven from the markets of the world!" Other Populists reacted by voting for a big navy. Speaking as president of the NAM, Theodore C. Search provided a candid summary of business thinking: "Many of our manufacturers have outgrown or are outgrowing their home markets and the expansion of our foreign trade is their only promise of relief." Senator Albert J. Beveridge phrased it more majestically: "American factories are making more than the American people can use; American soil is producing more than they can consume. Fate has written our policy for us; the trade of the world must and shall be ours."

Businessman F. L. Stetson voiced the fears of many of getting hemmed-in with his warning that "we are on the eve of a very dark night unless a return of commercial prosperity relieves popular discontent." Others argued that such overseas economic expansion was the only program that would enable them to eke out a profit under the staggering load of welfare legislation. Charles A. Conant, one of the first corporation intellectuals, provided a comprehensive overview: "New markets and new opportunities for investment must be found if surplus capital is to be profitably employed . . . if the entire fabric of the present economic order is not to be shaken by a social revolution."

Then, just as that combined analysis and program for action seemed to be verified by the dramatic jump in agricultural and steel exports during the late summer of 1897, it appeared to be threatened by European counteraction throughout the world. The resulting drive among Americans for militant diplomacy in Latin America and Asia had far more to do with the coming of the Spanish-American War than most historians have allowed. It was the crucial factor in the changing attitude of the large corporation leaders who were hesitant about military intervention in Cuba prior to the summer of 1897. Beginning in May 1897, and becoming very rapid and apparent through the winter of 1897-1898, key economic spokesmen shifted their position.

That movement was further accelerated by their growing distrust of the Cuban rebels, who appeared increasingly unreliable and generally unsatisfactory as allies, and by the new disposition among Cuban conservatives to accept American overlordship. As a result, a majority of American economic leaders were ready for war by mid-March 1898, some in terms of Cuba as the key to Latin America, perhaps even more with Asia in mind. President William McKinley may have given way to overwhelming pressure for war; but not only was that pressure as much economic as ideological, much of the ideology was counter-revolutionary and characterized by an economic definition of the world. The President made it perfectly clear, moreover, that neither he nor other leaders were going to war to turn the island over to the rebels.

A third influence exercised by the large corporation on the foreign policy of the 1890's was more indirect. Its attitude, policy proposals, and action served as data for influential intellectuals such as Brooks Adams who were driven by the same fear of economic stagnation and social revolution. The same factors reinforced the implicit and explicit conclusions that were drawn from the theory advanced by Frederick Jackson Turner, who explained America's past greatness as the result of such expansion. His frontier thesis stated that prosperity and democracy depended upon expansion; and Turner added a bit later that he was sure Americans would continue the process. Still others, such as the more conservative followers of Herbert Spencer, led by William Graham Sumner, advanced theories that defined such expansion as a natural right (and a natural law) under the principles of laissez-faire.

Those demands of the corporation community and other economic groups were synthesized with the theories of the intellectuals and the ideas of Roosevelt and Bryan by Secretary of State John Hay in his famous Open Door Notes of 1899 and 1900. Hay's policy was designed to secure equal opportunity for American economic power in such areas as China, and to prevent other advanced nations from carving up such regions into new colonies and spheres of influence. It is currently fashionable to dismiss the Open Door Notes as a naive failure, but that approach is seriously misleading in two vital respects.

First, the Open Door Notes ended the debate between the Imperialists and the Anti-Imperialists by subsuming the great majority of both groups in enthusiastic support for the idea that America's preponderant economic power would cast the world in a pro-American mold. A small group of Anti-Imperialists carried on their battle against a foreign policy of expansion for several years, but the issue itself was resolved by the Open Door Notes. The editors of the London *Times* immediately caught that significance of the Notes: "Even protectionist organs are for free trade in China, where freedom is for the benefit of American manufacturers. Even anti-Imperialists welcome an Imperial policy which contemplates no conquests but those of commerce." Seven lean years before, in the first shock of the Panic of 1893, the editors of *Harper's* had advocated the same policy in even blunter terms: "The United States will hold the key, unlocking the gates to the commerce of the world, and closing them to war. If we have fighting to do, it will be fighting to keep the peace."

The second important point about the Open Door Policy is that it became the strategy and tactics of America's expansion and security for the next two generations. If it be judged a failure, the verdict has to be cast in the subtle form of the failure of success. For the mid-century crisis of American diplomacy is in large measure defined by the fact that the Open Door Policy built an empire which is confronted by the specter of general and specific revolt. It may be useful, therefore, to trace the role of the large corporation in the implementation of the Open Door Policy.

2

The large industrial corporation was the most important economic institution in foreign affairs until Theodore Roosevelt failed (during the Russo-Japanese War) in his effort to open the door to all of Asia in one grand gesture by manipulating

Japan and Russia into exhaustion. It received most of the legislative attention, as in such matters as reform of the consular service and reciprocity treaties, and also was favored by the executive, as in Manchuria and Latin America. Roosevelt's classic blunder hurt the industrial corporation most in Asia, but it was challenged there and elsewhere by the large bankers for the next decade.

As with the standard interpretation of the debate between the Imperialists and the Anti-Imperialists, there is some—and probably more—value in the broadly accepted idea that the years after 1895 were characterized by the phenomenon of finance capitalism. Even so, the facts are by no means as clear as suggested by the stereotype. Rather, the evidence points toward a relatively short, vigorous struggle in which the bankers won and then lost the initiative in foreign affairs, though their subsequent actions affected American policy in many ways.

Basically, of course, the financiers were dependent upon the industrial corporation. The industrialists produced the goods which made the profits; and even the life insurance companies, which supplied the bankers with vast funds in the earlier period, collected their premiums from people with jobs. By 1923, at the very latest, the industrial corporation had asserted its economic primacy. Secondly, while the Open Door Policy could have been implemented by working through Japan or Russia, as well as in China directly, its object was to structure and control the development of weaker economies. Fundamentally, therefore, if not immediately, the policy defined the bankers as a tool to help the industrial corporation.

For their part, the bankers naturally stressed operations which would provide them with a steady return on investment. Ideally, and for that reason, they favored direct ties with foreign governments in preference to subordinate collaboration with industrial corporations. Until the Great Depression, therefore, they seldom cooperated directly in the program of overseas industrial expansion. But the crash forced them to accept such an approach, and after the mid-1930's they worked ever more closely with the industrialists, and with the government which pushed an industrial policy.

For those reasons, the struggle between the bankers and the industrialists was a complex and continuing process. In Latin America, Canada, Europe, and most underdeveloped regions, the industrial corporation established and maintained an early predominance: in those areas the bankers succeeded only as they functioned as a means to an industrial end. But the situation in Asia was not that clear. Until his death in September 1909, Edward A. Harriman led the industrialists and outmaneuvered the bankers dominated by the House of Morgan. But none of Harriman's immediate successors (save perhaps John Hays Hammond) were willing to sustain the policy of working through the Russians. Hence the only option was to fall back on the less satisfactory alternative of collaborating with the already entrenched Japanese while at the same time trying to extend America's position in China itself. Even if ultimately successful, that was a slow process because influence had first to be established in Japan. But that approach did give the House of Morgan, which stressed its connections in Tokyo, a kind of *de facto* control of the Open Door Policy in Asia unless and until the industrial corporations or the government committed themselves to a major effort in China proper.

President Woodrow Wilson did get the bankers to finance his chosen White Russians in the battle to overthrow the Bolshevik Revolution and simultaneously open the door into Siberia and Manchuria, but the House of Morgan remained adamant about a clear rupture with the Japanese. Herbert Hoover and Charles Evans Hughes also failed in their later efforts to break the veto wielded by the bankers. For one thing, the industrial corporation was heavily involved at home and elsewhere in the world during the 1920's, and could not undertake a large program in China. For another, China was in the throes of a revolution influenced by the Soviet Union, and that upheaval could be controlled only with the help of Japan. Probably most important of all, however, was the ideological dilemma faced by Hoover and Hughes. For while they wanted to exercise control over the operations of the bankers, and in that way push the Open Door Policy more vigorously in Asia and elsewhere, they did not want to set a precedent of the government defining and limiting property rights to that extensive degree. Expansion itself, after all, was designed primarily to sustain and rationalize the existing system. Forced to choose, they reluctantly acquiesced in Thomas Lamont's financial ties with Tokyo.

Thus there would appear to be four long-term characteristics of the struggle between the industrial and the financial corporation. First, the industrial corporation soon established its leadership in every area except Asia. In those regions the bankers succeeded only as they accepted their subordinate position. Second, the bankers made one major effort, in Latin America, to use foreign loans to strengthen themselves against the industrialists at home. That maneuver not only failed; it no doubt accelerated the bankers' domestic decline. Third, the House of Morgan's pro-Japanese policy became the *de facto* policy of the government in Asia for the next two decades, and was seriously considered as late as 1941. Fourth, the industrial corporation and the government ultimately took over financing the expansion of the Open Door system, and in that fashion settled the conflict in favor of the industrial corporation.

3

Except in Asia, however, the industrial corporation was the key element in the political economy of American foreign policy after 1895—and even there the Open Door Policy was ultimately interpreted from their point of view. A preview of that final emphasis on China proper came in 1913, when Wilson refused to support the bankers in a multi-national consortium loan to the Chinese government. Usually interpreted as a noble retreat from dollar diplomacy, the move was in fact nothing of the sort. The Wilson Administration opposed the loan for two reasons. First, and in the words of Secretary of State Bryan, because the United States would "not have a controlling voice" in it. Second, Wilson thought exports more important than loans to American prosperity and democracy.

Even more revealing, perhaps, was the relationship between the Wilson Administration and the National Council of Foreign Trade. Secretary of State Bryan and Secretary of Commerce

William Redfield were the major speakers during the first day of the Council's national convention on May 27, 1914. That date is significant, for it specifies the policy of the Wilson Administration at a time when it was clear that America was suffering a serious economic downturn, yet at an hour prior to the outbreak of World War I. Secretary Redfield, who had been president of the American Manufacturers Export Association and a vigorous advocate of overseas expansion before Wilson called him to the crusade for the New Freedom, led off with a broad outline of government policy. He assured the corporation leaders that "because we are strong, we are going out, you and I, into the markets of the world to get our share." Secretary of State Bryan spoke next. First he reminded the audience that President Wilson had already made it clear that it was official policy to "open the doors of all the weaker countries to an invasion of American capital and enterprise." Having made that point, Bryan concluded by telling the corporation leaders that "my Department is your department."

On the next day the convention left its downtown quarters for a special meeting in the East Room of the White House. President Wilson, who interpreted the frontier thesis and the crises of the 1890's and 1913-1914 as proof of the necessity of overseas economic expansion, had seen fit to take time from his more official duties to address the delegates. His purpose was to assure them that he gave full and active support to a mutual campaign to effect "the righteous conquest of foreign markets." Perhaps it was because some in his audience seemed startled by that candid statement of policy, but in any event Wilson went on to emphasize the point by remarking that such an objective was "one of the things we hold nearest to our heart." Though the war intervened to delay the program, the Wilson Administration carried through on such rhetoric with the Webb-Pomerene Law and the Edge Act, both designed to facilitate corporate expansion overseas, and with vigorous diplomacy to check opposition in Latin America and Asia.

That quiet gathering in the White House symbolized a vital integration of corporation and government thinking on the nature and role of overseas economic expansion. Accelerated and extended by the war itself (which also freed the industrial corporation from the last vestiges of banker control), that consensus asserted the thesis that such expansion was necessary for American prosperity. As was the case in the 1890's, the question of whether or not American leaders were driven by personal economic motives is rather beside the point. Clearly enough, the businessmen *qua* businessmen were, and it is less than helpful to gingerbread the obvious as the complex. As for the corporation leaders who went into the government, the intellectuals, or the more narrowly defined political leaders, they also entertained and acted upon an economic definition of reality. Overseas economic expansion was for them *the* solution for America's problems—be they social, political, or economic.

Of vital importance, therefore, was the concept of trade that had matured since the turn of the century. Far from being defined in the classical sense as the exchange of commodities and services between independent producers meeting in an open market, trade had come to be characterized as the control of markets for American exports and similar authority over raw materials for the production of those exports. In terms of personalities, the consensus was dramatically illustrated by the close and extensive collaboration between Wilson and Herbert Hoover, a corporation leader turned public servant during the war. In Hoover's words, he and Wilson "were always able to find a path ahead upon which to travel successfully together." They agreed upon the crucial importance of economic expansion through the policy of the Open Door, and also shared a preference for securing American objectives through the manipulation of food supplies and by other economic means.

Throughout the 1920's, moreover, American foreign policy was dominated by two corporation men: Hoover and Charles Evans Hughes. Hoover's approach was indicated by his transformation of the Department of Commerce from an organization concerned primarily with domestic affairs into an agency oriented toward overseas expansion; and by his curiously neglected thesis that "the hope of our commerce lies in the establishment of American firms abroad, distributing American goods under American direction, in the building of direct American financing and, above all, in the installation of American technology in Russian industries."

In his efforts to implement the crucial phase of that policy, Hoover tried to shinny on both sides of the street. He refused to let the bankers accept Russian gold but encouraged the large industrialists to take charge of Russia's industrial development. The tactics were less than successful. For one thing, the Russians were quite aware of Hoover's counter-revolutionary objective and interpreted it as verification of Marx's prophecy. For another, the Great Depression made many key industrialists (such as machine tool manufacturers) dependent upon the Russian market and prompted them to pressure Hoover to recognize the Soviet Union. Finally, and most ironic of all, American economic assistance did a great deal to strengthen the very government that Hoover wished to undermine. Neither Hoover nor his successors thought seriously of taking advantage of the pro-American orientation of one segment of Soviet leadership in order to develop and extend that early collaboration.

Hughes revealed his outlook in several ways. He extended the Open Door Policy to all European colonies and Eastern Europe (where such industrialists as W. Averell Harriman became very active). He developed the technique of selecting one large corporation within each industry (as with the Standard Oil Company) as the chosen instrument of such expansion. He initiated, with the vigorous promptings and assistance of the businessmen, a revision of the practice of military intervention in Latin America. Economic leaders favored a more moderate policy because, having established themselves in the region, they found that intervention often cost them more in ill will and the disruption of the marketplace than it gained them in other ways. Hoover carried on that work, which culminated in the Good Neighbor Policy of Franklin Delano Roosevelt and Cordell Hull. And, finally, Hoover and Hughes made it clear to the bankers that the government viewed loans principally as a device to penetrate and control markets for industrial exports and to secure control of key raw materials, and secondarily to establish American political authority in Europe.

Choosing in the arrogance of their decline to flout that warning, Morgan and other bankers tried to restore their earlier power by financing Latin American nations and Japan's penetration of northeast Asia. The strategy failed in Latin America. The bankers' desperately effective efforts to seduce unfaithful borrowers served only to accelerate and deepen their own domestic crisis after 1926. The results were not so clear-cut in Asia. Supported by some industrialists who found Japan a profitable market, and by various traders, the bankers kept alive the old alternative of putting the Open Door Policy into operation by working through and with the Japanese. Though seriously proposed as late as the summer of 1941 by such intellectuals as Harry Dexter White, as well as by Thomas Lamont and John Foster Dulles, that option of the Open Door was ultimately discarded in favor of direct involvment over China.

In the meantime, however, the majority of large corporations extended their overseas operations in Latin America, Europe, the Middle East, and Southeast Asia. First advocated in an organized and sustained fashion by the agrarians in the 1870's, and then pushed hard by the NAM in 1895, the principle of reciprocal trade treaties as a technique of building and integrating an American world system was finally adopted and legislated into operation by the Roosevelt Administration in 1934. That historic link between the decade of the 1890's and the New Deal was reinforced in several other ways. The principle of the unconditional most-favored-nation clause was a crucial part of the trade agreements program, for example, and New Deal leaders were quite aware that the unconditional most-favored-nation provision was the very crux of the Open Door Policy. It was simply a more austere and legal formulation of John Hay's phrase, "equality of commercial opportunity." And in planning and negotiating such trade treaties, New Deal policy-makers consciously sought to build an integrated American system of export markets and raw material supplies.

In another way, the drift toward formal Keynesian economics which characterized the New Deal served to reinforce the traditional American conception of an Open Door Empire. A Keynesian system need not literally be confined to one nation, but when it is extended it has to be done as a system—in this case an American system. For, by its very reliance upon various controls to stabilize the business cycle, the Keynesian approach cannot by definition even be attempted beyond the limits of such central authority. The climax of that aspect of American policy came in the sharp struggle between Lord Keynes and Harry Dexter White, both of whom understood the principle at stake and sought therefore to define the postwar international monetary organization in terms of their respective Keynesian systems.

Though largely overlooked by historians as well as by supporters of the New Deal itself, the liaison between the Roosevelt Administration and the large industrial corporation led to an extensive and intensive expansion of the American foreign economic system by 1939. It was broadly committed in Latin America, Europe, and the Middle East; and had defined its rubber and tin supplies (and others as well) almost exclusively in terms of the resources of Southeast Asia. Beginning in 1935, moreover, there was a revival of interest in China as the market of the future. Save for a small group led by Lamont and Dulles, and the corporations trading with Japan, the large corporation had by 1939 identified itself with an industrial outlook oriented more and more toward England and France, toward the dependencies still controlled by those nations, and toward other underdeveloped areas penetrated or threatened by the Axis powers.

4

The final integration of government, industrial, and financial thinking developed in the course of a serious and heated debate about what to do in response to the expansion of the Axis powers. Most corporation leaders entered the 1930's fearing another war as the midwife of international and domestic revolution. Bernard Baruch, for example, thought a war could make the world safe for democracy as he defined it, but he was impressed by the dangers of trying that approach a second time. Others thought a general war would "destroy our Western civilization," either directly or by forcing totalitarianism upon even the United States. For those reasons, as well as because of their initial attraction toward some features of the counter-revolutionary movements in Italy and Germany, many corporation leaders thought it wise to work out a compromise with those nations. The approach was balanced, however, by the feeling that recovery from the depression would enable America to set the terms of such arrangements and in other ways take the lead in world affairs and keeping the peace. That attitude, so similar to President Woodrow Wilson's initial response to World War I, seems also to have been shared at the outset of the 1930's by President Franklin Roosevelt.

Until about 1935, therefore, there was no serious disagreement over foreign policy between Roosevelt and the leadership of the large corporation. Even afterward, their differences did not flare up dramatically. Most corporations, for example, went along with the principle and practice of the moral embargo that Roosevelt began to use against the Axis. By 1937, however, the corporation community had split into two camps on the issue of foreign policy. That division can be understood most clearly as the result of three factors. First, the continued economic expansion of the Axis in Central and Eastern Europe, Latin America, and other underdeveloped areas led some corporation leaders to conclude that America's Open Door Empire was directly threatened. Second, some of them had realized that the New Deal was not a devilishly clever strategy of revolution, an awareness no doubt facilitated by Roosevelt's growing propensity to take them into his administration. Hence domestic considerations did not prompt them to resist the President's movement toward more active opposition to the Axis. Third, and as a direct consequence of the others, such corporation leaders came to identify democracy as well as economic welfare with the continued existence and expansion of the American system throughout the world.

Other corporation leaders opposed that estimate of the situation. Though to a lesser extent than earlier in the decade, they still thought that a compromise with Germany and Japan would help rather than hurt America's economic and political position in the world. Perhaps most important was their fear that victory in a war against the Axis would be purchased at the price of socialism at home. "It is fairly certain," concluded an important spokesman of the group, "that capitalism cannot survive American participation in this war." Others extended the analysis, seeing American involvement as leading to "the end of capitalism all over the world" and the consequent "spread of communism, socialism, or fascism in Europe and even in the United States." Tormented by that nightmare, such corporation leaders argued that America could and should avoid war by building and integrating an impregnable empire in the Western hemisphere, or that it could and should assert America's ultimate supremacy by waiting for the belligerents to exhaust themselves. Senator Harry S Truman and other political leaders shared the latter view. "The role of this great Republic," explained Truman in October 1939, "is to save civilization; we must keep out of war."

Ultimately, of course, most of those so-called isolationists concluded that such a policy would lead to socialism at home before it produced American predominance in the world. As they did so, particularly after the fall of France, they moved toward an acceptance of American belligerence in the war. In a curious way, the importance of that corporation opposition to an active anti-Axis policy is illuminated by reference to the public opinion polls which have been used by many scholars to justify Roosevelt's behind-the-scenes moves toward military involvement in the war. Such commentators suggest that Roosevelt actually lagged behind the public in acting on a pro-Allied policy. But if the polls are correct, then Roosevelt's hesitation has to be explained either as a misjudgment on his part of the climate of opinion or as the result of his own reluctance to go to war on two fronts.

If the first option is taken, and Roosevelt the master politician judged guilty of a grievous misestimate of public opinion, it would appear that the militant and vocal opposition manifested by the anti-war corporation leadership goes a long way to account for the President's mistake. For by 1939 and 1940 Roosevelt was courting the corporation community more than at any time in the previous five years. If, on the other hand, the fear of a two-front war is emphasized as an explanation for Roosevelt's actions, then the historical and immediate influence of the large corporation appears quite apparent. Approached from the 1890's, the issue became one of waiting to see whether or not the Japanese would move to seal off all of China.

In that context, the question faced by American policy-makers was whether or not to follow the bankers in making a deal with Japan—either in Asia or as a broad strategic move against Germany. In either case the role of the large corporation was very significant. For in failing to take the bankers' option, Roosevelt was left with the original emphasis placed on China by the industrial corporation and those intellectuals who interpreted prosperity and democracy in terms of such overseas expansion of the American economic system.

Perhaps it is wise, in concluding such an analysis, to emphasize the point that there are two questions involved in any discussion of American entry into World War II. The first is whether or not it was necessary for American survival. The second concerns how and why the nation entered it; in what fashion and on what grounds it was determined to be necessary; and the means employed to implement that decision. It may be the greater part of wisdom to conclude that the war was necessary for the survival of American society, but also to conclude that the conception of the world which accounted for the way it was entered was not a definition which strengthened American prosperity and democracy.

Whatever conclusion is preferred on that issue, it seems clear that the large corporation sustained and extended its influence in American foreign affairs after Pearl Harbor. For by mid-1943, when the issue of postwar foreign policy came to the fore and was thrashed out in Congressional hearings and departmental discussions, it was apparent that the Roosevelt Administration was dominated by men whose personal experience and intellectual outlook was conditioned by their careers as leaders or agents or students of the large corporation. Dean Acheson, Averell Harriman, Donald Nelson, Edward Stettinius, Adolph A. Berle, Jr., John Foster Dulles, Eric Johnston, William C. Foster, and James Forrestal are but the most obvious names from the top layer of American leadership in foreign affairs. Those men, and perhaps even Roosevelt himself, had concluded by 1944 that the policy of the Open Door offered the only way to ensure American prosperity and democracy.

Though divided over whether or not to modify America's long-term antagonism toward the Soviet Union and work out a post-war program in conjunction with Russian rulers, American leaders did agree that continued overseas economic expansion was absolutely essential. A few of those men, apparently led by Eric Johnston and Donald Nelson, saw Russia as an enormous market as well as a source of key raw materials. They argued that firm ties with Russia would end the threat of a domestic depression and also pave the way for international peace. From the spring of 1943 through 1944, Russian leaders responded favorably to that approach; first in direct talks with Johnston, then at the Teheran Conference, and finally by submitting a request for a large postwar loan from the United States. Though clearly derived from the axiom that vast overseas economic expansion was necessary to sustain the prosperity of the American system, and not from any romantic or seditious attachment to the Soviets or their revolution, the Johnston-Nelson program was blocked by a majority of American leaders. Some opponents stressed the importance of keeping the Russians weak; others were more specifically concerned with the problems of building what Assistant Secretary of State Acheson called "a successfully functioning political and economic system."

By 1944, indeed, so many American leaders were preoccupied with the specter of another major depression (or sliding back into the old one) that it is quite surprising to realize how little attention has been given to that fact in most accounts of recent American foreign policy. As early as January 1940, for that matter, representative leaders of America's large corporations began to define the crucial problem of the future in those terms. Their discussion of American policy in the context of World War II hinged on the question of how "to organize the economic resources of the world so as to make possible a return to the system of free enterprise in every country, and provide adequate economic opportunities to the so-called 'have not' powers." Having had the problem defined for them in those terms, the editors of *Fortune* devoted the next issue to the questions of "The Dispossessed" at home and a redefinition of "The U.S. Frontier."

From the candid admission that the American system was in serious trouble—"For nearly one-fourth of the population there is no economic system—and from the rest there is no answer"— the editors of *Fortune* drew three major conclusions. First, they acknowledged that "the U.S. economy has never proved that it can operate without the periodic injection of new and real wealth. The whole frontier saga, indeed, centered around this economic imperative." Second, and in consequence of that fact, the editors defined two new frontiers. A new emphasis on enlarged consumer sales at home would have to be paralleled by a tremendous expansion of "foreign trade and foreign investment." Secretary of State Hull's trade agreements program was "a step in the right direction"; but to "open up real frontiers, under a general policy of raising the standard of living of other countries, we shall have to go much further."

In outlining its conception of such a program, *Fortune* argued that "the analogy between the domestic frontier in 1787, when the Constitution was formed, and the present international frontier is perhaps not an idle one. The early expansion of the U.S. was based upon firm political principles; and it may be that further expansion must be based upon equally firm—and equally revolutionary—international principles." *Fortune's* third point emphasized the need for the corporate community to admit its earlier error of opposing the New Deal and go on to more extensive and vigorous leadership inside and outside of the government. Stressing the fact that the New Deal still faced nine million unemployed, the editors concluded that business leadership was essential if the American system was to sustain itself after the war.

Though they did not all agree with the latter specification in that remedy offered by *Fortune* in 1940, by 1943 a broad cross section of American leaders did accept the fact of crisis and did agree that the basic remedy was further overseas economic expansion. Senator Joseph C. O'Mahoney, for example, was highly disturbed by the question of what was to replace the government as the chief consumer of American production after the war.

"If that doesn't happen, it is impossible to see how a depression can be avoided much worse than any depression which the country has ever known."

Harold G. Moulton of The Brookings Institution supported that broad analysis, as did the Department of Labor specialist who pointed out that "the thing we have liked to refer to as the American standard of living is only possible in situations where two people in the family are working." Economist Robert Nathan and Senator Warren Austin also agreed: Avoiding a depression posed "quite a challenge" that could be met only by "assuring markets for the goods and services" produced by America's corporate economy. And William Green, testifying to labor's point of view, concluded that "we will have to, and ought to, find an increased market for much of our surplus production and that will be, I think, one of the problems that ought to be dealt with at the peace conference. I think that we ought to facilitate the sale and shipment of goods between nations to the end that they ought to be able to purchase here and we ought to be able to produce here what they need."

By September 1944, the government had developed a broad synthesis of those various interpretations and proposals. Assistant Secretary of State Acheson presented the analysis during the Congressional hearings on postwar economic policy and planning procedures. His point of departure was the threat of depression and the consequent necessity to sustain full employment. "If we do not do that," he warned, "it seems clear that we are in for a very bad time, so far as the economic and social position of the country is concerned. We cannot go through another ten years like the ten years at the end of the twenties and the beginning of the thirties, without having the most far-reaching consequences upon our economic and social system." "When we look at that problem," he continued, "we may say it is a problem of markets. . . . The important thing is markets. We have got to see that what the country produces is used and sold under financial arrangements which make its production possible. . . . You must look to foreign markets."

In an aside very reminiscent of a similar comment made by Brooks Adams at the turn of the century, Acheson admitted that "you could probably fix it so that everything produced here would be consumed here." But he asserted that such an approach would mean the end of democracy: "That would completely change our Constitution, our relations to property, human liberty, our very conceptions of law. And nobody contemplates that. Therefore, you find you must look to other markets and those markets are abroad." "We cannot have full employment and prosperity in the United States," he summarized, "without the foreign markets." As for the role of economic agreements in the peace settlement, Acheson shared the earlier conclusions of America's corporation leaders. They were vital to such a system because otherwise "it would really mean that we would be relying exclusively on the use of force. I don't believe that would work."

There were almost no references made in those discussions between 1940 and 1944 to the idea of helping poorer nations, or to the relevance of moral standards for foreign policy. The emphasis was on economic expansion and checking the Russians. Acheson had provided, in September 1944, an outline and overview of America's bipartisan foreign policy in the postwar years. While it is true that the program was later presented in a form that emphasized the threat from the Soviet Union more than any other factor, the fact remains that it was conceived in response to quite different dangers. It was originated and sustained as a program to prevent the stagnation of America's corporate economic and political system by industrializing the frontier thesis first advanced by Brooks Adams and Frederick Jackson Turner in 1893.

5

American diplomacy after World War II appears in many respects as a fulfillment of the eerie judgment offered by the editors of *Harper's* in 1893: "If we have fighting to do, it will be fighting to keep the peace." For, certainly, the sustained use of military force around the world, ostensibly to avoid war (and therefore only with reluctance spoken of as "war"), has been one of the central characteristics of the nation's foreign policy since

1945. And the phrase "fighting to keep the peace" has been used by every President and Secretary of State to justify and defend that activity.

The standard accounts of this Twenty Years of War After the War explain the phenomenon almost wholly in terms of the actions of the Soviet Union and the revolutionary movements in China and other countries. Liberals (and even some so-called radicals) have joined conservatives and reactionaries in promoting a devil theory of war that places the blame on a few individuals like Joseph Stalin, Mao Tse-tung, Fidel Castro, and Ho Chi Minh. That grossly oversimplified picture of reality won broad acceptance (or acquiescence) for two reasons. It is undeniable that many individuals and governments have manifested a steadily increasing resistance to the vast extension of American power and to the uses for which it has been employed. But the primary explanation lies in the beliefs held by most Americans concerning the naturalness, inevitability, necessity, desirability, and morality of the Americanization of the world. For, given those assumptions and attitudes, opposition to that course of events becomes either foolish, irrational, or evil.

What began in the late nineteenth century as a reasoned and coherent argument for the overseas expansion of the American marketplace for economic and benevolent purposes had become by the middle of the twentieth century an unreasoning article of faith. That intellectual and psychological transformation involving large numbers of ordinary American citizens should not, however, obscure the continuing central role of the corporation and its leadership in the making of American policy after 1945. The corporation political economy continued to enlarge its overseas operations in close cooperation with—and with great assistance from—the federal government.

The best study of that expansion has been offered by Harry Magdoff in *The Age of Imperialism*, where he concludes that "the size of the foreign market (for domestic and United States-owned foreign firms) is equal to approximately two-fifths the domestic output of farms, factories, and mines." He also makes it clear that the overseas sales operations have become relatively more important in manufacturing industries, and that the investment in foreign plants climbed to 17 percent of the domestic investment by 1965. In a similar way, foreign operations accounted for more than 20 percent of the after-taxes profits of American manufacturing firms in 1965.

The government itself provides figures that dramatize the importance of direct exports (*The Survey of Current Business,* November 1964). Topped by the companies that manufacture machinery for the construction, mining, and oil extraction industries, which export 26.9 percent of their output, there are fourteen major industries that export at least 9 percent of their production. Pointing out that most of the purchases made by the federal government are used for military operations directly connected with imperial activities, Magdoff concludes that the true economic importance of the American empire is even greater than indicated by those impressive figures for direct exports.

The increasing militarization of American foreign policy has often, if not usually, been explained as the result of a growing influence wielded by the armed forces within the government. The evidence strongly indicates, however, that the rising power of the military has resulted more from decisions made by civilians than from a successful push for independent decision-making authority by the generals and admirals. The Joint Chiefs of Staff have not been reluctant or backward, but the opening they exploited was provided by the coalition of corporation leaders, labor union officials, politicians, and intellectuals who defined the vital national interests of the country in terms of the necessity of the overseas expansion of the corporation political economy.

Given that imperial outlook, the only serious questions that remained open for debate concerned the tactical problems of the size of the American empire, and the techniques of establishing and maintaining control. At the end of World War II, one bipartisan group of American leaders advocated a policy of moderation and adaptation. Despite their vigorous disagreement on other issues (and their contrasting temperaments and styles), men like Senator Robert A. Taft, Secretary of Agriculture and Commerce Henry A. Wallace, and former President Herbert C. Hoover agreed that it was neither wise nor necessary for the

United States to police the entire globe, or to react as a frightened doe to revolutions and other changes throughout the world.

None of those men was an isolationist in any meaningful sense of that misused term. Hoover came the closest to advocating a general withdrawal and consolidation, yet his strategic perimeter was large enough to include Great Britain, parts of the Mediterranean, and all the Western Hemisphere. At the other extreme, Wallace was a traditional liberal reformer who saw the United States as the primary agent of benevolent progress for all men everywhere. What united those men, and the group of labor leaders, intellectuals, corporation executives, and ordinary citizens who responded to their proposals, was a skepticism about either the morality, the necessity, or the possibility of trying to set limits on the activities of the entire world. In a real sense, they were the heirs of the men who opposed President Woodrow Wilson's attempt to freeze or control all change through Article X of the League of Nations Covenant.

They were acting, that is to say, on the same perception that prompted Elihu Root's unanswerable critique of Wilson. In 1919 he charged that:

> If perpetual, [Article X] would be an attempt to preserve for all time unchanged the distribution of power and territory made in accordance with the views and exigencies of the Allies in this present juncture of affairs. It would necessarily be futile . . . It would not only be futile, it would be mischievous. Change and growth are the law of life, and no generation can impose its will in regard to the growth of nations and the distribution of power, upon succeeding generations.

And Taft added, in 1946 and 1947 that the attempt to do so might well incite or provoke the Russians to defend their interests through a resort to force.

The failure of Taft and the other moderates to win their battle to modify the militant and universal assertion of American power is largely explained by five factors. First, they composed a minority of the leadership of the corporation political economy. The majority, led by such men as Dean Acheson and W. Averell Harriman, favored the vigorous use of American power to consolidate

the existing empire, and to enlarge it by penetrating areas formerly controlled or dominated by Great Britain, France, and other
nations. Second, the great absolute and relative power at the
disposal of the majority of American leaders made it possible, at
the outset and in the short-run, to carry out such imperial operations without serious difficulties. Third, that power was adroitly
deployed behind the banner of anti-communism, a psychological
and political strategy that was as successful as it was commonplace. The imperial majority of American leaders recognized
that the populace would have to be re-aroused to sustain the
kind of activity (and its related costs) that they had supported
during the war. Senator Arthur Vandenberg was merely being
more candid than most of his colleagues when he remarked that
it would be necessary "to scarce hell out of the American people."
The specter of communism met that need.

The fourth element that contributed to the success of the
imperial majority was the great rationality and self-restraint of
the Russians. Without any question, American policy-makers
recognized the great importance of that factor from the outset,
though they took great pains to deny it in debates with their
critics, and to conceal it from the general public. It was not openly
discussed in any significant manner until the far-left wing of the
radical and communist movements used it as a weapon against
the Russians and others they felt were being too conservative.

In one sense, of course, the Russians had no choice. The gap
between their weakness and American strength was so great
that they could have done nothing else. That interpretation assumes, however, a degree of intelligence and self-control that is
far from commonplace in human affairs (as well as being denied
in connection with the Russians in official American rhetoric
about the Cold War). Yet the Soviet leaders displayed precisely
those characteristics. The restraint of the Russians was a central
—and very probably the crucial—factor in preventing a nuclear
war between 1945 and 1955. If they had acted otherwise, whether
from psychological illness or ideological ardor, the revolutionary
movements of the world would have suffered catastrophically—
along with the rest of the human race.

The final element that contributed to the victory of the imperial majority was the growing overseas resistance to American expansion. For, given the deeply entrenched tradition of American expansion with its strong element of righteousness about the effects of the resulting empire, and given the successful postwar definition of the renewed imperial thrust as an anti-communist defensive maneuver, the rising opposition to the United States could effectively be presented—at least in the short-run—as unjustified and evil aggression against the righteous. Thus America became the beleaguered defender of the true and the good.

There is some evidence to suggest that the Russian ability to recover from the war, the consolidation of the Chinese Revolution, and the failure to overthrow Castro in 1961 forced the more perceptive leaders of the corporation system to begin questioning the viability of American policy. Most observers have dated the beginning of that process to the administration of President John F. Kennedy. It seems more likely, however, that it started with President Dwight D. Eisenhower. He not only terminated the war in Korea, but he clearly restrained the *actions* of Secretary of State John Foster Dulles, who had been an advocate of the vigorous expansion of the corporation system ever since the years of the First World War, and who became a militant cold warrior after 1944.

The extension of the discussion during the aborted Kennedy Administration did serve to make it clear, moreover, that the debate concerned tactics far more than strategy, and that the expansionists still held control of the decision-making process. Kennedy no more intended to dismantle the American empire than Winston Churchill planned to revive the outlook and policy of the Little Englanders. The Kennedy group wanted an optimum empire, and it sought to achieve and maintain that objective through a greater reliance on the economic and ideological resources of the United States.

They were probably on the verge of trying to re-educate the American people to an understanding of the truth that they had belatedly come to comprehend: the United States could lose a Cuba without disrupting or endangering the empire. They understood that the economic loss was more than compensated for by continuing corporation expansion in Western Europe, and in other underdeveloped nations. And they realized that the military, political, and prestige factors could be handled within tolerable limits.

Kennedy seems to have sensed, however, that he faced a very difficult challenge. He was not only confronted with the problem of overcoming a strongly entrenched set of popular traditions and stereotypes, but also with the difficulty of changing a very similar pattern of thought and belief accepted by himself and other leaders of the corporation economy. If the accounts that have so far been offered are correct, then he was pessimistic about the prospects of significant improvement. He commented bluntly that Vietnam presented a challenge that he could not handle by withdrawal. He explained his inability to maneuver in terms of the impossibility of being re-elected if he failed to maintain the American presence, but it seems very likely that he also understood that such a decision would be bitterly opposed by many key leaders within his own administration, as well as by those in the Republican Party.

In a more fundamental respect, moreover, it appears highly probable that Kennedy himself was at best ambivalent about the wisdom of a less militant and energetic imperial policy. He never seriously attacked the explanation of America's dynamic growth, or the definition of its vital national interests, that had developed around the expanding political economy dominated by the large corporation. Instead, he persistently reiterated the classic goals of the old Progressive Movement: reform at home to improve and save the system coupled with the necessary and righteous extension of American power abroad.

Paradoxical as it may appear at first glance, Lyndon Baines Johnson was probably more inherently willing to follow a moderate foreign policy than either Presidents Truman or Kennedy. Had he been given an opportunity to establish himself as an effective and reforming President in his own right through the success of a domestic program, he might well have eased the United States out of the Vietnam quicksand. In any event, he never had that opportunity, *for the turning point came in the late summer of 1964 before he had been elected as his own man.*

Johnson was confronted with the necessity of making what

became a crucial decision between July and October 1964, the time when it became apparent that the Vietcong would achieve a military victory in the south unless the United States intervened directly with American troops and firepower. He was then thought of, and was acting, as the caretaker of the Kennedy Administration, which had significantly increased the number of American men in Vietnam shortly before the assassination. Johnson was also under vigorous attack by Barry Goldwater for being too soft on communism (the same charge that Kennedy had hurled at Richard Nixon and the Republicans during the 1960 campaign).

Johnson has often been charged, since that time, with being either cynical or dishonest in knowingly undertaking an open-ended expansion of the war while campaigning on the rhetoric of peace. That may be true, but there is enough evidence to at least suggest that Johnson may have been mistaken rather than dishonest. The President (along with other leaders) may very well have thought in August 1964 that a short, sharp deployment of a relatively small amount of American power would terminate the armed phase of Vietcong resistance as well as prevent an overt defeat in the south. He was mistaken, tragically mistaken, but by the time that became apparent the United States had become involved and psychologically committed beyond the point of an immediate reversal of policy.

The crucial point, of course, is that the mistake in judgment flowed directly from the analysis and attitude that had developed as part of the maturation of the corporation political economy. For, as held and acted on by the majority of American leaders, that view of the world had become so distorted and hardened that it not only overvalued the importance of Vietnam even to a capitalist economy (and to a super nuclear power), but its principal advocates had become almost completely incapable of recognizing and acting to correct the causes of its distortions and failures. The protagonists had lost operational awareness of the inherent limits of their approach to expansion, and of the dynamic resistance the operation of the system created *even when it functioned effectively.*

As a result, the re-education of the corporate oligarchy had to be initiated from the outside. *It had ceased to function intelligently or satisfactorily within its own framework.* The Teach-In Movement was the first phase of that effort to force the oligarchy to re-establish its connection with the real world. The most significant short-run effect of that action was to move the rational minority of the oligarchy—the Fulbrights, Kennans, and Gavins— to re-activate the critique of the majority that had first been undertaken by Taft, Wallace, and Hoover.

By the winter of 1965-1966, therefore, the central question had been defined as whether or not the rational minority of the oligarchy could modify American policy before it generated the kind of domestic and foreign opposition that would imperil the system itself. That remained the question in the winter of 1967-1968. Long praised and defended for its rationality, morality, and beneficent effectiveness, the corporation political economy had in truth reached the point where it might well produce irrational catastrophe for its own citizens as well as for those who existed as colonials within its empire.

The New Deal, New Frontiers, and the Cold War: A Re-examination of American Expansion, 1933-1945

by Lloyd C. Gardner

In the late summer of 1933, shortly after the conclusion of the first Roosevelt Congress and the adjournment of the London "World Economic Conference," Walter Lippmann began writing a series of lectures he would deliver the following spring at Harvard University and which were later published under the title *The Method of Freedom*.[1] Lippmann's remarks are still a useful take-off point for re-examining the origins and purposes of the New Deal. Of special interest to students of American foreign policy is the way Lippmann knit together an analysis of the breakdown of the international economy, or the "Great Society" as he called it, with traditional American frontier mythology and the outlook for the United States in a world rapidly returning to the narrow nationalism of medieval walled cities.

"The world economy having ceased to be self-adjusting," began the former *New Republic* editor, "men everywhere are bent upon establishing what controls they can within the orbit of their powers. Somehow or other they are determined to make a social order which will not be, as was the Great Society of the pre-war world, so unmanageable and so vulnerable."[2]

In thus pronouncing the end of an international era, so long dominated by Adam Smith laissez-faire rhetoric, so long dominated by Smith's countrymen through the Pax Britannica, Lippmann made the common observation that it had been the cannons of World War I which had blown apart the first Great Society. Actually, he was well aware that prewar tensions, caused in large part by the entrance of major competitors onto the outer frontiers of the international order, had already undermined a world system made up of loose arrangements, sustained more by routine than by design. Up to a point such contests could be absorbed in colonial competition; that point had been reached before the crisis in the European alliance system boiled over at Sarajevo. Lippmann himself suggested the essential contradiction between the rhetoric of free and equal competition in world marketplaces and the reality of international politics in the century before World War I. Stripped of its laissez-faire gloss, that history was "in considerable part the record of the struggle of various interested groups to carve out for themselves areas in which competition was limited for their own advantage."[3]

Empires, even if they came into being during supposed fits of absent-mindedness, are after all sustained with full mental and physical stamina for the advantage of the imperialist—not his rival. Until the 1890's America had a distinct advantage in this struggle: it had its own internal empire where the problems of ruling over an alien race were minimal, where raw materials and mineral resources were abundant. And as the leading edge of civilization pushed into the West, behind it grew up a single unified nation with needs to be filled and resources to be developed. In the post-Civil War period, a series of high tariffs protected that great empire from foreign competition.

Moreover, in the United States, as Lippmann observed, "the disinherited [had] . . . the opportunity to migrate and stake out their own inheritance. . . . The social disease of proletarianism is not serious where the frontier is still open. . . ."[4] The problem in 1934 had become how "to construct within the framework of our complicated machine civilization the moral equivalent to the opportunity to stake out private property in virgin territory."[5]

Before the 1890's, to extend these remarks in a somewhat different direction, the frontier had been the world to Americans. But as they turned to the world for a new frontier, the old international order was already strained by the rising power of Germany and Japan, and the almost desperate attempts by Russia to extend the Trans-Siberian Railroad to the borders of Manchuria and the Pacific Ocean. These forces all met in China in 1899 when John Hay issued the first Open Door Note to the Powers.

America's victory over weak Spanish forces in Cuba and the Philippines in 1898 apparently launched the United States onto the course of territorial imperialism. Yet in truth these possessions, though possibly of great value in themselves, were always thought of even by the most ardent imperialists as part of a larger purpose, be it material or moral. Thus Woodrow Wilson described the "Ideals of America" in 1902:

> The census takers of 1890 informed us, when their task was done, that they could no longer find any frontier upon this continent: that they must draw their maps as if the mighty process of settlement that had gone on, ceaseless, dramatic, the century through, were now ended and complete, the nation made from sea to sea. We had not pondered their report a single decade before we made new frontiers for ourselves beyond the seas, accounting the 7,000 miles of ocean that lie between us and the Philippine Islands no more than the 3,000 which once lay between us and the coasts of the Pacific.[6]

And, said Wilson, "the nation which yesterday intervened in the affairs of Cuba . . . today troubles the trade and the diplomacy of the world. . . ." American Far Eastern diplomacy, which, in Wilson's phrase, now "troubled" the world, was directed not toward sharing a slice of China, but toward maintaining the whole pie until United States interests could enjoy the most of it.[7]

In 1893 the domestic economy had taken another sharp downward turn in a business cycle that was becoming increasingly alarming to the nation's economic and political leaders. The depression found the railroads built (in fact overbuilt); in 1895 the American-China Development Company was organized. It proposed to carry out the next phase of American railway expansion in that country. Also in 1895, Secretary of State Richard Olney issued his famous challenge to British influence in South America. "Nervous Nellies" in the business community were worried by Olney's bold declaration, but most came to believe that Great Britain could not be allowed to "Africanize" Latin America. Out of their dual concern evolved the modern arbitration movement in the United States, led by expansionists such as Andrew Carnegie.[8] International arbitration was the only way, these men thought, to codify the loosely defined rules of the international order and to make way, most importantly, for the settlement of the future disputes which would inevitably occur with the stepped-up American commercial invasion of the world.[9]

"No just reason," exclaimed Senator John T. Morgan, a most enthusiastic expansionist from a major cotton exporting state, "can be given for a monastic policy which will shut up the energies of our people within a fixed limit, and compel them to trade within our present territory. This cannot be done without destroying the genius of our people."[10] The continuity of this and similar assumptions was startlingly revealed fifty years later in 1944 when Assistant Secretary of State Dean Acheson warned in phrases which echoed the 1890's: "We cannot go through another ten years like the ten years at the end of the twenties and the beginning of the thirties, without having the most far-reaching consequences upon our economic and social systems. . . . My contention is that we cannot have full employment and prosperity in the United States without the foreign markets."[11] Acheson's later statement of American foreign policy as "total diplomacy" was a revealing indication that foreign policy considerations had at last become the most important issues before the American people. Since the 1890's, when American prosperity and political well-being had first been defined in such terms, the trend had been growing stronger. Commercial expansion abroad, in this equation, equaled political democracy at home.

"The commercial opportunity," explained President William McKinley at the time America moved to take the Philippines, "which is naturally and inevitably associated with this new opening, depends less on large territorial possessions than upon an adequate commercial basis and upon broad and equal privileges."[12]

Thus America's colonial experiment remained a very limited one. Instead, American leaders predicted that commercial expansion, as long as the door remained open, would provide the United States with the economic advantages of a formal empire without the political responsibilities and moral liabilities connected with colonies. If conflicts arose, they could be settled by international arbitration.[13] The greatest difficulty for the United States turned out to be the problem of finding a nation to work with in Asia, to act as doorman. Japan was chosen after the

Russo-Japanese War, but the partnership was a troubled one from its early stages and was maintained by a series of *ad hoc* agreements. It came the closest to being resolved amicably in the decade following the Washington Naval Conference in 1921-1922. The decade which began with Japan's forward movement into Manchuria in 1931 demonstrated that even informal empires could indeed involve a nation in political and military entanglements.

The Japanese problem arose very forcefully at the outset of the New Deal. Despite the early common interpretation of the New Deal as revolutionary (which is at last giving way to more sophisticated analyses), the basic outlook of the New Dealers came down to the best way to reform American corporate society, not to revolutionize it. An alliance between Raymond Moley and Rexford Tugwell inside the famous Brain Trust presented a nationalistic program as the solution to America's depression-caused illness. As long as it was necessary to follow this regimen, these two said, the United States should not challenge Japan in Asia, nor should it attempt other remedies such as those offered by "internationalists" at the World Economic Conference.

Roosevelt followed the general outlines of this program, but to Moley and Tugwell's great disappointment he publicly backed Secretary of State Henry L. Stimson's doctrine of non-recognition of Japan's Manchurian conquest at a conference only days before he was inaugurated President.[14]

Thus the victory gained by Moley and Tugwell was an uncertain one. Yet it has misled later students of the New Deal, as indeed it did those "internationalists" most upset by early planning programs.[15] Though Rex Tugwell, for example, urged the fullest exploitation of the possibilities opened up by NRA-AAA national planning, though he asserted that such projects as the Civilian Conservation Corps were the beginnings of a moral equivalent to the frontier, as Lippmann had put it, or even to war, as William James had put it earlier, his influence waned while the advocates of a new attempt to reconstruct the Great Society, among them many former Brain Trusters, grew stronger and more persuasive.[16] Of course the Axis challenge from the mid-1930's helped to shape these events; so did the 1937-1938 recession, which struck down much of the progress toward domestic recovery. But we must not therefore assume that New Deal foreign policy was simply a reaction to immediate events, without considering more long-standing pressures upon American society and the continuing initiatives its leaders had put forth to overcome these problems since America came to industrial maturity.

Tugwell's 1933 ally, Adolf Berle, wrote several articles which revealed a murky ambivalence in New Deal philosophy and unresolved tensions within its wise men and prophets. In one article Berle asserted that "the heart of the Marxian argument on the economic side has never been answered. . . ." Production far outstrips the capacity to consume. Berle later changed his mind, but in the midst of the depression crisis he contended that the main aim of the New Deal was to open up greater markets for the businessman. "If there were another California to settle, or if we could, let us say, attempt the conquest of Africa," the businessman might "solve the difficulty by searching for dreams of empire and imperial markets." Since the United States was not an imperialistic nation, since there were no more frontier lands to settle at home, the New Deal had to supply both a moral and a material equivalent.[17]

More than creeping socialism, creeping ambivalence character-ized another article by this young philosopher of American cor-porate capitalism:

> The profit motive, essential in a developing country, has still a tre-mendous place in any economic civilization. For example, it must continue to function in developing new inventions; in pushing out the frontiers, *either geographically or scientifically:* in devising new forms of organizations. *It is not easy to think of a civilization which is not constantly pushing out its frontiers in terms of goods and services, though geography is beginning to be a restricted field* (emphasis is added).[18]

Although the problem was viewed from a slightly different per-spective by the later head of the NRA, Donald M. Richberg, the ambivalence remains noticeable. As Richberg saw it, the question was whether "here upon this continent, where our ancestors devised a new variety of political government which has developed lustily for over 150 years, we may have the courage and vision to develop a new variety of industrial self-government," or whether total control by political coercion would be inevitable. "That is the final issue of the recovery program." Or, as General Hugh Johnson, head of the NRA, put it: "We must substitute for the old safety valve of free land and new horizons a new safety valve of economic readjustment and direction of those great forces. There is no alternative to shipwreck. We are permanently in a new era."[19]

Always aware that over their shoulders even friendly critics were comparing their remedies for the depression with the "isms" then being practiced in Russia, Italy, and Germany, the New Dealers reacted to such charges by summoning up the traditions of American democratic theory and practice. But many of them linked the present experiments to the voluntarism of Jeffersonian individualism, ironically (and properly) associated with an expanding frontier since the Louisiana Purchase in 1803. To explain it another way, they did not assume they could recreate such conditions in America, but they did assume that the frontier spirit would carry the country through this period of adjustments.

It can be seen that the tensions and ambivalences in New Deal philosophy were giving way to paradox. And when the national planning of the so-called First New Deal failed to bring recovery, these questions were resolved in favor of New Frontiers. Even those who, in Professor Warren Susman's phrase, rejected the frontier thesis as a "useless past" totally unsuited for an intellectual foundation on which to build a present New Deal, remained deeply influenced by their own interpretations of that theme. Richberg and Hugh Johnson quite explicitly justified the dangerous course chosen in the NRA by the unique American national experience. They apparently believed that they still had a Western jackrabbit's foot left over from the last century for luck.[20]

The intra-nationalism of the most dedicated New Dealers, then, continually reckoned upon the outward thrust of frontier expansionism! Here indeed was a paradox. On the other hand, this position of temporary nationalism met a very clear assertion of immediate internationalism from Herbert Hoover, Henry L. Stimson, and Norman H. Davis. To this challenge the New Dealers replied that the nation had to come to terms with a closed frontier at home, cure the depression, and then take up the challenges of closing frontiers abroad. To oppose Japan's forward movement in Manchuria, Great Britain's imperial preference system, or Germany's new autarchy in Central Europe while the United States still remained depression-weakened, would be to attempt the most dangerous course of all, risking revolution at home and military defeat abroad.

Hoover had insisted that the only safe path out of the depression was through the London Economic Conference in 1933; Roosevelt's advisers warned against this course, though Raymond Moley seemingly became confused somewhere along the way when he tried unsuccessfully to patch up the Conference. He was repudiated, not primarily because Roosevelt had planned all along to drop a "bombshell" on any attempt at an international currency stabilization plan, but because "the logic of capitalism in crisis leads straight toward more barriers to trade, not less."[21]

Such was the credo of the Brain Trusters in 1933 and 1934, but it would still be mistaken to say that the "First New Deal" was truly isolationist. The partnership between government and industry in the NRA and between government and agriculture in the AAA, the economics of scarcity these arrangements produced, the attempt at a semi-planned society, the economic foreign policy of self-containment, or any other similar description of these years, are at most only three-quarter truths. Indeed, the most amazing thing about the First New Deal may finally turn out to be that Americans never really tested their frontier-built institutions against the standard of a frontierless society.

Henry A. Wallace, Roosevelt's first Secretary of Agriculture, was clearly and fundamentally opposed to scarcity economics and self-containment. A great deal of plain nonsense has been written about Wallace since his fall from "liberal" grace and his apostasy during 1948, when he ran for the Presidency on the Progressive Party's platform of greater efforts at "co-existence" with the Soviet Union. Not until Stalin's death could this position be argued with impunity in public, let alone in a Presidential cam-

paign. The Communist Party's participation in the 1948 campaign tainted the Wallace crusade in the popular mind. Since
then this Iowa-born agrarian thinker has been fair game for a
whole generation of sophisticated new conservatives as well as
super-sophisticated old liberals. Yet if there was one sustained
thought in Wallace's public statements, writings, and actions
from 1933 to 1946, it was the idea that American freedoms could
not be preserved for long in a frontierless society. The products
of our farms and factories had to have the world market.

"Capitalism was bound to reach a crisis," he wrote in *New
Frontiers* in 1934, "for capitalism during the previous 150 years
had been reinvigorated time and time again by the conquest of
new frontiers. . . ."[22] Whether put to the public by Wallace, or
Berle, or anyone else, the thesis was the same.

During World War II, Wallace made a number of trips for
President Roosevelt on behalf of Allied war aims and hopes for
the postwar world. His natural inclination to put these matters in
humanistic and idealistic phrases sometimes led him to rhetorical
excesses that provided his later opponents with abundant examples of his other-worldiness. These became especially useful to
"realists" like Secretary of Defense James Forrestal when the two
disagreed time and again in President Truman's Cabinet discussions over the way to meet the Soviet threat after the war.[23]

Even if one grants all that was said about Wallace's misreading
of Soviet intentions, he still emerges from this period as much
more than the simplistic do-gooder portrayed by caricatures
drawn by hard-nosed realists. Like his father—Henry C. Wallace,
Agriculture Secretary in the Harding Administration—Henry
Agard Wallace accepted the premise that agriculture was one
function in many in a generally corporatized society. He hoped
to preserve the farmer's integrity in this system, but increasingly
he realized that the whole society must prosper if the farmer
were both to contribute to that well-being and share in it.

Taking a look at the history of American wheat-growing and
its contribution to the foreign trade balance of the United States
in the past, Wallace wrote in *Foreign Affairs Quarterly* that after
the great fertile areas of the West really opened up, the natural
increase in population and export sales still took up the surpluses

—for a time. "Exports increased about as rapidly as our population from 1880 to 1905, then decreased to about one-half by 1913." Since that time, he pointed out, constant adjustments had to be made to protect all the agrarian interests of the country.

Wallace had taken this problem to a meeting of national leaders in the offices of the Council on Foreign Relations. These men, who published the *Foreign Affairs Quarterly* and who included former Secretary of State Henry L. Stimson, corporation lawyer John Foster Dulles, and the always-somewhere-near Walter Lippmann, heard the Secretary of Agriculture plead not for continued domestic allotments for farmers under the AAA, but for a way to accept a billion and a half dollars worth of imports annually so that farm exports could be maintained. It was either that or plow up forty million acres of good land or sixty to seventy million acres of marginal land.[24]

In the fall of 1933, the United States had recognized the Soviet Union. Many political and economic policy-makers hoped that this diplomatic gesture would improve exports to Russia. Wallace was one of a minority less enthusiastic about the idea, warning the President that it was "desirable that a formal agreement be reached with Russia as to the maximum quantity of wheat she will export during the current crop year."[25] Here was strong evidence that the Secretary of Agriculture not only vigorously upheld the farmer's rights vis-à-vis the manufacturer, but more significantly regarded the international market as the ultimate salvation for American agriculture.

Though sharply critical of foolish foreign loans in the 1920's, and doubtful that international trade could be restored quickly or easily, the Secretary wrote in *America Must Choose* that following World War I ". . . we yearned only to come home quietly, expand some more in our own way within our own borders and contend thereafter only among ourselves for the old spacious, separate spoils of 'normalcy.'

"That couldn't be."[26]

Former Secretary of State Stimson, who had also listened to Wallace at the council meeting, read *America Must Choose,* approved its thesis, and made use of the book in a national radio broadcast in support of his successor, Cordell Hull, and the 1934

Reciprocal Trade Agreements Act: "Mr. Wallace frankly points out the dangers and difficulties which will be before us if we adopt . . . compulsory government control of production and marketing . . . ; the suppression of our hereditary institutions and love of freedom; and, worst of all, the stifling of individual free thought and speech which is a necessary accompaniment of the process if we carry national planning to its full conclusion."[27]

The passage of the Reciprocal Trade Agreements Act in 1934 marked the return to the search for world frontiers. Roosevelt, it should be pointed out, was skeptical of his Secretary of State's more optimistic claims in the early years of the New Deal. World trade never really was restored before World War II—but the direction he approved and had set by the State Department led away from intra-nationalism.

After Congressional action, Hull brought into the State Department Professor Francis B. Sayre, who became his chief emissary to the American intellectual and corporate elite (many of whom also had some doubts about the wisdom of the Reciprocal Trade Agreements program). Sayre wrote confidently in *America Must Act:* "Full American domestic recovery lies through world recovery. That is why we must press aggressively, by means of our own trade program, for the return not only by us but by other countries as well to policies based upon equality of commercial treatment to all and the termination of the system of special privilege and discrimination."[28]

The problem, of course, was not that American businessmen did not want greater foreign markets but that they hated to give up any of a depression-shrunk domestic market to achieve that goal. A future feast has little appeal to the man concentrating on the protection of his meager supplies against an outside threat.

By 1940 the situation had changed in many respects. If general pessimism about the reconstruction of the pre-World War I Great Society was in the ascendance in the early 1930's, a different mood characterized the final years of that fateful decade. There was, first of all, a growing determination to end the Axis threat to United States interests in Europe, Asia, and even Latin America. Of special interest here, however, was a feeling that went beyond such grim thoughts. As against the stubbornness of do-

mestic troubles, American leaders *believed* in their capacity to
meet this threat, and to overcome it. After the severe downturn
in the economy in 1937-1938, everyone in the Administration
noted Franklin Roosevelt's personal despair at the situation,
which he increasingly linked to the world situation (in any number of ways). He once told Morgenthau, Secretary of the Treasury,
that fascism was indeed making gains throughout the world.
"Brazil was veering that way. Take the situation in the United
States, he said. Four or five people might get together, talk it over,
and decide they had to have their own man in Washington. Even
though he said every so often that he wanted business to make
a profit and that he believed in property rights, business did not
believe him."[29]

Another time he made the link in a different way. Referring to
Cordell Hull's great faith in his Reciprocity program, Roosevelt
told Morgenthau, "Henry, these trade treaties are just too
goddamned slow. The world is marching too fast. They're just
too slow."[30]

The Axis challenge allowed American leaders to turn their
eyes from the domestic scene. As they did, they returned at once
to the old frontier thesis. If the United States took advantage of
the situation, this was the chance to establish a new international
political and economic Great Society.

Hull's trade treaties had been too slow, too slow either to restore American international commerce or to prevent the complete breakdown of international society. What America needed
was a policy to restore an open world at once. Soon after rejoining
the Executive branch of the federal government as Secretary of
War, Henry L. Stimson wrote to a noted American liberal that
he agreed fully "as to the importance of freedom of trade in the
present distracted world." After the revolutionary war in the
colonies, the new American statesmen, he continued, had failed
to write a proper constitution. The result was rising internal
tariffs which blocked the nation's prosperity. This situation
worsened until with the Constitutional Convention of 1787 they
found a remedy "which forbade tariff barriers and enforced free
trade as well as a common and sound currency." Stimson believed

that one of the great failures at Versailles had been that no one "suggested such a remedy after the Great War."[31]

Using a different analogy from United States history, he drove home the same point on a different occasion: In 1860 Lincoln had said that the country could not endure half slave and half free; in 1940 "we are forced to recognize this truth in respect to the world at large. That world cannot endure permanently half slave and half free. . . ."[32]

At the time Stimson became Secretary of War, in a display of bipartisan support for the Administration's opposition to the Axis, other policy-makers expressed similar views about the pre-war and postwar world. For example, a group of political, economic, and intellectual leaders came together under the auspices of *Fortune* magazine to discuss self-containment as an answer to the Axis challenge. They agreed that it was impossible without greatly reduced living standards and regimentation. Moreover, "American mass production would sacrifice some of the advantages arising out of large capital investment and technological skills, which can be fully realized only in a constantly expanding market."[33] And Henry Wallace stated in *The American Choice* that with Hitlerite methods controlling and curtailing world trade it was impossible for the United States "to get an adequate outflow of exports. . . . An increase of governmental intervention is inevitable."[34]

As the sounds of war came closer, this antagonism to Axis trade methods grew. The point here is not that the United States opposed Germany and Japan solely or even primarily *because* of narrow economic reasons; what is of more concern is how policy-makers viewed America's place in the postwar era. That question involved the momentary problem of Axis trade and economic policies; it also was tied up in their interpretation of past American experience and their projections about the future of American institutions.

American leaders often associated the aggressiveness of Axis commercial policies with "closed" societies. Since they viewed increased regimentation at home in a not dissimilar fashion, it would have been surprising if this had not happened. Both conservative critics of the New Deal (and it was in this period that Dean Acheson and Will Clayton both rejoined the Democratic coalition behind Roosevelt in the White House) and liberals could agree on the need to oppose the Axis. Their agreement had intellectual roots in the frontier thesis; their interpretation of the situation in 1940 conformed not only to the ease with which Americans had moved into the West in the century past, but also to the modern needs of agriculture and corporate capitalism.

Perhaps the term "closed" society needs some clarification to drive the point home. I use it here to mean the same or similar things on several different levels. The world in 1933, for example, appeared to New Deal leaders to be breaking down in such a fashion. Cordell Hull said that the British Empire under the Ottawa Preference System was closing "like an oyster shell."[35] And when the United States set about the task of restoring an "open" world in the postwar period, the Administration believed that Great Britain and its Empire, more than any other nation or area, were the key to the situation.

The New Deal, especially to critics, had sacrificed many of the freedoms of the "open" society at home in combating the depression. This may have been necessary, but conservatives and liberals alike felt the task of restoring an open world would be a more congenial task than further regimenting and "closing" American society. American opposition to Japan in the Far East was based on the Open Door Policy. The Japanese Co-Prosperity Sphere was the prime example of an attempt to fence off and hold in feudal subjugation an area which had always been thought of as America's farthest western frontier.

Similarly, the loss of major trading areas to Germany was a two-fold danger. Secretary Stimson's chief aide and speech writer, John J. McCloy, outlined this dual challenge in a final draft of one of these speeches: "With German control of the buyers of Europe and her practice of governmental control of all trade, it would be well within her power as well as the pattern she has thus far displayed, to shut off our trade with Europe, with South America and with the Far East."

So much for the immediate threat, he continued, "but more important than this, a victorious Germany could compel us to

spend year after year billions of dollars for our defense. . . .
What we now speak of as emergency expenditures would become
normal. All of which would lead to restrictions and the economic
and governmental controls which we abhor. In short, the fruits
of the economic gains which we have made in the last century
would be lost."[36]

McCloy went on to describe the fruits of the "last century" in
the human realm. They were: freedom, freedom of mind, spirit,
and body. It was necessary to protect the new frontiers, but they
could be protected only as a result of protecting the *past* frontier:
both its material and moral heritage.

Postwar planning began with such assumptions. Though nearly
everyone agreed that the Reciprocal Trade Agreements program
had been right in principle, it was, as Roosevelt had said, "too
goddamned slow." What was needed was some way to expand
the principle into broad reality. Still, Hull could be pleased that
he had outlasted the intra-nationalists and the NRA-AAA planning of the first two years of the New Deal. "The camel is not
too bright," he said to aides, "is slow moving and ruminating,
but after all—it carried a greater burden than a whole group of
asses."[37]

Central to such plans, however, was the problem of persuading
Great Britain to do away with the Ottawa Preferences and similar
appraches to the postwar world.[38] Washington feared that, instead
of being abandoned by British planners, the Ottawa system would
in fact be closed even tighter, as part of a British "New Deal."
Such concern spurred American policy-makers to make an effort
to get from London a pledge that all international discrimina-
tions would be discussed, pointing toward an end of bilateral
and imperial trade schemes. (Now the most powerful trading
nation in the world, as Britain had been the century before, the
United States asserted against its old economic rival the same
kinds of free-trade arguments British statesmen had once employed to have their way in an open world. The irony was perfect.) Though something approximating such a pledge was forced
on Great Britain in Article VII of the master Lend-Lease agreement of 1942, few in the State Department believed that the
matter could rest there without still firmer commitments and the

creation of actual international institutions to assure the restoration of the Great Society.

Certainly Lord Keynes' visit to Washington in the summer of 1941 did little to relieve such fears among State Department planners. The British economist and Treasury official gave Washington little hope that his countrymen would see their way to prosperity after the war by following the American blueprint for restored world trade. Certainly he did not. "This is just one more evidence," remarked one State Department officer, "that the future is clouding up rapidly and that despite the war the Hitlerian commercial policy will probably be adopted by Great Britain."[39]

The problem of world trade restoration was also discussed at Argentia, when Roosevelt and Prime Minister Winston Churchill sought to put out a joint statement of war aims to counter Axis proposals and propaganda. In Article IV of the Atlantic Charter there were references to postwar economic policy—but these were hedged by Churchill, who thus managed to put off even the limited commitment London later accepted in the Lend-Lease agreement.[40]

Even so, President Roosevelt tried to use the Atlantic Charter and his discussions with the Prime Minister when he talked with the Japanese Ambassador Tokyo had sent in a last-ditch attempt to avoid war with the United States. "The President elaborated on the point that, with regard to the question of non-discrimination," reported Ambassador Nomura, "he had agreed with Churchill . . . to abolish the economic limitations throughout the world; that he opposed Germany because Germany followed a policy contrary to this idea; and that he wished that the principle of non-discrimination would be applied throughout the world."[41]

Roosevelt obviously overstated any economic agreement he had reached with Churchill earlier.[42] Moreover, the President's comments on German trade policy were as much and probably more relevant to a description of American opposition to Japanese forward movements in Asia. Since 1931, when Secretary of State Stimson had first tried to dissuade Tokyo from its Manchurian ventures, using the Washington Naval Treaties of 1921-

1922 as the basis of a Japanese-American contractual arrangement in the Far East, succeeding policy-makers had all emphasized the reasonableness of non-discrimination and the Open Door Policy. Far from retreating out of Manchuria, however, Japan had then gone on into North China in the mid- and late 1930's. Secretary Hull told the special Congressional committee which later investigated the Pearl Harbor attack that Japanese attempts to establish a feudal overlordship in China had been at the center of the whole Japanese-American dispute:

> I had been trying to see whether it was humanly possible to find any way to approach the Japanese and prevail on them to abandon the movement of conquest. We had been urging the Japanese to consider their own future from the standpoint of political, economic and social aspects. The people of China were living on a very low standard. Japan, if it should conquer China, would keep China bled white and would not have the capital to aid in restoring purchasing power and social welfare. It meant everything for the development of that half of the world's population to use the capital of all nations such as the United States and other countries, in helping China, for example, to develop internal improvements and increase its purchasing power.[43]

Since early in the century, American Secretaries of State had known that the so-called Great China market would always remain a Marco Polo mirage at the other end of the Pacific Ocean unless the Chinese government was (1) strong enough to carry out reforms and modernize the weak central administration of the country; (2) secure from outside dangers from Russia and Japan; and (3) able to draw upon the major capital exporting countries to provide money for the basic facilities which would, in Hull's phrase, "increase its purchasing power." Japan's goals in Asia, it seemed to Washington, were to shut off China from the rest of the world and impose a special economic feudalism upon the whole area. And from that vantage point, Japan might then go on to dominate all of Southeast Asia. Most Americans expected that Japan would fail ultimately—but in the meantime Chinese development would have been set back perhaps irretrievably (at least under capitalism, for Hull specifically warned the Japanese of the bolshevist threat to China), but certainly longer than the United States was prepared to wait. "A war against America's best customer in Asia," wrote William L. Neumann recently, "was also a war for potentially the greatest future customer."[44] And, he might well have added, that was the Great American Dream of the century—which turned into the Great American Nightmare of the next two decades.

But even before the Japanese actually attacked Pearl Harbor, Washington had intervened dramatically in British-Russian discussions over postwar Europe. When Germany attacked the Soviet Union in the summer of 1941, the Nazi-Soviet Pact was pushed off the diplomatic chess table. A new player, Anthony Eden, went to Moscow to arrange the pieces for a new game. Witnessing this development in Washington, State Department officials grew worried that territorial and political agreements would be made to the detriment of American interests. And even though many policy-makers thought Germany would overrun Russia quite quickly, concern about Russian expansion, with British acquiescence, was an unspoken subject at the Atlantic Conference shortly thereafter. Fearing that an Anglo-Russian Treaty would be signed giving the Soviets a free hand in Eastern and Central Europe, Washington made known its strong opposition to such a pact on December 5, 1941—two days before the Japanese finally pushed the United States directly into the war.[45]

Instead of such political bargaining over the spoils, America offered Russia massive military aid—and a second front in Europe. But having taken up a hand in what had now become a three-handed poker game, more to American liking than the subtleties of chess, Roosevelt was not able to deliver a second front until 1944. Whatever the reason for this delay, whether military or political, it is now quite clear that the United States was opposed to any Anglo-Russian agreement that would bring the "Russian system considerably west of Vienna."[46] At war's end this issue centered in the future of Poland. That unhappy country came to symbolize both the cause of war with Germany, and chances for future Big Three cooperation. If it could be rebuilt on the ashes of World War II, a few United States policy-makers thought Russia might become an important customer for "surplus plant and equipment." Such hopes had been in back of the original 1933 decision to end the first "cold war" with the Soviet Union. In that decade they had not been realized.

By 1944 the vast expansion of American heavy industry threatened serious surpluses in the immediate postwar years.[47] Fully aware of this development and the general problem of preventing a new inflation-depression cycle at war's end, Roosevelt moved closer to Secretary Hull's original 1933 position. Both insisted that the major task for American planners was to re-establish the international system which had been smashed to pieces by the two wars.[48] Of course the reformers and the advances in general social security made by the New Deal were not to be abandoned; the President made it quite clear even during the war that they would have to be improved.* The Full Employment Act of 1946 was the culmination of New Deal efforts in this direction. Even conservative Republicans, though not without a good deal of internal dissension, had come around to this position by the 1940 Presidential campaign. At stake more than anything else that year was which party could better administer the reforms.†

"But it seems pretty clear," President Roosevelt assured newsmen after the Cairo and Teheran conferences, "that we must plan for, and help to bring about, an expanded economy which will result in more security . . . so that the conditions of 1932 and won't come back again."[49]

How this economy could expand when the country converted its war-swollen factories to peacetime endeavors became the para-

_____

* British Economic negotiators constantly warned their American opposites during the war that if England were to follow Washington's lead on international trade policies, there must be an assured commitment by the United States to maintaining the social security measures of the New Deal so that American businessmen and farmers would not be tempted to make up for recessions at home through export dumping. On the other hand, American planners assumed they must have constantly increasing exports to maintain full production and employment. (See Richard N. Gardner, *Sterling-Dollar Diplomacy*, for details.)

† The 1964 Republican candidate Barry Goldwater, the most conservative in several elections, tried mightily (if unsuccessfully) to dispel the notion that he would tamper with social security. By 1964 the New Deal had become an accepted foundation for both major political parties in the United States.

mount issue.[50] "So far as I know," Assistant Secretary of State Acheson advised Congress, "no group which has studied this problem, and there have been many, as you know, has ever believed that our domestic markets could absorb our entire production under our present system."[51]

A return to the NRA-AAA was thus said to be impossible. Roosevelt was haunted by this problem. After a trip to Hawaii and Alaska he explored with the Cabinet any possibilities for increased settlement of the latter "by returned veterans *and others.*" What kinds of crops could be grown in that climate, he asked the Agriculture and Interior Departments?[52] Farther away from the continental United States were still other frontiers which Roosevelt now thought the State Department had been slow to develop and exploit. Scolding the Department for not having acted sooner, the President suggested a plan for a world "Conservation Conference" to which each of the United Nations would send delegates. From that meeting, "we could get world information which is now lacking, and in a short period of time could begin a program to build up non-buying nations into good customers."[53]

The State Department was not lax, however, in setting forth United States determination to expand the Open Door Policy to the world. When a French diplomat opposed the American intrusion into the Levant question in the spring of 1945, arguing that United States economic power "had now become so colossal that if the Open Door Policy were followed . . . others would be unable to compete with us," he was cut off with the remark "that equality of opportunity was high on our list of war aims and that we had no intention of fighting this war and then abandoning our objectives."[54]

In a more persuasive vein, the United States led in the planning for several international conferences on postwar economic problems in 1944 and 1945. The most famous of these was the Bretton Woods Conference held in New Hampshire in the summer of 1944. Here delegates from all the United Nations, including the Soviet Union, assembled under the guidance of the United States Treasury Department to see if Anglo-American suggestions could not be formulated and put into operation through the creation of international institutions. It was hoped that the problems of bringing into full participation planned economies like that of Russia—or possibly planned Empires, if the British Commonwealth persisted in its "New Deal"—along with other nations could be overcome.[55]

Eventually the delegates agreed on the need for two major new institutions: the International Monetary Fund (IMF) and the International Bank for Reconstruction and Development (IBRD). Secretary of the Treasury Henry Morgenthau said later that he hoped "to erect new institutions which would be instrumentalities of sovereign governments and not of private financial interests."[56] To United States planners who had worked with Morgenthau, this declaration did not mean that since capitalism had failed to maintain the old international system, Bretton Woods was an attempt to legislate some new form of socialism internationally. It did mean that the state had to replace the invisible hand of Adam Smith. In 1933 the United States had similarly "national-ized" its own exporters through the creation of the Export-Import Bank. It had "nationalized" them in the sense that the United States began loaning credits to foreign nations to buy American goods instead of leaving the task up to private banks. It "na-tionalized" them in a different way also, in that the problems of the exporter now became national problems. Though this might have been true for many years prior to 1933 and the New Deal, it is well to note that the formal creation of the Export-Import Bank was a recognition of that situation by the New Deal. And this was further proof that even the intra-nationalism of that period was questionable.

Morgenthau made all this absolutely clear to Roosevelt and the Conference itself during its opening sessions: "The chief purpose of the Bank for International Reconstruction and De-velopment is to guarantee private loans made through the usual investment channels."[57]

The Bretton Woods proposals had, in Morgenthau's mind, an even larger purpose.[58] They were the culmination of the New Deal—its transformation into an international attack on poverty, unemployment, and world depression. Both motives were juxta-posed in other New Dealers as well, including Adolf Berle of the

First New Deal and Harry Hopkins of the so-called Second New Deal. The *bête-noire* of American conservatism in the late 1930's, Hopkins made the change from relief administrator to Secretary of Commerce, and then to special assistant to the President at the war-time conferences of the Big Three, with remarkable skill and perfect poise. And at the end of it all he and the former Liberty-Leaguer Will Clayton were in substantial agreement. Hopkins wrote to his fellow postwar planner, Clayton, now an Assistant Secretary of State: "I just cannot understand what is going through the minds of those fellows who wash up foreign trade in such cavalier manner. It seems to me they are quite unrealistic about what makes the wheels go round." And in a magazine article entitled "What Victory Will Bring Us," Hopkins expressed himself on foreign trade and investment almost as strongly as an earlier defender of private rights under the Fourteenth Amendment.[59]

At this point it would be well to pick up some of the later activities of Henry Wallace, for he is one of the strongest ties between 1933 and 1945 in American foreign policy thinking and planning. The Treasury Department recruited him to speak for the Bretton Woods program, providing him with speech drafts. "There can be no permanent prosperity in American heavy industry," he informed a meeting of "progressive" businessmen on November 2, 1944, "unless the world is the market. American heavy industry is the backbone of the consumer goods industry. The two together constitute jobs for all."[60]

Anything which Hopkins and Wallace were for, however, was still anathema to some conservatives. The more xenophobic, especially those whose trade patterns did not include much foreign commerce, were doubtful. Moreover, New Dealers stressed the reformist aspects of the new programs, giving opponents a chance to attack the international do-goodism of all postwar planning, including that of the United Nations. To counter this attack the Administration lined up powerful support from the American Banker's Association, the National Grange and other farm organizations, and the great labor unions. And the new Secretary of State, Edward R. Stettinius, a former U.S. Steel executive, refuted the charge several times, as in the following statement at Chicago: "Once in a while one of my business friends speaks to me of Government planning as if it were either ridiculous or dangerous. I reply that when I was in business planning was fundamental to successful management and I don't suppose things have changed since." Having settled that, the Secretary of State concluded: "The core of our whole post-war foreign economic program is the expansion of private trade and the encouragement of private enterprise, with such assistance as is required from the Government to maintain high levels of production and employment." [61]

The IMF and the International Bank, as well as the extension of the Reciprocal Trade Agreements Act, the increase in lending funds for the Export-Import Bank, and even the United Nations Organization itself, were all posited, in Washington's view, upon the foundation of an open world. An open world where America could constantly expand its foreign trade and investment under a generalized Open Door Policy supported by these international institutions was the primary goal of economic postwar planning. "In the field of international relations," Secretary of State James Byrnes said on August 26, 1945, "we have joined in a cooperative endeavor to construct an expanding world economy based on the liberal principles of private enterprise, non-discrimination, and reduced barriers to trade. The importance which we attach to this task derives from the firm conviction that a durable peace cannot be built on an economic foundation of exclusive blocs, discriminatory policies, prohibitive barriers, autarchy, and economic warfare." [62]

The closed economic blocs which Germany and Japan had attempted to expand into great spheres of influence had been crushed; Great Britain had been persuaded, sometimes with logic, sometimes with blunt pressure, to give up extreme Imperial planning in favor of an American-led international system. [63] In its heyday, England had led the world in demanding a free trade system; now the United States had taken on that role. But there was more than sentiment in this new relationship. Churchill's government, as well as the Labour government which succeeded it in the summer of 1945, depended upon the United States for political and military support as well.

What about Russia? Where did the totally planned economy of the Soviet system fit into Anglo-American postwar plans? As suggested above, there were some officials in Washington (not at all of the bleeding heart, liberal, or parlor-pink nightmares of Whittaker Chambers, *et al.*) who looked upon Russia as a possible outlet for heavy goods exports in the postwar transition period. More important to American plans, however, was the question of how Russia would take to the whole system. If the Soviets proved agreeable, matters would go much more smoothly and so Russia had been asked to many of the 1944 preparatory conferences.

There were many who thought that the chances for such agreement were pretty slim and felt that the Soviet system was just as dangerous, perhaps more so, than either the German or Japanese. In between these positions, most American policymakers shared Cordell Hull's deep suspicions about the Soviet Union. Even in 1933, when the United States had needed every foreign market it could secure, Hull had been doubtful about diplomatic recognition; he never lost these fears.[64]

It didn't help matters that because of such distrust, Russia had never been brought into the Anglo-American secret about the development of the atomic bomb. If the Allies did not trust one another enough to open contacts on this matter of creating a weapon capable of destroying cities, it was unlikely that other matters could be easily resolved.

In this clouded atmsophere, the Polish and Eastern European questions arose. Since 1942 the United States had promised a second front against Germany as an alternative to political bargaining. Not until very late in the game, June 1944, could this promise be fulfilled, but already disagreements had arisen about the Italian surrender. In the summer of 1944, Churchill decided that the political question could not be put off. In the fall of 1944, the British Prime Minister and Stalin struck a bargain over the Balkans. The United States held aloof.

Then, in January 1945, the Polish question came to a head. To many in the West it mattered little whether the Russians were trying to colonize Poland for security reasons or for international communism. The end result would be the same. After Roosevelt died, President Truman sent Harry Hopkins on a special mission to Moscow to find out just what the Soviet Union did intend. The Polish question, Hopkins told the Russian Premier, was symbolic rather than material. "Our whole foreign policy has been reoriented, reimplemented," Dean Acheson was telling the American people in a radio broadcast about this time. "It's not simply the charter, but the whole pattern of cooperation that has emerged—Bretton Woods, the reciprocal trade act, and the others—that will really make it possible to deal with some of the causes of wars and depressions."[65]

Following a temporary agreement on the composition of a new Polish government, the United States tried to make this pattern work in that country. These plans failed. The United States had once again wanted an Open Door Policy and continuation of traditional reciprocal trade treaties, so essential to the functioning of multilateral international commerce.[66]

Russian Foreign Minister V. M. Molotov answered the demand for equal access to Poland and Eastern Europe in a 1946 statement on the national rights of Eastern European countries; rights, of course, which the Soviets had more concern about in rhetoric than in policy, as they would demonstrate brutally over the next decades.

The principle of so-called equal opportunity has become a favorite topic of late. What, it is argued, could be better than this principle, which would establish equal opportunity for all states without discrimination? . . . Let us discuss the principle of equality seriously and honestly. . . .

[Take] Rumania, enfeebled by the war, or Yugoslavia, ruined by the German and Italian fascists, and the United States of America, whose wealth has grown immensely during the war, and you will clearly see what the implementation of the principle of "equal opportunity" would mean in practice. Imagine, under these circumstances, that in this same Rumania or Yugoslavia, or in some other war-weakened state, you have this so-called equal opportunity for, let us say, American capital—that is, the opportunity for it to penetrate unhindered into Rumanian industry, or Yugoslav industry and so forth: what, then, will remain of Rumania's national industry, or of Yugoslavia's national industry?[67]

In the first weeks after Roosevelt's death, there were still two or three in the cabinet who argued that Russian cooperation with the United States might still be a possibility under certain conditions. Henry Morgenthau was one: he believed that the United States should extend to Russia credits equaling the six billion dollars granted to Great Britain. But his plan was based on the assumption that Russia would grant the United States guaranteed access to certain strategic raw materials and commit itself to purchases of consumer goods in this country. The proposal, he argued, would constitute a "major step in your program to provide 60 million jobs in the postwar period."[68]

Henry Wallace, now Secretary of Commerce, was another. But he also assumed that Russia was interested in furthering American plans for the Great Society. To begin with, Wallace wanted commercial air stops in Siberia in order to open the door to Asia once and for all.[69]

In the reassessment of the politico-military situation undertaken shortly after Roosevelt's death, Truman's advisers more and more doubted the wisdom of encouraging Russia to enter the Far Eastern war. Those who had some idea of the power of nuclear weaponry wanted to reverse the position taken after Pearl Harbor. Ironically enough, the atomic bombs dropped on Japan telescoped Asian difficulties, especially in China, and did not get the war over before the Russians could enter Manchuria. If anything, the atomic bomb actually lessened chances for stability in Asia.

Despite doubts expressed by Morgenthau, Wallace, and even Henry L. Stimson upon occasion, it was quickly decided to insist upon a hard line against Russia in Eastern Europe.[70] There was a genuine fear of Russian-inspired communist revolutions spreading from that area into Western Europe. Though not willing to try and push the Red Army out of areas it had won from the Nazis, Truman told Molotov as early as April 23, 1945, that unless Russia came to terms on the Polish issue—i.e., accepted the British-U.S. understanding of the Yalta agreement on that country's government—and worked with the Western allies at the San Francisco Conference, Washington would go ahead with post-war plans without the Soviet Union.[71]

And while the Administration was not willing to challenge the Red Army directly in 1945, it could not be said that the United States simply yielded a sphere of influence to Stalin without any fuss at all. The Morgenthau proposal for a multi-billion-dollar credit to Russia, as well as a similar application from the Russians themselves, were pushed into the background and then lost. Plans for selling heavy goods to Russia thus had to be abandoned; indeed, ways of curtailing strategic trade items soon began to be considered. An attempt to secure international control of atomic energy, as proposed by the United States at the United Nations, thus had very little chance from the beginning.

In these circumstances, the American effort to rebuild Europe from the ashes of World War II took on political significance long before the Marshall Plan. By February 1947, however, the situation had reached crisis proportions. "There are many signs that the world is approaching this year the greatest crisis since the turn in the tide of the war in November 1942," wrote a State Department aide to Senator William Benton.

It is primarily an economic crisis centered in Britain and Empire, France, Greece and China. . . . If these areas are allowed to spiral downwards into economic anarchy, then at best they will drop out of the United States orbit and try an independent nationalistic policy; at most they will swing into the Russian orbit. We will then face the world alone. What will be the cost in dollars and cents of our armaments and of our economic isolation? I do not see how we could possibly avoid a depression far greater than that of 1929-1932 and crushing taxes to pay for the direct commitments we would be forced to make around the world.[72]

This conflict had already begun by the time of the Potsdam Conference in July 1945. There had been exchanges over the future of Anglo-American oil interests in Rumania, and proposals to put economic pressure on Russia to protect those properties.[73] One development led to another. Secretary Stimson complained: "The Russian policy on booty in Eastern Germany is rather

oriental. It is bound to force us to preserve the economy in Western Germany in close cooperation with the British, so as to
avoid conditions in our areas which, in the last analysis, neither
British nor American public opinion would long tolerate."[74]

Every analysis, in fact, from that of John J. McCloy in 1940
that "the fruits of the economic gains which we have made in the
last century would be lost," to Dean Acheson's in 1944 and 1945
that, "It's not simply the charter, but the whole pattern . . . that
will make it possible to deal with some of the causes of wars and
depressions," to that in 1947, "What will be the cost in dollars
and cents of our armaments and of our economic isolation?"—
every analysis pointed in the same direction.

At Potsdam Truman refused all of Stalin's attempts to secure
final diplomatic recognition of his "friendly" states in Eastern
Europe. The Russian Premier just as firmly drew the line against
the American proposal for internationalization of major European waterways. Across these lines, Cold War formations were
being drawn into battle array. Truman was "very greatly reinforced" by news that the atomic bomb had been tested successfully in New Mexcio. And Stimson recalled that he was now
confident of "sustaining the Open Door Policy."[75]

And that feeling was not limited to China. "Every time the
Soviet Union extends its power over another area or state," wrote
William C. Bullitt in 1946, "the United States and Great Britain
lose another normal market."[76] Bullitt had been America's first
Ambassador to the Soviet Union. He had gone to Moscow full of
hopes, but grew disillusioned with the impossibility of dealing
profitably with Soviet monopolies in foreign trade or with the
Russian government in any way. The atomic bomb had not
preserved the Open Door Policy, which helped to move Bullitt
politically from the "Left" to the "Right." Other American
liberals, although they did not move in this direction, shared
variations of the same feeling. "The San Francisco Charter is
promising in its possibilities," Oswald Garrison Villard wrote to
Cordell Hull, "but I think you will agree with me that it will fail
to achieve its end if economic nationalism is not done away with
and every barrier to freedom of trade removed."[77]

This meeting of "Left" and "Right"—between Bullitt and

Villard, between Will Clayton and Harry Hopkins—on the crucial question of postwar economic policy would soon overshadow smaller differences among them.

There was already, I would suggest, a consensus in 1945, not necessarily at the level of immediate agreement on the way to meet the Russian-Communist challenge, that an open frontier must be maintained. For some it was mainly a simple concern that American foreign trade be expanded to prevent a new depression; for others it was equally a question of opposition to totalitarianism. But both groups shared a belief in values associated in their minds with an "open society." In American experience this had always been connected with expansion—expansion into new frontiers. This consensus was as present in 1933 as it was in 1945. Sometimes it created tensions among and within American policy-makers, yet it was always the dominant motif. It was indeed a collective memory of American society, one that haunted the present and future as well.

On September 12, 1946, Secretary of Commerce Henry A. Wallace went to New York to address a rally of progressives who were deeply disturbed by the breakdown in Soviet-American relations. Most of them believed it was the result of a triumph of "reaction" in America. Wallace was one of the few New Dealers left in power, and his statements seemed to make him their ally. The outlines of the "Containment Thesis" were already visible at the time Wallace spoke in Madison Square Garden. To fellow Cabinet members, Wallace was too far outside those outlines. His speech that evening confirmed their desire to be rid of the man.

Almost anything he had said, one comes to feel, would have had such an effect. But Wallace did say that he believed cooperation with Russia had not been given a fair chance; that "getting tough . . . never brought anything real and lasting—whether for schoolyard bullies or businessmen or world powers. The tougher we get, the tougher the Russians will get."

Hinting that reactionary elements in the United States actually were behind many of the troubles in relations between the two countries, Wallace pleaded for a "spirit of openmindedness and flexible give-and-take." This speech so infuriated Secretary of

State James F. Byrnes and Secretary of the Navy Forrestal that it brought about Wallace's immediate resignation. His removal purified and completed the development of the Cold War policy.

To stop there (as is often done), however, is to give a bad and misleading interpretation of the Madison Square Garden speech. The Secretary of Commerce had also said: "We cannot permit the door to be closed against our trade in Eastern Europe any more than we can in China."[78] While he was willing to see the world divided politically, he could not abandon all his other assumptions about the world market and the international frontier. And no matter how Wallace (and many other opponents of the Cold War) tried to square this circle, those running the American foreign policy machine always had the final word; for how could the United States maintain the Open Door without the "Containment Thesis" and the strategic military force to back it up?

It was a wrenching experience for American liberalism; Wallace, like many others, was besieged on one side by his conviction that the United States must try harder to get along with the Soviets, and on the other by his typical reliance upon "Newer" Frontiers. "I want to say that I have considerable sympathy with Herbert Hoover's problem as Secretary of Commerce right now," he told Congressmen at the hearing on his nomination to that post,

> because . . . I am going to go all-out . . . to foster and develop trade. . . . I am going to use those powers [of the Department] to the maximum to get an increase in foreign trade and, undoubtedly, there will be a great excess for . . . five or . . . ten years . . . of exports over imports, and here I would be contributing perhaps as much as any single individual in the United States in doing exactly the same thing I criticized . . . back in . . . the Twenties. I say, from the standpoint of the United States and the whole world, that the thing ought to be done. . . .[79]

On a later occasion, Wallace denounced Chiang Kai-shek for fostering "a backward feudal rule which has kept China's 400,-000,000 from being the good customers they should be. . . ."[80] Following Commerce Secretary Wallace's economic advice, the

United States increased its annual exports by more than 100 percent between 1945 and 1957, from $10,097 million to $20,989 million. More significantly, this last figure was more than ten times the 1933 total of $2,061 million. Great as these figures were, however, the percentage totals of American exports as compared to the Gross National Product actually declined from 4.9 percent to 4.7 percent.[81] America's economy after 1945 reached unprecedented levels of prosperity, but it was always bolstered by government spending, especially in the defense sector. Export figures by themselves do not reveal the whole impact of the vast overseas expansion upon the American economy since the war. American direct investments help to fill in the picture: In 1946 these totaled $7.2 billion, slightly less than 1929; by 1950 that figure had climbed to $11.8 billion, by 1955 to $19.3 billion, by 1959 to $29.7 billion. Moreover, most of this investment was going into manufacturing and petroleum.[82] Total investments, including foreign securities and government investments, rose from $18,693 million in 1946 to $64,779 million in 1959.[83]

No less than American businessmen, American liberals insisted that there was only one path to human liberation—of the body and of the spirit—the modified free enterprise New Deal, New Frontier, Great Society way. Americans were occasionally embarrassed when such requirements were written into foreign aid programs too blatantly, or when Pentagon representatives openly peddled arms exports to help maintain the balance of payments. Until the Vietnam War, however, few challenged the basic premise. But by the mid-1960's, the United States had been fighting for more than twenty-five years in Asia, the oldest of the New Frontiers. There was some evidence that a new re-examination of old assumptions and premises might be underway. What directions American policy might take, if it could free itself from the jungles and swamps of Indo-China, was very much an open question. One thing seemed clear: the continued outward push of the American economy was now confronted not by rival imperialisms as in the 1930's so much as by the nationalist and communist revolutions of the 1960's. The old answers offered by American policy-makers in the former era were no longer applicable.

Notes

1. Walter Lippmann, *The Method of Freedom* (New York, 1934).
2. *Ibid.,* p. 23.
3. *Ibid.,* p. 27.
4. *Ibid.,* pp. 105-106.
5. *Ibid.*
6. Reprinted in Lloyd C. Gardner, ed., *A Different Frontier: Selected Readings in the Foundations of American Economic Expansion* (Chicago: Quadrangle Books, 1966), pp. 132-133.
7. *Ibid.*
8. For an introduction to this idea, see Walter LaFeber, "The American Business Community and Cleveland's Venezuelan Message," *Business History Review,* Winter 1960, pp. 393-402.
9. See Gardner, *A Different Frontier,* Parts II and III.
10. Quoted in *A Different Frontier,* p. 90.
11. Quoted in William Appleman Williams, *The Tragedy of American Diplomacy* (New York: Delta Books, 1962), p. 148.
12. Quoted in Thomas McCormick, "Insular Imperialism and the Open Door: The China Market and the Spanish-American War," *Pacific Historical Review,* May 1963, pp. 155-169.
13. On this point, see Joseph Schumpeter, *Imperialism and Social Classes* (New York: Meridian, 1955), pp. 72-73.
14. Lloyd C. Gardner, *Economic Aspects of New Deal Diplomacy* (Madison: University of Wisconsin Press, 1964), p. 21.
15. Professor Elliot A. Rosen in his excellent article, "Intranationalism vs. Internationalism," *Political Science Quarterly,* June 1966, pp. 274-296, has now given us the most detailed study of the Brain Trust victory over an increasingly "wobbly" Franklin Roosevelt and internationalists such as Norman Davis and Henry L. Stimson. But we must not go too far with this idea. The basic disagreement was a tactical one, even though each side warned of dire results if the other's tactics were adopted. As Rosen says: "The brain trusters believed that international negotiations could succeed only after domestic conditions had been improved here and abroad." The present author also took this position in *Economic Aspects of New Deal Diplomacy,* Chaps. I and II.
16. Rexford Tugwell, *The Battle for Democracy* (New York: Columbia University Press, 1935), p. 75. See also his article, "The New Deal: The Available Instruments of Governmental Power," in *Western Political Quarterly,* December 1949, pp. 545-580. Of all the major New Deal

figures, Tugwell was clearly the most consistent advocate of national planning.

17. A. A. Berle, "Business and Government," *Scribners*, November 1934, pp. 258-265. See also A. A. Berle, "What's Behind the Recovery Laws," *Scribners*, September 1933, pp. 129-135; "High Finance: Master or Servant," *Yale Review*, September 1933, pp. 20-43; "Ready Money," *Survey Graphic*, April 14, 1934, pp. 625-626.

18. "Private Business and Public Opinion," *Scribners*, February 1934, pp. 81-87.

19. "Progress Under the National Industrial Recovery Act," *Academy of Political Science Proceedings*, January 1934, pp. 393-401.

20. Warren I. Susman, "The Useless Past: American Intellectuals and the Frontier Thesis: 1910-1930," *Bucknell Review*, March 1963, pp. 1-21. Susman points to a pioneering effort by Curtis P. Nettels to relate the frontier theme to what New Dealers were saying and doing in the latter's article, "Frederick Jackson Turner and the New Deal," *Wisconsin Magazine of History*, March 1934, pp. 257-265.

21. George Soule, "The New Internationalism," *Harper's*, February 1934, pp. 357-366. New Dealers considered nonsensical such statements as the following one on the floor of Congress by Millard Tydings: "In my judgment, the unemployment today is directly attributable to the loss of the foreign market, because the calculations work out exactly to an apex. . . . And when we get back $5,000,000,000 a year worth of new orders we will put back to work 10,000,000 people who are now out of employment." *Congressional Record*, April 24, 1933, 73rd Cong., 1st sess., vol. 77, part 2, p. 2236. Later on, however, many of them made something of the same kind of equation.

22. The following will introduce the reader to some of Wallace's writings on the subject: *America Must Choose* (1934); *New Frontiers* (1934); *The American Choice* (1940); *Sixty-Million Jobs* (1945).

23. See Forrestal's comments in a "Memorandum of a Cabinet Meeting," September 21, 1945, in Walter Millis, ed., *The Forrestal Diaries* (New York: Viking Press, 1951), pp. 95-96

24. Henry A. Wallace, "American Agriculture and World Markets," *Foreign Affairs Quartely*, January 1934, pp. 216-230; Diary Entry, October 27, 1933 in The Papers of Henry L. Stimson, Sterling Library, Yale University, New Haven, Connecticut (hereafter called *Stimson MSS.*).

25. Wallace to F.D.R., November 7, 1935: National Archives of the United States, Washington, D.C., State Department file no. 711.61/322.

26. *America Must Choose*, p. 5.

27. Radio Address, April 29, 1934. Quoted in Henry L. Stimson and McGeorge Bundy, *On Active Duty in Peace and War* (New York: Harper Brothers, 1948), p. 299.

28. Francis B. Sayre, *America Must Choose* (Boston: World Peace Foundation, 1936), pp. 36-37.

29. John M. Blum, *From the Morgenthau Diaries* (Boston: Houghton Mifflin, 1959), p. 392-393.

30. *Ibid.,* p. 524.

31. Stimson to White, January 2, 1940: *Stimson MSS.*

32. Gardner, *Economic Aspects of New Deal Diplomacy,* p. 152.

33. "The Fifth Fortune Round Table," *Fortune,* January 1940, pp. 70-72.

34. Wallace, *The American Choice,* p. 141.

35. Gardner, *Economic Aspects of New Deal Diplomacy,* p. 106.

36. Speech draft, August 1941: *Stimson MSS.*

37. "Notes on a Visit to Washington, July 10-12, 1941," in The Papers of J. Pierrepont Moffat, Houghton Library, Harvard University, Cambridge, Massachusetts (hereafter called *Moffat MSS.).*

38. See the discussions and debates as reviewed in Richard N. Gardner, *Sterling-Dollar Diplomacy* (Oxford: Oxford University Press, 1956), especially Chaps. I-IV.

39. Moffat Notes, July 10-12, 1941: *Moffat MSS.*

40. Moffat Notes, September 24, 1941: *Ibid.* Accounts of the Atlantic Charter conversations are plentiful. The most dramatic may be Eliot Roosevelt, *As He Saw It* (New York: Asia Publishing House, 1947). But for that reason these recollections should be treated carefully. See Gardner, *Economic Aspects of New Deal Diplomacy,* pp. 171-173.

41. Nomura to Tokyo, November 10, 1941: Joint Committee on the Investigation of the Pearl Harbor Attack, *Hearings,* 79th Cong., 1st Sess. (39 parts; Washington, 1948), part 12, pp. 115-116.

42. Notes, September 24, 1941: *Moffat MSS.* Hull felt strongly "that the President and Welles did not get a sufficient commitment from Churchill in Point IV of the Atlantic Charter to bind Britain to economic liberalism."

43. Pearl Harbor Attack, *Hearings,* part 2, p. 413.

44. *America Encounters Japan: From Perry to MacArthur* (New York: Harper Colophon Books, 1965), p. 227. And see all of Chapter XI for this paradoxical—yet persistent—American attitude about China and the Far East.

45. Gardner, *Economic Aspects of New Deal Diplomacy,* pp. 295-302.

46. *Ibid.*

47. Lauchlin Currie, Foreign Economic Administration, to Harry L. Hopkins, December 31, 1943: The Papers of Harry L. Hopkins, Franklin D. Roosevelt Library, Hyde Park, New York (hereafter called *Hopkins MSS.*). On this point, see also Herbert Feis, *Churchill, Roosevelt, Stalin: The War They Waged and the Peace They Sought* (Princeton: Princeton University Press, 1957), pp. 641, 644.

48. See Diary Entry, December 18, 1940: *Stimson MSS.*

49. Press Conference No. 929, December 28, 1943: The Papers of Franklin D. Roosevelt, Franklin D. Roosevelt Library, Hyde Park, New York (hereafter called *Roosevelt MSS.*).

50. Cf. C. Hartley Gratton and George R. Leighton, "The Future of Foreign Trade," *Harper's*, August 1944, pp. 193-202. Donald M. Nelson is quoted here: "Unless we can develop a broad export market for capital goods, I don't see the opportunity for them to be prosperous. We've got to have them in a healthy condition if the entire economy is to be prosperous." See also Herbert Feis, "Economics and Peace," *Foreign Policy Reports*, April 1944, pp. 14-19. William L. Clayton, former Liberty-Leaguer turned New Deal internationalist told the 1943 National Foreign Trade Convention that the alternative to greater foreign trade was "to turn our country into an armed camp, police the seven seas, tighten our belts, and live by ration books for the next century or so." *Foreign Commerce Weekly*, November 20, 1943, p. 11. These are merely representative articles. A detailed discussion is in Gardner, *Economic Aspects of New Deal Diplomacy*, chap. XIII.

51. Special Committee on Post-War Economic Policy and Planning, *Economic Problems of the Transition Period*, 78th Cong., 2nd Sess. (Washington, 1945), pp. 1081-1082.

52. Memorandum for the Secretary of War: Notes of a Cabinet Meeting, August 18, 1944: *Stimson MSS.*

53. F.D.R. to Under-Secretary of State, November 22, 1944: *Roosevelt MSS.*

54. Memorandum, March 10, 1945: The Papers of Joseph Grew, Harvard University, Cambridge, Massachusetts.

55. Cf. Gardner, *Sterling-Dollar Diplomacy.*

56. *New York Herald-Tribune*, March 31, 1946; quoted in *Ibid.*, p. 76.

57. Morgenthau to F.D.R., July 23, 1944: *Roosevelt MSS.*

58. See Morgenthau, "Bretton Woods and International Cooperation," *Foreign Affairs Quarterly*, January 1945, pp. 182-194.

59. Clayton to Hopkins, November 18, 1944 and Hopkins to Clayton, November 20, 1944: *Hopkins MSS*. And see Hopkins's article, "What Victory Will Bring Us," *American Magazine,* January 1944, pp. 1 ff.

60. Quoted in the *Congressional Record,* 79th Cong., 1st Sess., vol. 91, part 10 (appendix), pp. 47-48.

61. *Congressional Record,* vol. 91, part 11, pp. 1656-1658.

62. State Department, *Bulletin,* August 26, 1945, pp. 279-280.

63. In England, left-wing economist Thomas Balogh was highly critical of Keynes's conversion. See "The League of Nations on Post-War Foreign Trade," *Economics Journal,* June 1944, pp. 256-261 and "Britain's Foreign Trade," *Economics Journal,* March 1948, pp. 74-85.

64. Gardner, *Economic Aspects of New Deal Diplomacy,* pp. 314-315.

65. State Department, *Bulletin,* August 5, 1945, pp. 181-188.

66. Gardner, *Economic Aspects of New Deal Diplomacy,* pp. 311-313.

67. V. M. Molotov, *Problems of Foreign Policy: Speeches and Statements,* April 1945-November 1948 (Moscow, 1949), pp. 207-214.

68. Gardner, *Economic Aspects of New Deal Diplomacy,* p. 315.

69. *Sixty-Million Jobs,* pp. 74-75, 138.

70. For details on the crucial cabinet meeting of April 23, 1945, see Stimson Diary for that date: *Stimson MSS*.

71. *Ibid.,* and Gardner, *Economic Aspects of New Deal Diplomacy,* p. 308.

72. Joseph M. James to William Benton, February 26, 1947; cited in Henry Berger, "A Conservative Critique of Containment," in David Horowitz, ed. *Containment and Revolution* (Boston: The Beacon Press, 1967).

73. See Herbert Feis, "Political Aspects of Foreign Loans," *Foreign Affairs Quarterly,* July 1945, pp. 609-619.

74. Memorandum for the President, July 22, 1945: *Stimson MSS*.

75. Notes for Diary, July 15-24, 1945: *Ibid.*

76. *The Great Globe Itself* (New York: Scribners, 1946), p. 121.

77. Villard to Hull, August 2, 1945: The Papers of Oswald Garrison Villard, Houghton Library, Harvard University, Cambridge, Massachusetts.

78. Reprinted in Norman Graebner, *Ideas and Diplomacy* (New York: Oxford University Press, 1964), pp. 701-705.

79. *New York Times,* January 26, 1945.

80. *Ibid.,* May 22, 1948.

81. From tables in *The Statistical History of the United States: From Colonial Times to the Present* (New York: Horizon Press, 1965), pp. 537, 542.

82. From tables in Raymond Mikesell, ed., *U.S. Private and Government Investment Abroad* (Eugene: University of Oregon Press, 1962), pp. 55, 56.

83. *Ibid.*

Business Planners and America's Postwar Expansion
by David W. Eakins

In his essay, Lloyd Gardner discusses an important element of
the thought of key New Deal officials: the attainment of New
Frontiers abroad as a solution to overproduction and unemployment at home. During the war many government officials both of
the "left" and the "right" came to agree, Gardner says, that the
government could sustain American prosperity only by helping
to expand overseas trade and investment. The unrelenting pursuit of that expansionist objective later provided the impetus
behind (and gave the real content to) the Cold War.

By 1945, new consensus among policy-makers on the magical
foreign solution for the achievement of domestic prosperity had
been reached. That consensus was not simply the outcome of
discussions among government officials; its source was also in
the business community. It came out of a working coalition of
corporate liberal businessmen, government officials, and academi-
cians, all of whom often played several of those roles simultaneously. A number of businessmen, for example, entered
government service after a term on the New Deal's Business
Advisory Council, while academics lent their expertise to both
business and government in the shaping of corporate liberal
policies. The businessmen involved frequently supported (in
fact, often helped draw up and implement) major New Deal
measures. Their liberalism was grounded in a class-conscious
desire to sustain and stabilize a healthy American capitalist
system. They were not primarily concerned with humanitarianism
or the rhetoric of political liberalism, but desired policy changes
in order to guarantee profits for the American corporation.
To these men reform meant government-supported economic
growth and an end to depression and class warfare; it meant a

corporatist cooperation among government, business, farmers, and labor.

However, these corporate liberals also feared an expanded New Deal type of planning that would concentrate on a domestic solution to domestic problems and in the immediate postwar years these men worked out a plan that would accomplish the sort of economic growth they wanted. They proposed the "nationalization" of the American export industry; but even that, they felt, was not enough. Capital had to be exported on a much larger scale than that provided by the orthodox expansion of trade. The solution developed by the corporate liberal coalition of businessmen, government officials, and academic experts was foreign aid. The politics of Cold War not only initially sold the new program, but also provided the enduring context of crisis in which the program could exist on the scale necessary for success. Having shaped the program, the business-led corporate liberals were called upon to administer it. Their program was secure. So, too, was their hegemony.

The history of the planning of the postwar economic expansion is best understood by viewing some of the business-created agencies that planned it. These were private organizations such as the National Planning Association, the Twentieth Century Fund, and the Committee for Economic Development. They were all organized by corporate liberal businessmen (two at the end of the Progressive Era and one during World War II) and were widely acknowledged as impartial and objective research groups. They served as a meeting ground for business, the government, and the academic expert. The significance of these groups is not only their role as planners of postwar economic policy, but also the part they played in implementing that policy.

Two of these groups were involved in postwar planning even before Pearl Harbor; the third, the Committee for Economic Development, was organized a few months after the war began. The National Planning Association and the Twentieth Century Fund had supported most of the New Deal program, but the NPA, which was organized as the National Economic and Social Planning Association in 1934, had been critical of the New

Deal for not engaging in more far-reaching national planning. However, the outbreak of war in Europe and the impact of defense spending on the depression economy brought a change of emphasis in the organization. In early 1941 businessmen William L. Batt and Charles E. Wilson took over the group, changed its name to the National Planning Association, and concentrated on planning for America's new role in the postwar world. Although both NPA and the Twentieth Century Fund were dominated and financed by businessmen, their policy studies were produced by committees of businessmen, labor leaders, government officials, and, sometimes, farm organization leaders.

The Committee for Economic Development, on the other hand, was established out of a desire to raise an unadulterated business voice in discussions of postwar planning. Roosevelt's conservative Texan Secretary of Commerce Jesse Jones was a key figure in its creation. He feared that if business did not create a national organization to develop a postwar program based on what industry "can do for itself," then it "will find that many others are prepared with plans which may or may not embrace the business point of view."[1] This did not imply, however, a rejection of business-government cooperation. It was, after all, the Secretary of Commerce who took the lead in urging businessmen to define the course of postwar planning. Moreover, the Committee for Economic Development was the direct result of business participation in the New Deal, and it was constituted, with only one or two exceptions, from the membership of the Business Advisory Council of the Department of Commerce.

That council, which functioned from its creation in 1933 until 1935 as the Business Advisory and Planning Council, was composed of some sixty business leaders who served without pay. It was charged with considering questions raised by the President and the Secretary of Commerce, and with acting "as a clearing house for industrial views on governmental matters which affect business."[2] The first council chairman was the ubiquitous Owen D. Young; early members included such men as Henry I. Harriman and his son W. Averell Harriman, Pierre S. DuPont, Charles F. Kettering, Gerard Swope, E. R. Stettinius, Juan Trippe, William L. Clayton, William L. Batt, Henry S.

Dennison, Ralph Flanders, Marion Folsom, T. J. Watson, and Donald Nelson. The group was originally seen as a pool of talent to staff the Industrial Advisory Board of the National Recovery Administration,[3] whose administrative board was also headed by a council member (S. Clay Williams, Council Chairman for 1934), as was the Agricultural Adjustment Administration (Chester C. Davis). Other council members held posts on the advisory body responsible for the drafting of the Social Security Act, on the first National Labor Board, the National Resources Planning Board, the Export-Import Bank, and on a number of other government agencies during the 1930's. Council members literally flooded into government posts during World War II. Thomas B. McCabe, a CED graduate of the council, estimated in 1949 (when he was serving as chairman of the Board of Governors of the Federal Reserve System) that the Business Advisory Council had supplied "almost 100 men from industry to government since 1933."[4] It was this business-government cooperation in policy-making and the feeling that businessmen could shape the direction of postwar planning that stimulated the formation of the Committee for Economic Development. As S. Clay Williams wrote Jesse Jones, CED promised "a new comfort and effectiveness in the relationships of government and business."[5]

The early activities of CED further demonstrated that "new comfort." After the incorporation of the committee in September 1942, Carroll Wilson was granted a paid leave of absence from his important post as director of the Commerce Department's Bureau of Foreign and Domestic Commerce to serve as executive secretary and assistant treasurer of CED. The committee was given a number of rooms on the fifth floor of the Commerce Department building so that it could be close to the office of the Undersecretary of Commerce, Wayne C. Taylor, who spent much of his time working with CED. CED trustee Will Clayton exemplified another aspect of the relationship with government. From 1940 to 1942, while he and others were in the process of organizing the group, he served as a vice-president of the Export-Import Bank, and in 1942 he became an Assistant Secretary of Commerce. Later he moved to the State Department as Undersecretary for Economic Affairs.

CED immediately engaged in a variety of well-publicized activities and issued a series of studies and reports on the problems of reconversion and full employment. Political liberals were at first dismayed. "Look Who's Planning!" cried an article in the *New Republic* of July 1943 in which the author attempted to equate CED with the National Association of Manufacturers and the National Industrial Conference Board. "Rich Man's Tax Program" was the label pinned on CED tax proposals by another *New Republic* writer. But a rebuttal to that article by the CED researcher, University of Wisconsin Professor Harold M. Groves, was printed without comment, and in subsequent months the *New Republic* found things to praise about CED—including its proposals on the Bretton Woods Conference in 1944. By 1945 the criticism had faded away.[6] The *Nation* carried one critical editorial in 1944 on the CED tax proposals but dropped the subject after printing Keith Hutchinson's good-humored piece, "Heresy in High Places," in October 1945. The CED report, "Toward More Jobs and More Freedom," was not only an important document, Hutchinson wrote, but it was "historic" because "it provides proof that some of the basic concepts of Keynesian economics have at last penetrated into the upper stratum of American business society." He concluded by reporting that conservative economist Henry Hazlitt found the report a "'most disheartening development' and I . . . understand his dismay. When economic heresy spreads to such quarters, where is it going to stop?"[7]

This "economic heresy," which was shared by all the corporate liberal policy-planning groups, was largely motivated by fear of a postwar depression. If full employment was to be maintained after the war (and any other alternative was unthinkable), then peacetime jobs had to be found for twenty million defense workers and ten million servicemen. Moreover, the shift would have to be made quickly—possibly within a year or two. New Dealer Leon Henderson emphasized the awesome nature of this task: "We have never been able to re-employ, even on the upbeam, more than four million men in one year."[8]

A second and intimately related problem was how to use

the productive capacity created by the stimulus of war. That capacity, it should be recalled, had not come into being automatically. Before Pearl Harbor the business community had been divided on the question of developing basic war production. At the outset of the defense effort, the National Planning Association pointed out in its *Guides for Postwar Planning* (November 1941) that some businessmen feared a postwar "depression making even 1929-33 a tea party by comparison. 'Business as usual,' " the NPA asserted, "became a slogan that identified industrial reluctance to expand." The NPA authors commented caustically that those "businessmen who had learned how to survive profitably in a society with ten million or more unemployed had nightmares envisioning the possibility of excess plant capacity and high fixed charges when 'normalcy returned.' "[9]

This reluctance evaporated, however, as the war brought "cost plus" contracts, federal financing of nearly half of the war production plant, the confidence of patriotism, and unprecedented civilian support of the war effort. During 1944, the last full year of the war, the Gross National Product climbed to $211 billion. This was a real increase of 60 percent over 1940, even though federal expenditures accounted for nearly half this sum.[10] The compelling questions for postwar planners concerned the level of national income that could be sustained when federal war spending dropped off, and whether or not the gap could be filled by private investment and consumption.

Given the years of depression pessimism, the forecasts of the corporate liberal groups were relatively optimistic. For example, in late 1943 Gardiner Means, who had become an economist for the Committee for Economic Development, predicted a GNP of $135 to $145 billion in the immediate postwar years. This amounted to a drop in the wartime high, but was substantially higher than the defense-stimulated $100 billion GNP of 1940. During and shortly after the war the Twentieth Century Fund forecast a GNP of $177 billion by 1950.[11] H. Christian Sonne, chairman of the National Planning Association, and Beardsley Ruml, one of the founding members of CED and a vice-chairman of NPA's Business Committee on National Policy, drew up a proposed national fiscal program that assumed a GNP of about

$165 billion in the immediate postwar period.[12] Unemployment estimates were also relatively optimistic. It must be remembered that in 1940, when employment was on the upswing, there were still over eight million unemployed. But both CED and the Twentieth Century Fund anticipated a figure no higher than three million jobless in the postwar transition period.[13]

The most significant feature of these postwar projections, however, was their acceptance of high federal peacetime spending. In 1944 both CED and NPA estimated (and hoped for) federal postwar spending of $18 billion annually.[14] These figures were remarkably high when compared to previous peacetime government spending, even though they are considerably lower than even the very lowest federal expenditure ($33 billion) on the eve of the Cold War. The largest federal expenditure during the New Deal years had been a comparatively modest $8.5 billion in 1939.[15]

The assumption underlying the thinking of the business planners was that prosperity could not be sustained by private investment and consumption. This assumption and its corollaries were explored, in one instance, by a symposium of economists called together by the Twentieth Century Fund in the last year of the war. The Fund chose eight economists to represent "the whole spectrum of responsible economic opinion," which was defined as running from the conservative Benjamin M. Anderson of the University of California to the liberal Keynesian Harvard economist Alvin H. Hansen (who had also become a trustee of the National Planning Association at the time of its corporate liberal business takeover). These men were asked the following major questions: whether private enterprise and investment could take care of postwar reconversion and employment; what short-range compensatory role—if any—the government should play; and what long-run functions the government should assume. All agreed that the government was properly committed to the maintenance of a high national income. All but Anderson favored federal deficit spending during a depression. All but Anderson agreed that the federal government should assume responsibility for, but not necessarily guarantee, full employment.[16]

It was generally agreed that compensatory spending offered the best mechanism for discharging the government's new responsibility. This was accepted even by those economists who attacked what they termed "deficit spending" and the Keynes-Hansen "stagnation thesis." Howard S. Ellis, a University of California economist and the assistant director of research for the Federal Reserve System, was one of those who rejected the stagnation thesis. He read it to mean "that private enterprise cannot possibly provide investment sufficient to maintain high-level employment." This led him to conclude that spokesmen for the stagnation thesis foresaw the "demise of private enterprise."[17] And yet even Ellis, along with most of his symposium colleagues, believed that it was the responsibility of *government* to support full employment, to prepare in advance public works to offset depression, and to provide liberal unemployment benefits and an extension of social security to support consumption. None of the economists advocated permanent federal spending over and above federal income from taxation, but nearly all agreed that the government must engage in compensatory or "anti-cyclical deficit spending."[18] Ellis and the others who rejected the stagnation argument were saying that "private enterprise" *could* provide investment sufficient for full employment; but, in case it did *not,* government should close the gap.

Thus there was a coming to terms between the avowed Keynesians and those who renounced Keynes but who acknowledged the validity of the Keynesian solution if they were proved wrong. By their actions, the corporate liberal businessmen were acknowledging Keynes and the fact of stagnation as well. Ruml and Sonne, for example, were not alone in believing that in the postwar years the government should disburse over twice the amount spent in the most spendthrift years of the New Deal.

This summary of one particular symposium gives some idea of the range of opinion among corporate liberals at the time. Corporate liberal businessmen were generally agreed that the government should continue to help sustain full production and employment, but most of them were opposed to more internal planning—that is, to an expanded New Deal at home—and did not fully agree on the efficacy of foreign trade as the solution to their problems. It gradually became clear, however, that corporate liberals were not simply content with an enhanced government role in the economy and they began to demand government support for new approaches to economic expansion abroad. Much of this demand was focused in corporate liberal policy research groups.

When Jesse Jones had established the Committee for Economic Development he had expected it to concentrate almost exclusively on the domestic aspects of reconversion and full employment, but the businessmen of CED moved rapidly beyond Jones' program to demonstrate that the "new comfort and effectiveness in the relationships of government and business" included cooperation on the expansion of foreign trade. Assistant Secretary of Commerce Will Clayton told his fellow CED trustees in April 1943: "It is terribly important to keep in mind that measures adopted for the conducting of international trade are likely to have a very important bearing on the whole future of free enterprise domestically." He insisted that "the international problem is far too important for the Committee to treat as a stepchild."[19]*

In 1943 economist Calvin B. Hoover, Dean of the Duke University Graduate School, was commissioned to head a CED research project on "International Problems After the War." Hoover's group produced a paper, "International Trade, Foreign Investment and Domestic Employment," which CED published in

---

* The trustees agreed with Clayton. They had previously, in fact, asked CED Chairman Paul Hoffman to set up an Inter-American Committee to provide information on Latin American trade and investment possibilities. The functioning of that committee provides an interesting example of further CED-government cooperation. CED worked in phase with Nelson Rockefeller, head of the State Department's office of Inter-American Affairs, in setting up the committee in December 1942. "Simultaneously," CED Vice-Chairman William Benton told the CED trustees, Rockefeller "appointed a United States Commission for Inter-American Development. So far there is complete identity of membership on the two committees." The chairman of both groups was Eric Johnston, president of the United States Chamber of Commerce. Benton added that the commission was "to be financed entirely by Government." It "seemed soundest," he remarked with unintended humor, "not to tie in CED with the United States Commission any closer than it now is." "The Trustees may be sure of one thing," Paul Hoffman remarked in a similar vein, "C.E.D.'s own Inter-American Committee has no Government money whatever."[20]

1945. In a draft paper a year earlier, Hoover had urged CED cooperation with the government in a new international program for the postwar period, and had proposed wholehearted support for American participation in an international bank and monetary fund to be discussed at Bretton Woods that summer. CED carried through on Hoover's recommendations.[21]

Determined to avoid another period of instability in world trade such as that which followed World War I, business liberals encouraged large-scale government support of a postwar rebuilding of world trade, and the re-establishment and strengthening of private investment abroad. The multi-national conference at Bretton Woods in the summer of 1944 fit in well with their plans. The conference proposed an International Bank for Reconstruction and Development (the World Bank) and an International Monetary Fund. The World Bank would—because private capital was insufficient for the task—grant long-term loans for reconstruction in various war-torn nations. It would be capitalized at a maximum of $10 billion, with the United States contributing something over $1 billion. The International Monetary Fund would lend money to nations confronted with temporary foreign trade difficulties, in order to stabilize world currency. The United States would contribute approximately one-third of the projected $8.8 billion fund. The general purpose of both agencies was to restore world trade; American businessmen would, of course, benefit directly.

The American business community did not give unqualified support to the new agencies. The concept behind them was broadly accepted, but there were disputes over details. The International Monetary Fund received most of the criticism. As CED and NPA officer Beardsley Ruml later remarked, "the bankers of the country were almost unanimous that the Monetary Fund, since it involved the exchange of currencies as a matter of right, would be subject to improper use, resulting in the unbalancing of its accounts and in the freezing of its resources as soon as its hard currencies, particularly dollars, were exhausted." Ruml was worried because he felt that an "international agreement on any postwar financial program" was doubtful if American participation in the Bank and the Fund was defeated in Congress.[22] Members of the CED promptly testified before House and Senate committees in support of the Bretton Woods proposals and their most important contribution was to suggest a minor compromise in the plans that won the support of American bankers. All parties finally accepted the CED suggestion that the World Bank charter could be interpreted as authorizing "stabilization loans." The bankers were satisfied that the Fund would not be subject to reckless use by other nations.[23]

The World Bank was not subjected to as much criticism because it was expected to give close scrutiny to its loans for reconstruction and development. Furthermore, it was clear that the United States would be in effective control of the Bank* and that the Bank would function to encourage private investment Loans would be granted only if recipient governments followed "sound" policies: from the outset the World Bank "threatened to withhold loans in order to 'encourage' governments to pass legislation more favorable to private foreign investors, to control inflation, to pay private external debts, to avoid government-owned enterprises [and] to improve the 'climate of investment' in other ways. . . ."[24]

The businessmen of CED had demonstrated that they knew how to operate in the political arena. Emanuel Goldenweiser, the articulate director of research for the Federal Reserve System, wryly noted that the CED proposal about the World Bank, while it offered an effective strategy, had very little substantive merit because it tried "to distinguish and make clear lines" between loans, currency transactions, and gifts, which could not really be done. Goldenweiser wrote that the proposal "probably won't do any *harm*"—providing the World Bank was well managed, and "was welcome" as a "political or parliamentary move." He concluded that "it may be that some of the first-class brains behind it deliberately undertook the role of moderators and reconcilers. They seem to have accomplished their purpose."[25] Obtaining

---

* The directors of the World Bank have subsequently elected only Americans to that agency's presidency. President Lyndon Johnson's virtual appointment of Robert MacNamara to that post illustrates an even greater degree of United States direction—Johnson did not bother even to go through the motions of giving a choice to the directors.

acceptance of the Bretton Woods plans was, of course, the CED purpose. After Congress ratified the proposals, President Truman singled out CED for praise for its part in saving the agreements from defeat.[26]

But there was still considerable discussion about the various problems connected with Will Clayton's view of expanded foreign trade as the salvation of the private enterprise system. In 1944, Benjamin Higgins, the former head economist of the New Deal's Federal Works Agency, urged the expansion of the New Deal, insisting that the national income could be maintained only by increased internal spending and *not* by expanding exports. There was, he wrote, "an important difference between spending on domestic public works and spending on exports." Other nations would benefit if the United States maintained full employment by domestic public works, he explained (and he assumed stagnation without it), because national income would rise and America would buy more abroad. This would raise the national income of other countries, which in turn would increase their ability to buy American exports. But if America was to "start from the other direction, and try to maintain full employment here by an export surplus, there will be import surpluses elsewhere—which will tend to reduce the national income of other countries, thereby diminishing their ability to go on importing from us."[27]

There was substantial agreement within CED during the later war years on the validity of Higgins' broad analysis, although not on his advocacy of public works spending. Calvin Hoover and Gardiner Means also believed that expanded trade could only come as a by-product of a domestic program of full employment. Hoover admitted that foreign trade was important, but held that it was not as important to the United States "as it is to a large number of other countries." The chief contribution to a revival of foreign trade, he felt, would have to come first and foremost from a domestic program of "substantially full employment."[28] Gardiner Means, writing at the same time (1944), concluded that after a more or less prosperous postwar transition period the United States would be confronted with the same problems it had faced in the 1930's. He anticipated two major problems. The first was how to maintain markets, and the solution, Means cautioned, would *not* be found in expanding markets, it would be found in the transformation of a "potential into an actual domestic market." The second problem concerned "corporate concentration." In his view, this was "not monopoly *per se*," but the imperfect competition, the administered and insensitive prices, and the low wage rates that resulted from oligopoly. Means therefore laid heavy stress on domestic policy in his recommendations.[29] But neither Means nor Hoover were willing to advocate the large-scale government spending on domestic programs that unreconstructed planners like Higgins were proposing.

In his 1945 study for CED, *International Trade and Domestic Employment*, Hoover made a rather contradictory analysis that, nevertheless, ended up by supporting new foreign expansion. Hoover wrote that CED favored international agreements that would expand all national incomes, but he insisted that the advantages of foreign trade did not consist in offsetting ' excess capacity" in the United States. For "if there truly existed a chronic inability to sell all we produce, then the whole theory of international trade would have to be revised." On the other hand, he also argued that the United States should encourage international specialization and take the lead in pushing such a program.[30] In the context of American productive might that specialization meant, of course, that the United States would have an enormous comparative advantage in capturing the markets of the world. A program of international specialization led by the United States would result in an unparalleled expansion of foreign trade.

Others were less reluctant to make explicit avowal of the new opportunities abroad. In 1945, Herbert Feis, a State Department adviser on International Economic Affairs, wrote that he saw "a great reversal of attitude" regarding foreign investment and trade. Feis suggested that the war itself had introduced a new attitude that came in part from a growth of "our understanding of our international political position," and in part "from a sense of economic need." During the war the United States had served as the central source of war equipment, food, and raw materials for the Allies and a continuing flow of American products after the war seemed to many nations to be "indispensable to their recovery and progress." This need created a "magnetic field of attraction for our capital" which would bring about "the marriage between surplus and need." Feis acknowledged the existence of surplus and assumed that there would be considerable government aid in "any adequate foreign investment program."[31] He was far more optimistic about the boost which would be given the economy by encouraging foreign trade than were Higgins, or CED's Means and Hoover. But Feis had not confronted the central dilemma in the expansion of foreign trade that Higgins and, to a lesser extent, Means and Hoover had recognized. In the long run, a nation could sell more to foreigners only by eventually buying more from foreigners. Failure to recognize that hard fact of international economic life meant that the problem might be deferred, but it could not be escaped. The corporate liberals could not have their cake and eat it too.

In 1944, the National Planning Association offered a foreign economic policy plan on the scale of that proposed by Secretary of State George C. Marshall three years later. It called for a great expansion of government-supported foreign investment, and it did so strictly on the basis of American domestic needs, using, of course, none of the later justifications that were to be based on a Cold War with Russia. The NPA's Committee on International Policy (constituted in December 1943 from members of its Business, Agriculture, and Labor Committees on National Policy) published the report, *America's New Opportunities in World Trade,* in November 1944. Significantly, the report was grounded on the very assumption of economic surplus that men like Calvin Hoover rejected. The report asserted that at the end of the war the United States "will have an enormous backlog of idle and underemployed capital at home, and a capital formation capacity which will greatly exceed the amount of new capital which can currently be absorbed by domestic business. . . . We will have a capital equipment industry nearly twice the size which would be needed domestically under the most fortuitous conditions of full employment and nearly equal to the task of supplying world needs." Because of its wartime industrial expansion, the United States could meet both foreign and domestic demand. Moreover, the NPA committee reported, "this idle capital must be used if full employment is to be maintained."

The report argued that if "this potential export demand" was to be made effective, "financial aid would have to be forthcoming from the United States." The report dovetailed this aid requirement with domestic American needs: "At home we will be searching simultaneously for means to invest $5 to $10 billions of current savings for which normally effective domestic demand cannot be foreseen." By 1950, the report continued, foreign needs for American goods and capital would probably equal American "surplus productive capacity and savings." The level of that surplus would be "in the range of $7-$8 billions annually." Such a figure, the authors pointed out, was "very high." Furthermore, it was "quite out of line with our past trade volume and capital export experience."[32]

The NPA experts then discussed what had to be done to take advantage of the new opportunities. They concluded that in order to meet its own and world needs the United States would have to increase its merchandise exports to $10 billion a year by 1950. (This was twice the value of exports in the best peacetime years of 1929 and 1941.) The problem was, however, that according to the Committee's own estimates, the United States would be spending only $6 billion on *imports* by 1950, leaving foreigners $4 billion short of what they needed if they were to buy the full $10 billion of American exports.* The NPA recognized that private enterprise could not export enough capital to maintain the level of American merchandise exports that would be needed for full production and employment at home. The government would have to help by providing some investment funds and by exercising "general supervision" over both private and public American investment abroad.

---

* The NPA estimates were very close to the actual trade balance of the early 1950's. Merchandise exports were $12 billion in 1949—down to $10 billion in the recession year of 1950—but ranging from $14 to $15 billion in the five years following. Merchandise imports in that period (except for the unusual $1 billion gap in 1950) ranged from $4 to $5 billion below exports. If inflation is taken into account, the figures are even closer to the NPA projection.

The report offered a number of proposals both to increase that capital export, and to provide security for such a large degree of private investment abroad: The United States should support the World Bank and the International Monetary Fund; the powers of the Export-Import Bank and the Reconstruction Finance Corporation should be expanded to underwrite private capital equipment exports as well as foreign investments by American corporations; formal safeguards for American operations should be secured through diplomatic negotiations, and should cover foreign expropriation of American assets and other discrimination; where private capital could not be secured, "and where reasons of national interest" indicated support for projects not backed by the World Bank, large long-term loans should be granted by the government. Even more sweeping was the NPA proposal to create a Foreign Investment Commission composed of representatives of the State, Commerce, and Treasury Departments, the Securities Exchange Commission, the Export-Import Bank, and the Reconstruction Finance Corporation, "to coordinate information and exercise general supervision over American investment from all sources, whether public or private or joint public and private."[33]

Imports, of course, would eventually have to be increased. This could be accomplished through a selective lowering of tariffs, building stockpiles of raw materials, and, in the long run, through cooperative efforts by agriculture, business, labor, and government "to shift American capital and labor to fields of enterprise where the United States enjoys comparative advantage."[34] This was a tough program designed to put the nation on a competitive footing with state-controlled economies abroad. It was also a rather traditional free trade program, but one that rested on a neo-mercantilist base.

The NPA committee was aware that some American businessmen would disagree with the details of their foreign trade program. Such disagreement, the report concluded (in terms that were to be used increasingly during the years to come), stemmed from an "inability to agree upon what our interests are, or to organize a concerted will to put defined aims into operation."[35]

Although *America's New Opportunities in World Trade* contained a somewhat bolder foreign trade program than that proposed in the late New Deal, it said nothing fundamentally new. Nor did it demonstrate how to sell more exports abroad without buying the equivalent amount of imports. But in 1947, a few months before the announcement of the Marshall Plan, one group of businessmen, academics, and labor officials did publish a report that suggested a new solution. The report, *Rebuilding the World Economy—America's Role in Foreign Trade and Investment,* was a summary of an earlier investigation by the Twentieth Century Fund's Committee on Foreign Economic Relations. The report was significant in that it represented a composite view of the positions taken by the leadership of the Congress of Industrial Organizations, the American Federation of Labor, the National Planning Association, the Committee for Economic Development, and the Council on Foreign Relations. The TCF report indicated that an extremely influential body of men was coming to an agreement on the relative importance of foreign trade and investment and on a program for its realization.

The Fund committee, citing figures to illustrate the relationship, concluded that foreign trade provided a vital boost to the domestic economy: Persons employed in the production of exports had come to comprise 6.6 percent of the total working force by 1937. If employment in such areas as construction, public utilities, and the service trades was excluded (leaving agriculture, manufacturing, transportation, and mining) the percentage was even higher: 12.4 in 1929, 5.9 in 1935, and 9.6 in 1937. To maintain a high percentage of employment in export production was crucial, but it could not be maintained, the committee argued, unless the United States revived postwar trade by exporting capital. The benefits were clear. First, it would be "simply profitable in pecuniary terms"; second, it might improve the national income "by raising and maintaining domestic employment at a high level"; third (and here the new impact of the Cold War was emerging), it "might encourage the kind of economic and political world that the United States would like to see prevail."[36]

It was at this point that the corporate liberals of the Twentieth Century Fund Committee suggested a new way in which exports could be dramatically and painlessly expanded. They began by denying that foreign lending was the best means of quickly exporting capital. Lending money abroad was, at least in theory, a "poor device to secure full employment" because of the repayment problems it created. Lending would have to be maintained and continually *increased* because not only would the debt be amortized, but there would also be a need for additional dollars to permit the payment of interest and dividends on the original loans. Yet the committee was not adamant: "If capital exports assist [in bringing economic reconstruction] . . . then, within limits, the price is worth paying without regard to the possibility of future repayment." Here the committee added the magic new ingredient. Not only was "future repayment" of diminishing concern, but "in fact, an outright gift, plainly labeled as such, may be the best solution in certain circumstances."[37] This was the new concept of foreign aid that was to be further spelled out by corporate liberal planners in the Marshall Plan. The outright granting of dollars to other nations offered a solution both to the repayment problem and to the problem of an imbalance of trade that had worried Means and Hoover in 1945. Those dollars had to be spent in the United States, sooner or later, and meant, of course, an expansion of the public sector of the economy, but not in an internal, or New Deal, direction. It was a new domestic tax that was to be used to finance American exports as the means to full employment.

Business liberals were moving toward the "concerted will" the National Planning Association had called for in 1944. But that will was made effective only in the context of the intensified Cold War of mid-1947. It did not come evenly. In fact, for a relatively brief period in 1946 some corporate liberals, including a number of CED spokesmen, felt that public spending abroad could be reduced. Lend-Lease was cut sharply and the United Nations Relief and Rehabilitation Agency was disbanded. After the $3 billion American loan to Great Britain many leaders felt that European production was returning to normal. Finally, the pent-up consumer demand of the war years created a far larger domestic American market than had been anticipated.

President Truman reflected this short-lived optimism in June 1946 when he created the Committee for Financing Foreign

Trade composed of twelve bankers and industrialists and chaired by Winthrop Aldrich of the Chase National Bank. Truman emphasized the temporary character of government lending for financing foreign trade, and directed the committee to work closely with the National Advisory Council on International Monetary and Finance Problems.* The two groups were to encourage the quick return of foreign commerce and foreign investments to private channels. The Aldrich Committee, the Advisory Council, and the Export-Import Bank all felt that government financing could be cut drastically by the end of 1946. This view was based on the belief that private capital would welcome the opportunity to provide funds for foreign borrowers through the World Bank. In addition, no extraordinary problems were anticipated. European recovery seemed to be proceeding at a steady pace, and the World Bank and the International Monetary Fund appeared adequate to the task of maintaining that essentially normal recovery.[38]

But even as this planning proceeded, political considerations were increasingly influencing American foreign spending—as they had done in the cutting of Lend-Lease and the elimination of UNRRA—and there were signs that European recovery was not continuing as smoothly as it had begun. Secretary of State James F. Byrnes made explicit what was already practice when he announced in October 1946 that future lending would be determined by need *and* "friendship." (A case in point was the 1946 cancellation of a $50-million loan to Czechoslovakia after that nation joined the Soviet Union in charging the United States with "dollar diplomacy."[39]) The dramatic shift came with the inauguration of large-scale economic aid under the Truman Doctrine in March 1947, after the British announcement that their own military and economic aid to Greece and Turkey would be withdrawn. Congress voted large foreign aid appropriations with uncharacteristic speed in response to the declaration that it was

---

* The Advisory Council had been established by Congress to coordinate American activities growing out of the Bretton Woods agreements and other foreign trade problems. It had the same composition as the Advisory Board of the Export-Import Bank, except that the Secretary of the Treasury acted as chairman of the council.

necessary to repel "totalitarian aggression." Then, in June, in a speech at Harvard University that drew upon the thoughts of such advisers as Charles Bohlen, Dean Acheson, and Undersecretary of State for Economic Affairs Will Clayton—as well as his own—Secretary of State George C. Marshall outlined the Marshall Plan.[40]

The Marshall Plan cannot, however, be understood or explained solely as a product of the Cold War, although it can be argued that massive foreign aid would not have been politically feasible without its stimulus. To put it another way, the political crisis was at root an economic crisis. The status of European economic reconstruction looked very different in 1947 than it had the year before. "At first," as Clayton explained, "the recovery went even faster than after World War I." But during the winter of 1946-1947, underlying weaknesses were exposed. Severe weather, in which "floods washed away top soil and drowned livestock," was followed by drought.[41] Production in some countries had reached prewar levels, but recovery was uneven. There were general coal and power shortages, and although the heavy investment necessary to restore output in capital goods was achieved in the first year, it could not be sustained. Moreover, American assistance was an uncoordinated, *ad hoc* kind of aid to individual countries, and even then, as was the case with Great Britain (under the conditions that encumbered the large credit granted in 1946) it did not solve the exchange problem. As for the International Monetary Fund, it "played only a minor role in the . . . five years" after its founding. The World Bank provided only "a fraction of the transitional assistance needed." Furthermore, as a Brookings Institution study noted, the American contribution in "removing trade barriers did not come up to expectations." And finally, American price increases in 1946 had already placed an additional burden on the dollar-short Allied economies.[42]

This was the essential—and usually neglected—context in which it became clear that the atom bomb had neither reopened Eastern Europe to Western capital nor blunted the Communist appeal in Western Europe itself. French Communists, who comprised France's largest political party, began to oppose government policy in May 1947. A wave of strikes ensued and a Third Force opposition arose that attempted to steer a neutral course between Russia and the United States. The most serious Communist threat in Western Europe appeared in inflation-ridden Italy where it appeared likely that the Communist Party would be victorious in the April 1948 elections. American political, business, and labor leaders reacted against the spread of "totalitarian aggression" and "tyranny" with vivid rhetoric and expressed concern about the "eclipse of freedom." Such phrases were used frequently, and they were, of course, believed by the men who intoned them. But the business leadership reveal themselves to have been *most* concerned with the *economic* meaning of this political threat in Western Europe

A Brookings analysis* of American foreign assistance clearly revealed the economic basis for the political antagonism. The problem of European recovery, the authors explained, involved more than the recovery of production in separate countries. If the highly specialized system of European production was to be rebuilt, then the intricate trade relations both within Europe and between Europe and the rest of the world would have to be restored. Not only would it be necessary to increase the total volume of trade, but adjustments to new patterns of trade would have to be made to accommodate to the changes in production in individual countries. The Brookings experts realized that "success in this direction . . . depended on the establishment of *political stability and the acceptance of a code of international financial integrity that would be conducive to foreign investment"* (emphasis added).[43]

Thus "political stability," "financial integrity," and foreign investment became both the means and the end of European recovery. Communist victories, whether electoral or not, were seen as ending, or at the very least drastically reducing, foreign investment from the West, and thereby destroying the viability of the entire system.

Once again, the point should not be misunderstood or distorted. American businessmen and politicians were certainly op-

---

* Although The Brookings Institution took a conservative stance on domestic policy in this period, its position on foreign policy paralleled that taken by the corporate liberal CED, NPA, and TCF.

posed, by experience and ideology, to the non-economic aspects of communism. This antagonism was reinforced by their habit of equating all communism—and even socialism—with the Soviet system. Such an attitude helps explain their willingness to act so quickly and militantly, and it was a view that was strengthened by the rhetoric of various government officials.

But political anti-communism was not the central motivation. Will Clayton* cut to the heart of the matter in a speech to the New York Citizens Committee on the Marshall Plan in December 1947: "The Marshall Plan is not a relief program; it is a recovery program for Western Europe. Hence our interests rather than our humanitarian instincts should be mainly considered. . . ." If the United States did not provide this aid, Clayton warned, "the Iron Curtain would then move westward at least to the English Channel. Consider what this would mean to us in economic terms alone. A blackout of the European market could compel radical readjustments in our entire economic structure . . . changes which could hardly be made under our democratic free enterprise system."[44]

Clayton's argument had meanwhile been accepted within the Committee for Economic Development. This commitment led to CED's leadership becoming deeply involved in the development and administration of the Marshall Plan. After Marshall's speech, President Truman asked for the creation of a committee of "distinguished citizens" which would propose specific recommendations to implement the Secretary of State's general plan. This "President's Committee on Foreign Aid" was chaired by a graduate of the Business Advisory Council, Secretary of Commerce Averell Harriman. And it was the Harriman Committee that had the most to say in the final drafting of the Economic Cooperation Act of 1948. Nearly half of its nineteen members were connected with CED: of the nine businessmen, five (including Paul Hoffman) were CED trustees; three of the six academic representatives

---

* Clayton had been adding to his policy-making credentials. In addition to his duties as Undersecretary of State for Economic Affairs, he was also chairman of the United States Delegation to the United Nations Conference on Trade and Employment at Havana. and an alternate governor of the World Bank.

were from the CED Research Advisory Board. In addition to the
eight CED members, the executive secretary of the Harriman
Committee was Richard Bissell, Jr., who had been close to CED
from its birth, when he helped formulate the original plans as
an aide to Jesse Jones in the Commerce Department.[45]

The Harriman Committee's overwhelming emphasis was on
direct government underwriting of a vastly expanded aid program. The committee urged an expenditure of $5.75 billion the
first year (the Republican-controlled Congress appropriated $5.3
billion with very little fuss) and a total of $12 to $17 billion over
a four-year period. The committee further recommended that
Europe be encouraged to develop its own resources and to tear
down barriers to private trade and investment; that American
private investment in Europe be encouraged; and that a clear dis-
tinction be made between aid for relief (items such as food, coal,
and fertilizers), which should be given in the form of outright
grants, and reconstruction aid, which should be a combination
of grants and long- and short-term loans administered through
the Export-Import Bank. Congress responded, in the Economic
Cooperation Act, by specifying that loans should comprise only
$1 billion of the first $5.3 billion appropriation.[46]

While the Harriman Committee was preparing its report, CED
was at work on the specific problems of European aid. By this
time the issue had largely become one of how the aid should be
administered. Wayne C. Taylor (who had left the Department
of Commerce with Jesse Jones in 1945 and had served as president of the Export-Import Bank until 1946), took charge of a
CED research and policy group on European aid. Taylor also
agreed to work with a similar body organized by the National
Planning Association.[47] And, in a move that further integrated
the private and government groups, Senator Arthur Vandenberg
(chairman of the Senate Foreign Relations Committee) asked The
Brookings Institution to submit a report to the Senate on the
administration of foreign aid.[48]

A ticklish legislative problem arose at this point; it was solved
by the compromise proposals of two of these corporate-liberal
groups. The Administration wanted the European Recovery Program to be handled through the State Department, while Con-

gress insisted on the creation of a new government corporation headed by businessmen. (Both Brookings and CED later took credit for supplying the compromise, and in reality the organizations did suggest essentially similar plans.[49]) Congress was satisfied by the creation of a separate Economic Cooperation Administration, while the Administration won an important point in that the ECA was directed to cooperate with the State Department. Once it was made unofficially clear that the new agency would be headed by a man of business experience, the Economic Cooperation Act was passed on April 2, 1948. This met the deadline urged by President Truman, which allowed the Administration to use the legislation to influence the Italian elections scheduled for April 18.[50] CED chairman Paul Hoffman—a Republican businessman who was acceptable to Truman (they had conferred together on other matters) as well as to Senator Vandenberg—was chosen as the ECA administrator. On Hoffman's recommendation, Harriman, a Democrat, was appointed as a special ECA roving ambassador to Europe. The other top officials of ECA were largely recruited from the CED staff and officers. These included Wayne Taylor, W. L. Batt (both also active in the National Planning Association), Edward Mason, Calvin Hoover, William C. Foster, J. D. Zellerbach, and Richard Bissell, Jr. Thus the officers of the Committee for Economic Development had not only helped formulate the Marshall Plan, but were also almost uniquely responsible for carrying it out.

The agreement that corporate liberals had reached in 1945 on the saving qualities of foreign trade was institutionalized in the new program in 1947. Massive infusions of dollar aid abroad solved the foreign trade problem, which in turn solved the problem of full production at home. The Economic Cooperation Act signified a recognition of that fact and marked out a postwar course that has been followed ever since. The form and magnitude of external spending has changed somewhat over the years but the essential purpose of the mechanism has remained the same. With the Korean War, aids and grants of the Marshall Plan type took a back seat to the new Military Assistance Program, but the result was the same. Grants still went to foreigners to buy—in this case and subsequently—military hardware in the

United States. American efforts to build up the economies of the underdeveloped nations—as in the Point Four, Alliance for Progress, and other programs—have similarly provided dollars to be spent in the United States. In those areas of relatively insecure sovereignty, however, American conditions have been more stringent, the developing economies have been integrated more securely with the American system, fewer grants and more loans have been given, and more openings for United States investment have been demanded than was the case with the aid granted to the large industrialized nations.[51] And, despite its supposed slashing in Congress, the level of foreign aid has continued high. Senator Wayne Morse, for example, insisted in 1967 that foreign aid has not been cut at all. Funds appropriated for the Agency for International Development, Food for Peace, the Asian Bank, the Inter-American Bank, and the International Development Association, he reported, amounted to over $4 billion for 1967. In addition to that sort of foreign aid were military aid, support for United Nations programs, private investment abroad, and World Bank subscriptions sold to private investors—all of which worked to increase the dollar flow abroad and to support domestic production. The "real object" for most foreign aid in recent years, Morse argued, "is to acquire and keep as many foreign aid clients as possible, so the process of transferring resources can serve to give American aid, intelligence, and military officials a foothold in these countries and a real or imagined lever in their affairs." Senator Morse held that the foreign aid bureaucracy and "the American industry which regards it as another federal subsidy" will seek to perpetuate foreign aid "as an end in itself."[52]

Whether a large-scale foreign aid program, as it presently exists, will continue is a moot point. The corporate liberal planners who began to work out the system during World War II were aware of the political potential in foreign aid—in the sense that it would help create "the kind of economic and political world that the United States would like to see prevail." But their scheme had broader implications. It stemmed, first of all, from a well-learned lesson of the New Deal, that it was the duty of government to prevent the stagnation of the capitalist economy by large-scale compensatory spending. But that spending, if "free enterprise" at home was to be saved, had to be largely directed abroad. The world market would—with government help—support the needed American economic growth. But when it became clear in 1946-1947 that the expected expansion of overseas opportunities was not forthcoming, foreign aid emerged to provide an elegantly symmetrical answer to several dilemmas. It was a form of government compensatory spending that avoided revived New Deal spending at home. It could be made to open the way for new investment in grateful nations. It would re-establish a stable capitalist world economy. It would strengthen Western Europe in the face of a rising communist political threat—it would, that is, check the communist threat to American economic expansion abroad. And the high cost of the program could also be publicly justified on the basis of European suffering, American guilt, and American humanitarianism. The foreign aid solution of direct grants was at its best, however, in meeting a tough technical problem in international economics: how to expand exports without in turn buying more imports. Foreign aid seemed a foolproof solution to a host of problems. It has, in fact, worked for many years—but at a price. Foreigners have paid a high political and economic price for the various forms of American capital exports; but Americans have had to pay by deferring (for nearly thirty years, now) their own solution to their own problems at home.

Will Clayton and Dean Acheson were probably right. To have turned inward to solve American problems—to allow foreigners to choose their own course—might very well have meant, as Will Clayton put it, "radical readjustments in our entire economic structure . . . changes which could hardly be made under our democratic free enterprise system." These men were fearful of the expanded New Deal solution to continued economic growth precisely because they felt that such a program would be compelled to move far beyond the most radical projections of New Deal planners. But we live in a world in which continued United States economic growth has led to an increasingly brutal and brutalizing imperialism abroad and to a nation on the verge of flames at home. Under these circumstances, might not the only rational option left be the very alternative so dreaded by our corporate-liberal policy-makers? Might it not, in fact, be the very height of "realism" to return to the vision that is a part of an honored American radical tradition? That is, to self-consciously and deliberately choose to move toward the cooperative Commonwealth?

Notes

1. Jesse Jones to S. Clay Williams, June 25, 1942, National Archives, Washington, D.C., RG 40, Department of Commerce file no. 102517/36.
2. "National Emergency Council," *United States Government Manual* (Washington, D.C., 1936), p. 114A.
3. *Twenty-Fourth Annual Report of the Secretary of Commerce* (Washington, D.C., 1936), p. 6.
4. Thomas B. McCabe, "The Committee for Economic Development—Its Past, Present and Future," an address to the Board of Trustees, Committee for Economic Development, November 19, 1949 (pamphlet, New York, 1949), p. 6.
5. S. Clay Williams to Jesse Jones, July 2, 1942, National Archives, Washington, D.C., RG 40, Department of Commerce file no. 102517/36.
6. *New Republic,* July 26, 1943, pp. 104-106; October 16, 1944, p. 481; December 25, 1944, p. 71; March 26, 1945, p. 405.
7. Keith Hutchinson, "Heresy in High Places," *Nation,* October 27, 1945, p. 431.
8. Leon Henderson, "Enterprise in Postwar America," in Arnold Zurcher and Richmond Page, eds., *Postwar Goals and Economic Reconstruction* (New York: New York University Press, 1945), p. 14.
9. National Planning Association, *Guides for Postwar Planning,* Planning Pamphlet No. 8 (Washington, D.C., November 1941), p. 3.
10. *Annual Report of the Council of Economic Advisers,* 1963 (Washington, D.C., 1963), pp. 171, 172.
11. J. Frederic Dewhurst et al., *America's Needs and Resources* (New York: Twentieth Century Fund, 1947), p. 72.
12. Beardsley Ruml and H. Christian Sonne, *Fiscal and Monetary Policy,* Planning Pamphlet No. 35 (Washington, D.C., July 1944), p. 9.
13. Committee for Economic Development, *American Industry Looks*

Ahead (Washington, D.C., 1945), p. 3; Dewhurst, *America's Needs and Resources,* p. 74.

14. Ruml and Sonne, *Fiscal and Monetary Policy,* p. 9; Ruml, "National Fiscal Policy," a lecture at Princeton University, May 2, 1950 (mimeographed, New York, 1950) pp. 6, 8; Harold M. Groves, *Production, Jobs, and Taxes* (New York: McGraw Hill, 1944), p. 9.

15. *Annual Report of the Council of Economic Advisers,* 1963, p. 238.

16. Paul T. Homan and Fritz Machlup, eds., *Financing American Prosperity—A Symposium of Economists* (New York: Twentieth Century Fund, 1945), pp. v, 4-5, 454, 488.

17. *Ibid.,* p. 129.

18. *Ibid.,* pp. 487-493.

19. "Minutes of Third Quarterly Trustees Meeting, CED, April 13, 1943," NA, RG 40, General Records of the Department of Commerce, Special Correspondence File of Jesse Jones.

20. *Ibid.*

21. Karl Schriftgiesser, *Business Comes of Age* (New York: Harper & Row, 1960), p. 118.

22. Beardsley Ruml, "International Economic Relations," lecture at Princeton University, May 8, 1950 (mimeographed, New York, 1950), p. 8.

23. *Ibid.,* p. 9.

24. David A. Baldwin, *Economic Development and American Foreign Policy, 1943-62* (Chicago: University of Chicago Press, 1966), p. 50.

25. Emanuel A. Goldenweiser, Memorandum "CED says Q.E.E. by E.A.G." (n.d.), Emanuel A. Goldenweiser Papers, Library of Congress.

26. Calvin B. Hoover, *International Trade and Domestic Employment* (New York: McGraw Hill, 1945), p. ix.

27. Benjamin Higgins, "Public Works and Our Postwar Economy," in Zurcher and Page, eds., *Postwar Goals and Economic Reconstruction,* pp. 79-80.

28. Calvin B. Hoover, "American Foreign Trade and Investment," in Zurcher and Page, pp. 287, 297; *International Trade and Domestic Employment,* pp. 13, 14.

29. Gardiner Means, "How May Business Enterprise Be Expanded After the War," in Zurcher and Page, pp. 107-110.

30. Hoover, *International Trade and Domestic Employment,* pp. 5, 14, 20.

31. Herbert Feis, "The Investment of American Capital Abroad," in Zurcher and Page, eds., *America's Place in the World Economy* (New York, 1945), pp. 73-76, 92.

32. National Planning Association Committee on International Policy, *America's New Opportunities in World Trade* (NPA Planning Pamphlets No. 37-38, November 1944), pp. 20, 59-60.

33. *Ibid.*, pp. 67-77.

34. *Ibid.*, pp. 64-71.

35. *Ibid.*, p. 73.

36. Norman S. Buchanan and Frederich A. Lutz, *Rebuilding the World Economy: America's Role in Foreign Trade and Investment* (New York: Twentieth Century Fund, 1945), pp. 73-76.

37. *Ibid.*, pp. 228-229.

38. Cleona Lewis, *The United States and Foreign Investment Problems* (Washington, D.C.: The Brookings Institution, 1948), pp. 202-203, 208-209.

39. *Ibid.*, p. 211.

40. Hans A. Schmitt, *The Path to European Union: From the Marshall Plan to the Common Market* (Baton Rouge: Louisiana State University Press, 1962), p. 20.

41. Will Clayton, cited in *ibid.*, pp. 17-18.

42. William Adams Brown, Jr. and Redvers Opie, *American Foreign Assistance* (Washington, D.C.: The Brookings Institution, 1953), pp. 114-119.

43. *Ibid.*, p. 119.

44. Will Clayton, Address to Citizens Committee on the Marshall Plan, New York, December 8, 1947, Department of State Press Release No. 977, Tom Connally Papers, Library of Congress.

45. Schriftgiesser, *Business Comes of Age*, p. 128.

46. Brown and Opie, *American Foreign Assistance*, pp. 138, 149, 151.

47. Schriftgiesser, *Business Comes of Age*, pp. 129-131.

48. Brown and Opie, *American Foreign Assistance*, p. 153.

49. Ruml, "International Economic Relations," p. 11; Schriftgiesser, *Business Comes of Age*, pp. 131-133; Brown and Opie, *American Foreign Assistance*, pp. 153-155.

50. Brown and Opie, *American Foreign Assistance*, p. 145.

51. See Baldwin, *Economic Development and American Foreign Policy*, for a discussion of the programs in underdeveloped areas.

52. Senator Wayne Morse, letter to the editor, *Challenge: The Magazine of Economic Affairs*, March-April 1967, p. 6.

Economic Effects of the Cold War
by Joseph D. Phillips

The purpose of this essay is to consider the impact of the Cold War on the structure and performance of the U.S. economy and, to a lesser extent, on the economies of other Western industrial countries. On the "Western" side, the Cold War may be said to be that phase of the effort to contain and, if possible, to wipe out socialist systems in the period following World War II, although the effort itself had begun long before and had become a major concern of state policy in the capitalist countries following the establishment of the first socialist system after the Bolshevik Revolution in 1917. Other state policy concerns had resulted in conflicts among the capitalist powers, characteristic of imperialism, which had in the end produced the "wrong war." The necessity of saving themselves from the aggrandisement of the Axis powers, the most aggressive of the capitalist states, forced the others to ally themselves temporarily with the Soviet Union, then the only socialist society. The extension and strengthening of socialist systems in Europe and in China as a consequence of World War II and their internal development intensified the already implacable hatred of socialism in the ruling circles of the capitalist countries and their determination to roll it back if possible and in any case to prevent its spread.

The principal aspects of the Cold War that have had an important impact on the economies of the capitalist countries are (1) the continuing very large military expenditures of the United States and, on a smaller scale, of Great Britain, West Germany, and France; (2) the expenditures of the United States in the form of grants and loans for the reconstruction of the war-devastated economies of its capitalist World War II allies and former enemies; (3) the organization of various economic unions in Europe, particularly the Common Market, in an attempt to create a larger political entity with which to confront the Soviet bloc; (4) the restrictions on trade with the socialist countries imposed at the insistence of the United States; (5) the break-up of the old colonial empires and their partial replacement by neo-colonialist forms of exploitation and control under American hegemony; (6) the foreign aid, economic and military, extended primarily in the form of loans and secondarily as grants to the economically underdeveloped countries, many of them newly independent, by the United States and the other capitalist countries; (7) the vast expansion of the role of giant multi-national, even supra-national, corporations, primarily U.S.-based; (8) the increasing integration of government and business, partly as a consequence of these developments and partly as a result of the need to deal with the contradictions inherent in them.

Military Expenditures

The impact of U.S. military expenditures on effective demand, and thus on the level of employment and output, has obviously been very great. It pulled the American economy out of the Great Depression when all else had failed. The New Deal had increased government spending by some 70 percent in the face of tenacious resistance, but 17 percent of the labor force was still unemployed in 1939. By 1944 government purchases of goods and services were seven times greater than they had been in 1939 and unemployment averaged 1.2 percent. The cutback in military spending at the end of the war was replaced by a sharp expansion in civilian spending reflecting the shortage of consumer goods and the accumulation of liquid savings during the war. The moderate decline in business soon turned into a reconversion boom which was still under way when the Cold War, with its inevitable accompaniment of limited "hot" wars, began to have its effect.

The table below indicates in broad terms the relation between military spending and the level of U.S. economic activity in the past two decades. The sharp increase in military spending and its percentage of the Gross National Product at the time of the Korean War is associated with a marked increase in the GNP and a marked decrease in the rate of unemployment. The cutback in arms expenditures in 1954 was in turn accompanied by a stand-still in the GNP and a sharp rise in unemployment. Military spending was maintained at about $40 billion from 1954 to 1955 and about $45 billion from 1957 to 1960, and it stayed close to 10 percent of GNP. Baran and Sweezy have contended that "the difference between the deep stagnation of the 1930's and the relative prosperity of the 1950's is fully accounted for by the vast military outlays of the 50's."[1] It would be difficult to disprove this contention, which has been made in substance by many other economists. However, it is clear that these outlays have not eliminated the tendency of the U.S. economy to generate periods of expansion and contraction that are not closely related to changes in military outlays. The 10 percent increase in military spending in 1957 over 1956 did not prevent the contraction of 1957-1958, and the 7 percent increase between 1960 and 1961 was accompanied by a rise in unemployment.

The expansion of military expenditures by the Kennedy Administration raised the total to $51.6 billion in 1962. It seems to have remained close to that level during the following three years, but when the essentially military outlays on space research and technology (which in terms of the administrative budget rose from $145 million in fiscal year 1959 to $5.1 billion in fiscal year 1965) are added, a significant increase is evident. This expansion no doubt was largely responsible for the rapid rise in GNP and the decline in unemployment in these years, although the tax cut in 1964 was also a factor.

The sharp increase in expenditures in 1965, 1967 and 1968 resulting from the war in Vietnam has not only reduced the unemployment rate to the lowest level since the Korean War, but has also released strong inflationary pressures. The U.S. Department of Labor has estimated that the escalation of the Vietnam War created more than one million jobs in the two years preceding mid-1967. These jobs accounted for 23 percent of the total increase of more than four million jobs since 1965.[2] Defense work in fiscal year 1967 accounted for 4.1 million jobs, or 5.9 percent of the nation's total civilian employment compared with 3.0 million, or 4.7 percent, in fiscal year 1965. These estimates "do not include the income multiplier or accelerator effects which

U.S. Gross National Product, Military Expenditures, and Unemployment Rate, 1947-1967

	GNP (in billions of dollars)	Military expenditures (in billions of dollars)	(as percent of GNP)	Unemployment rate
1947	231.3	9.1	3.9	3.9
1948	257.6	10.7	4.2	3.8
1949	256.5	13.3	5.2	5.9
1950	284.8	14.1	5.0	5.3
1951	328.4	33.6	10.2	3.3
1952	345.5	45.9	13.3	3.1
1953	364.6	48.7	13.4	2.9
1954	364.8	41.2	11.3	5.6
1955	398.0	38.6	9.7	4.4
1956	419.2	40.3	9.6	4.2
1957	441.1	44.2	10.0	4.3
1958	447.3	45.9	10.3	6.8
1959	483.6	46.0	9.5	5.5
1960	503.8	44.9	8.9	5.6
1961	520.1	47.8	9.2	5.7
1962	560.3	51.6	9.2	5.6
1963	590.5	50.8	8.6	5.7
1964	632.4	50.0	7.9	5.2
1965	683.9	50.1	7.3	4.6
1966	743.3	60.5	8.1	3.8
1967	789.7	72.4	9.2	3.8
1968	865.7	78.0	9.0	3.6

Sources: *Economic Report of the President,* January 1969, pp. 227, 252; *Survey of Current Business,* July 1969, p. 9.

induce further consumption and investment purchases."[3] Nor do they include the increase in military personnel from 2.7 million to 3.4 million. The increased civilian employment reflects a rise from 2.1 million to 3.0 million in estimated employment of wage and salary workers in the private sector attributable to military expenditures and an increase from 900 thousand to 1.1 million in Department of Defense civilian employment in the United States for military functions. It was estimated that each billion dollars of defense purchases from the private sector would create 82,000 jobs in fiscal year 1965 and 73,000 jobs in fiscal year 1967, the decline being due to higher prices and increased productivity.

The estimated distribution of private employment attributable to military expenditures in fiscal year 1967 by aggregate industry sectors indicates that aircraft and parts manufacturing accounted for 16 percent; radio, television, and communications equipment for 7.5 percent; ordnance and accessories for 6.2 percent; and manufacturing as a whole for 68 percent. The estimate for services is 25.8 percent of the total, of which transportation and warehousing accounted for 6.9 percent and wholesale and retail trade for 5.6 percent. These industry groupings accounted for about the same percentages of the increase in private employment resulting from the Vietnam build-up, except that the shares of ordnance and transportation were somewhat higher and those of the others were slightly lower. In general, the employment generated by military procurement was fairly broadly distributed over a wide range of industries with few accounting for more than 5 percent of the total.

Of course, the percentage of total employment within particular aggregate industry sectors that was attributable to military expenditures varied greatly among industries. In ordnance it amounted to 64.8 percent in fiscal year 1967, in aircraft to 59.1 percent, and in manufacturing as a whole to 10.5 percent. In a range of industries, including some in mining and others in the services category, the estimates indicate that significant shares of total employment were attributable to military spending, reflecting sales that probably contributed even larger shares to profits.

The concentration of U.S. military procurement in contracts with a relatively few large firms has been documented in Department of Defense publications, Congressional hearings, and the writings of a number of economists. The table below indicates the percentage of U.S. military prime contracts going to the largest 100 recipients, the largest 50, and those firms classified as small business (generally less than 500 employees. The higher degree of concentration beginning with fiscal year 1958 is attributed to the impact of space-age technology and the decline in fiscal year 1965 to a drop in missile procurement and a rise in awards for the more diversified military material required by the Vietnam build-up.

There has been, of course, some turnover from year to year among the corporations making up the 50 or 100 largest prime contract recipients. Firms disappear from the list, only to reappear on that of a later year. After adjustment for mergers, joint ventures, and transfers of assets, only thirteen of the firms on the 1957 list of the fifty largest contract recipients were not on the comparable list for 1964 and only four of these were not among the top 100 that year.[4] Changes in both rank and dollar value of contract awards to the firms on the lists also occurs. All these changes primarily reflect changes in the product mix demanded by the Department of Defense.

A considerable spreading of military procurement spending takes place through subcontracting. The percentage of military contract payments received by reporting prime contractors which they paid to their first-tier subcontractors ranged between 47 percent and 55 percent in the fiscal years 1957 to 1963. The percentage going to firms classified as small businesses ranged between 18 and 21 percent in the same years.[5] However, subcontracting does not seem to alter the degree of concentration in military procurement awards. Complete data on the recipients of subcontracts are not available, but it is known that "most of the major prime contractors are also substantial subcontractors."[6] One study compared the concentration ratios for prime contracts received by fifty-eight major contractors with ratios for their net military business after adding subcontracts received and subtracting those given and found the degrees of concentration to be similar.[7]

The profits obtained from this highly concentrated military business have generally been greater than those derived from domestic civilian production, despite protestations to the contrary. In some cases they have been truly fantastic. The 1956 Aircraft Production and Profits Hearings conducted by a subcommittee of the House Armed Services Committee revealed typical before-tax profits of aircraft manufacturers amounting to more than 50 percent of their net worth in the period 1952-1955. Boeing obtained 68.3 percent and Lockhead 74.1 percent

Distribution of U.S. Military Prime Contract Awards

Period	Largest 100	Largest 50	Small Business
June 1940/Sept. 1944 (WW II)*	67.2	57.6	
July 1950/June 1953 (Korean War)	64.0	56.3	
Jan. 1955/June 1957	67.4	59.5	
FY 1957	68.4	59.8	19.8
FY 1958	74.2	66.9	17.1
FY 1959	73.8	65.3	16.6
FY 1960	73.4	64.8	16.1
FY 1961	74.2	65.8	15.9
FY 1962	72.3	63.4	17.7
FY 1963	73.9	65.6	15.8†
FY 1964	73.4	65.8	17.2†
FY 1965	68.9	61.2	19.6†

* The figure for World War II is based on prime contracts of $50,000 or more and excludes procurement of food. The more recent series are based on contracts of $10,000 or more, including food. Thus, neither coverage nor base is strictly comparable.

† Because of a change in reporting coverage, the ratios starting with FY 1963 are not comparable with those for prior years. On a comparable basis, the FY 1963 ratio is 16.5 percent; those for FY 1964 and FY 1965 are not available.

Source: William L. Baldwin, *The Structure of the Defense Market, 1955-1964* (Durham, N. C.: Duke University Press, 1967), p. 9.

in 1953. Figures for the Allison Motors Division of General Motors indicate a return of more than 200 percent per year on fixed capital invested in the engine division over a five-year period. Another House Armed Services subcommittee brought out in its 1960 hearings numerous examples of overcharges reported by the General Accounting Office and by the Renegotiation Board.[8] Comptroller General Joseph Campbell testified that $1 billion in total overcharges on negotiated procurement by the Department of Defense would not be an unreasonable estimate for the period February 1957-March 1961.[9]

In most cases the giant corporations which are the principal recipients of military prime contracts are also engaged in civilian production, so it is difficult to obtain accurate data on their profits from military production. The allocation of overhead costs between their civilian and military production provides considerable opportunity for inflating the total costs of the latter. Profit rates on that part of their assets or net worth used in military production are still more difficult to obtain because of the problem of separating out the assets of their civilian production. However, it is possible to compare the profit rates of corporations heavily involved in military production with those of other corporations. The table below compares the overall after-tax rate of return on stockholders' equity for four groups of publicly owned profit-seeking corporations among the fifty largest prime contractors and for all U.S. manufacturing corporations, except newspapers, in 1957 and 1962. The groups are based on the primary product of the firms, including their civilian business.

	1957	1962
Publicly owned profit-seeking firms among the fifty largest military prime contractors*		
I. Aircraft and propulsion	16.96	12.67
II. Electronics	13.23	12.07
III. Others, except petroleum refiners	14.71	16.06
IV. Petroleum refiners	13.44	10.51
All U.S. manufacturing corporations†	11.0	9.8

  * Omitting A.T.&.T.
  † Except newspapers.

Source: Baldwin, *The Structure of the Defense Market,* pp. 181, 183.

Only the rates of return for the aircraft and propulsion group can be considered rates earned primarily on military business; the other three groups derived less than half of their sales revenue from military business. The decline in the rate for the aircraft and propulsion group reflects not only the decline experienced by all manufacturing corporations, but also the losses incurred on civilian aircraft production by several of the corporations in this group. The rise in the rate for the third group would be converted into a decline if General Motors were omitted.

These data give only a partial indication of the profitability of military procurement awards because many forms of hidden profits are excluded.[10] However, they are sufficient to make clear why some of the largest corporations in the United States urge the expansion of military expenditures and go to great lengths to increase their share in the total. Generals and admirals are hired upon their retirement from the service to help increase the sales of their corporate employers to the Pentagon. Those still in service are flattered, catered to, and cajoled for the same purpose. Jimmy Ling, head of Ling-Temco-Vaught, one of the most successful military contractors, has told how his company studies the Pentagon promotion lists to see which officers will be likely candidates for the top positions and then picks their brains to get insights into the kinds of weaponry that might be emphasized if a particular officer became chief of staff.

The giant corporations that receive the bulk of military procurement contracts are not the only force outside the Department of Defense that presses for the maintenance and expansion of military spending. The location of their military production facilities creates a host of other supporters. Workers employed in these facilities come to see their livelihood as a function of the orders their employers obtain. Smaller businessmen emerge and expand on the flow of spending generated. Local and state government officials and Congressmen find their political careers dependent on the continued prosperity deriving from the production of these establishments.

The geographic distribution of military production has been quite uneven. Some states have had a much larger share than others, and particular areas within states have become very vulnerable to changes in military expenditure. In 1959 California had an estimated 940,000 people employed by the Department of Defense and by firms working on military production. This amounted to 19 percent of total non-agricultural employment. The comparable proportion for Washington was 22 percent, for Arizona 17 percent, and for Maryland 16 percent; on the other hand, for Wisconsin and West Virginia it was less than 3 percent.[11]

The distribution of military procurement awards by regions is subject to marked shifts. To some extent these shifts reflect efforts to stimulate economic activity in depressed areas. To a greater extent they reflect regional differences in political influence in Washington at different times. However, the most important factor is the changing product mix desired by the Pentagon. Limited "hot" wars, such as the Korean and the Vietnam wars, favor areas producing the more conventional armaments used in such conflicts; the missile build-up led to a marked increase in awards to California and Florida. The table below shows the percentage distribution of military prime contracts in three different periods. Far greater shifts than those shown have occurred, of course, among smaller areas within each region. Inevitably, such changes result in great expansion in some areas and contraction in others and at times particular areas experience first rapid expansion, then sharp contraction in their economic activity. There can be little doubt that the rapidity of change in procurement patterns has introduced an element of instability at the local level and in the individual family which is related to some of the most pressing social problems of American life.

Research and Development

The Cold War has come to dominate research and development in the United States. It is the reason for the major part of the funds provided by the federal government, which constitute roughly two-thirds of all expenditures in this field. A large fraction of these funds goes for R & D in nuclear weapons, military planes, and other armament. Another large fraction is devoted to the space program, much of which has a clearly miliary orientation. Even that part of the space program which may have no conceivable military purpose is largely motivated by the Cold War: it is intended to provide spectacular scientific achievements that will enhance the prestige of the United States in the struggle with the socialist countries for allegiance

Percentage of Military Prime Contract Awards
by Region for Selected Periods

Region	World War II	Korean War	Fiscal 1961
East North Central	32.4	27.4	11.8
Middle Atlantic	23.6	25.1	19.9
West North Central	5.6	6.8	5.8
South Central	8.8	6.4	8.2
New England	8.9	8.1	10.5
South Atlantic	7.2	7.6	10.6
Pacific	12.3	17.9	26.9
Mountain	1.2	0.7	5.7
Alaska & Hawaii	—	—	.6
Grand totals	100.0	100.0	100.0

Source: U.S. Department of Defense, *The Changing Patterns of Defense Procurement,* June 1962, Table II. Cited in Perlo, *Militarism and Industry,* p. 109

throughout the world and offers little direct enhancement of the material welfare of the American people—nor is any such enhancement intended.*

Only token sums have been appropriated by the federal government for research in such problem areas as urban transportation, air and water pollution, mental health, slum clearance, race relations, and a host of others which bear directly on the quality of American life. These do not seem to be clearly related to the Cold War and therefore receive much less material support from the Administration, Congress, and organs of public opinion than do military and space programs, although their effect on the outcome of the Cold War may be more decisive in the long run.

Total funds for research and development in the United States increased from about $10 billion in 1957 to about $20

---

* Many scientists have welcomed the large expenditures on the space program as providing a means for acquiring knowledge about the universe that would otherwise have been obtained much more slowly. However, others in the scientific community have lamented the disproportionate amounts going into space research compared with funds available for investigation in areas of knowledge of more consequence to human welfare.

billion in 1965. Federal R & D expenditures, primarily for military and space projects, contributed greatly to this expansion. Most of these federal funds were provided by the Department of Defense (DOD) and the National Aeronautics and Space Administration (NASA). DOD accounted for 47 percent of all federal obligations for R & D in fiscal year 1966 and NASA for 32 percent.[12]

Funds for industrial R & D performance rose from $7.7 billion in 1957 to $14.2 billion in 1965, although its share in the total declined from 78 percent to about 70 percent. The federal government's contribution to industrial R & D performance increased over this period from $4.3 billion (56 percent) to $7.8 billion (55 percent). The bulk of all funds for industrial R & D are accounted for by five leading industries: in 1965 two of these—aircraft and missiles, and electrical equipment and communication—had 58 percent of the total, and these two plus three others—chemicals and allied products, motor vehicles and other transportation equipment, and machinery—had 85 percent. The share of the first two in funds furnished by the federal government was much higher, amounting to more than four-fifths of the total; 88 percent of the funds for R & D in aircraft and missiles and 62 percent of the funds for R & D in the electrical equipment and communications industry were furnished by the federal government.[13]

The concentration of experimental, development, test, and research (EDTR) work performed for the Department of Defense by private corporations is more pronounced than that of military procurement as a whole. EDTR increased from 13.5 percent of total military procurement in fiscal year 1956 to 25.7 percent in fiscal year 1961 and thereafter declined slowly to 21.4 percent in fiscal year 1964, but the share of EDTR awards going to firms classified as small business dropped from 5.7 percent in fiscal year 1956 to 2.9 percent in fiscal year 1961 and then rose to 3.7 in fiscal year 1964.[14] The latter figures contrast with the 17 to 21 percent of military prime contracts going to firms classified as small business. The concentration of EDTR awards in a few firms is brought out in the comparison of fiscal year 1962 with overall military procurement in the table below.

The figures in parentheses show the percentage of EDTR awards to the firms with the largest percentage of overall procurement. It is clear that the firms that lead in overall procurement also lead in EDTR awards and that they get a larger percentage of the latter than they do of the former.

	Percentage of total awards accounted for by the largest:				
	firm	*4 firms*	*8 firms*	*20 firms*	*50 firms*
EDTR	8.3	31.2	50.6	72.4	87.2
	(8.2)	(31.2)	(48.1)	(65.7)	(80.5)
Overall procurement	5.6	18.7	30.0	46.5	63.4

Source: Baldwin, *The Structure of the Defense Market*, pp. 115-116.

Some authorities have seen the vast expenditures on Cold War R & D as a threat to the general development of productivity in the American economy. Seymour Melman calls this threat the "depletion of production."[15] He cites much evidence of the diversion of skilled scientific and engineering personnel from producer- and consumer-goods industries to armament and space programs as a result of higher salaries. In his view, this diversion is related to the outmoded physical plant of much of the American economy. However, it would seem that he has underestimated the fall-out of technical progress applicable to many fields and deriving from R & D in armament and space programs. Certainly European political and industrial leaders are convinced that the giant American-based corporations have acquired an enormous lead in technology over European companies as a result of their participation in the R & D programs financed on such a gigantic scale by the U.S. government. It may be that this technological advantage shows to a greater degree in the overseas plants of the American-based corporations, but, if this is true, it cannot be explained as the result of the diversion of skilled scientific and engineering manpower to armament and space programs.

A very real consequence of the federal government's greatly increased expenditures on R & D and their concentration in contracts with a relatively few giant American corporations has been the reinforcement of the dominant position of these enterprises in the U.S. economy and in that of the rest of the "free" world. They have obtained technological knowledge of enormous value, often protected by patent rights, and have reaped profits in the process. They have acquired experience in the management of large research divisions and have built up extensive organizations of engineers and scientists. It is not surprising that they increasingly push into areas of research, policy formulation, and other operations traditionally considered to be the realm of government or of non-profit institutions. Thus a number of large manufacturing corporations have contracted with the federal government to operate training camps for the poverty program, and aircraft and other corporations in California have been given contracts by the state government to analyze and propose solutions to such problems as juvenile delinquency. Recently, International Business Machines, Westinghouse, Philco (Ford), Minnesota Mining and Manufacturing, and other corporations vied for a government contract to develop three single-semester courses for the U.S. Naval Academy.[16] This trend, if it continues, would carry the process of integration of government and business to a new plane.

Foreign Investment by the Multi-national Corporation

The dominant business institution of contemporary capitalist society is the giant supra-national corporation. It is no longer sufficient to recognize that the giant corporation has become the characteristic vehicle of monopoly capitalism in all the principal industrial nations outside the socialist sector of the world. Nor is it enough to appreciate the role of the giant corporation domiciled in one or another advanced capitalist country in the imperialist domination of colonial and neo-colonial regions of the world. The internationalization of business which is now taking place is projecting the giant corporation with its holdings scattered about the world beyond the control of any specific national government. The organizational basis for this stage of capitalist development has been created in a large number of corporate entities. Only the formal legal reflection of this development remains.

This new stage of monopoly capitalism has been well described by George W. Ball, an Undersecretary of State in two administrations. Now the chairman of the foreign operations branch of Lehman Brothers, one of the leading Wall Street investment banking houses, he is said to feel himself to be part of an emerging industrial structure that some day will transcend national boundaries. "Before many years we may see supranational companies incorporated under treaty arrangements, without a domicile in any particular nation-state."[17] He emphasizes the fact that

> modern business—sustained and reinforced by modern technology—has outgrown the constrictive limits of the antiquated political structures in which most of the world is organized . . . the explosion of business beyond national borders will tend to create needs and pressures that can alter political structures to fit the requirements of modern man far more adequately than the present crazy-quilt of small national states. And meanwhile, commercial, monetary, and antitrust policies—and even the domiciliary supervision of earth-straddling corporations—will have to be increasingly entrusted to supranational institutions.[18]

Of course, the major thrust of this internationalization of business comes from corporations that got their start in the United States. As the leading capitalist power, with the richest hinterland in which to develop, it had provided the base for the creation of the largest corporate giants well before World War II. Protected from the disruption and destruction of actual combat, the largest American corporations flourished on wartime orders and close integration in government operations. New giants were created.

Today, according to Raymond Vernon, "nearly half of *Fortunes'* 500 largest U.S. companies . . . have extensive overseas investments in plants, mines, or oil fields, representing an aggregate stake that is on the order of $50 billion. A score or two of these large companies now have a third or more of their total assets abroad; even a greater number derive a third or more of their total income from foreign sales through one channel or another."[19] Some of these corporations had acquired extensive properties abroad well before World War II, and a considerable number had some direct foreign investments. The big push, however, came after World War II. The value of U.S. direct investments abroad increased from $7.2 billion in 1946 to $54.6 billion in 1966. This has been predominantly an activity of very large corporations. In 1957, the most recent year for which such information is available, forty-five firms, each with direct investments abroad valued at $100 million or over, accounted for 57 percent of the total value of all U.S. direct investments in foreign countries. At that time the Department of Commerce listed only 2,812 corporate and non-corporate reporters of direct investments abroad.[20]

These direct investments in plants, mines, oil fields, plantations, and other facilities have generally been very profitable for their American corporate owners. In 1966 "earnings on direct investment abroad (before U.S. taxes) were about $5.76 billion or 11.7 percent of the invested capital; including receipts of royalties and fees, the yield was about 13.75 percent."[21] The rates of return on investments in the advanced capitalist countries tend to be lower than the average. Those obtained from oil fields and mines in the underdeveloped countries are often truly fantastic—57 percent in the Middle East, 63 percent in Libya, 27 percent in Peru, and 17 percent in Venezuela in 1966. The income returned to the parent companies in the United States typically exceeds the flow of direct investment capital from the United States to these countries. The table below reveals the relation between these flows for different regions during the period 1950-1965.

Thus parent corporations took back in earnings about $13 billion more over this period than flowed out from their treasuries as capital for direct investments abroad. Despite this, the value of these direct investments abroad rose from $11.8 billion in 1950 to $49.3 billion at the end of 1965.

The large overseas investments of a relatively small number of giant American corporations and the very profitable returns obtained from them are intimately linked with the Cold War.

	Europe	Canada	Latin America	All others	Total
			(in billions of dollars)		
Flow of direct investments from U.S.	$8.1	$6.8	$3.8	$5.2	$23.9
Income on this capital transferred to U.S.	5.5	5.9	11.3	14.3	37.0
Difference (+ or −)	+2.6	+0.9	−7.5	−9.1	−13.1

Source: Henry Magdoff. *The Age of Imperialism* (New York: Monthly Review Press, 1969), p. 198.

Their continued existence depends on the continued existence of regimes based on private property in the countries in which the investments are located. Socialist revolutions must be prevented at all costs. Socialism must be wiped out or undermined in Vietnam, in China, in Cuba, in Eastern Europe, and in the U.S.S.R. if at all possible, and these regions must be reclaimed for private enterprise.

To this end, leading American business circles have been instrumental in the formulation and implementation of government policies involving the use of both the "carrot" and the "stick." The Marshall Plan was developed to revive the faltering Western European societies and thus prevent their conversion to socialism. American troops in Europe and the restoration of the West German army were the "stick" that could be used against revolutions in Western Europe and, if the opportunity arose, in support of counter-revolutions in Eastern Europe. Aid programs in other parts of the world were supported less out of a concern with development in the poorer countries than with meeting short-term political crises. Where aid and/or the CIA failed, military intervention by American troops was called for. The muscle for this program to guarantee that this really become the "American Century" required vast arms expenditures, 275 major base complexes in 31 countries and more than 1,400 foreign bases of all kinds, and more than one million American troops abroad and a larger number in the United

States. Despite their general antipathy to government expenditures, no significant number of businessmen has questioned the tremendous sums spent for military purposes. Although the opposition to American military actions in Vietnam has come to include nearly half the population, few if any of the top business leaders have voiced any criticism.

The Integration of Business and Government

The Cold War has increased the integration of the great corporations and the government in the United States beyond that known other than in periods of full mobilization for war. This integration has developed primarily in conjunction with government procurement of military equipment and the research and development associated with it, and with the promotion of specific corporate and general state interests in the international sphere. It is manifest in the movement of top corporate officials into federal policy-making positions regardless of which party is in power and the reverse movement of leading government personnel, particularly general officers of the armed services, into the upper echelons of corporate management. A surprising indication of concern over this phenomenon, which his administration had in no way combated, was expressed by President Eisenhower near the end of his second term when he warned of the danger arising from the military-industrial complex. More specific and critical accounts have been given by C. Wright Mills and Fred J. Cook, among others.[22]

Military procurement and research and development contracts give rise to particularly strong incentives to develop close relations between corporate and government officials. In general both groups have a mutual interest in urging larger appropriations for military equipment. The corporations have found that retired general officers often make valuable corporate officials as a result of their knowledge of Pentagon requirements and their contacts in the military hierarchy. Military executives are keenly aware of the special knowledge and capabilities possessed by corporations. The Department of Defense maintains an elaborate public relations organization and uses it effectively to cultivate the support of the business community. Corporations organize institutes, such as the Mobility Forums sponsored annually by the Allison Division of General Motors, at which leading corporation executives, military officers, and others gather to discuss matters of mutual interest and to get acquainted. Of course, not all is sweetness and light. The rivalry can be bitter when a choice has to be made between two planes, for example, with millions or perhaps billions of dollars in orders riding on the decision. Then the fur can fly, as ever Secretaries of Defense have learned. But the general picture is one of increasing integration.

International policy, particularly where—as is usually the case —corporate interests are affected, is one aspect of government to which members of leading business circles are eager to lend their services. Top officials of investment banking houses or large corporations are frequently called in for special assignments. Sometimes they become Undersecretaries of State or even top dogs. The regular personnel of the Department of State, however, are well schooled to advance their interests. In the example drawn from the communications industry that follows, it is difficult to distinguish the industry men from the government men without the help of labels.

The communications industry affords perhaps the most striking example of the way the Cold War has contributed to the process of the growing domination of American society and much of the rest of the world by giant corporations and their integration with government. Of course, this industry has long been characterized by very large private corporate organizations with close ties to government. The American Telephone and Telegraph Company was the largest corporation in the world well before the Cold War, and its intimate association with federal and state government has been inherent in the grants of monopoly it has received. Similarly, International Telephone and Telegraph, Radio Corporation of America and its subsidiary, National Broadcasting Corporation, Columbia Broadcasting Corporation, and American Broadcasting Company, as well as a number of cable companies, motion picture producing and distributing enterprises, and newspaper, magazine, and book publishing corporations, have long since become corporate giants more or less deeply involved with the federal government.

In some cases this involvement derived primarily from the government's role as the dispenser of privileged and protected positions to broadcasting stations owned by, or affiliated with, giant corporations for the exclusive use of particular frequencies in the radio spectrum. Closely related was the federal government's role at international conferences in promoting the interests of these private enterprises—as well as those of its own agencies—in the allocation of frequencies in the radio spectrum.[23] In other cases the close association of the private giants with the government was based mainly on the readiness of the latter to exert pressure on foreign governments in the interest of its clients—for example, to secure removal of barriers to the unrestrained flow of motion pictures made by United States companies. In still other cases the overt relationship with the government was largely the consequence of the market it provided for the products of the corporation.

However, the pre-World War II development of these phenomena has been dwarfed by their efflorescense in the Cold War. In the prewar era, the U.S. communications industry was primarily concerned with the exploitation of the internal market. Although the motion picture industry had important foreign sales and IT & T and the cable companies had significant foreign facilities, the almost exclusive orientation of the advertising by U.S. corporations to the domestic market kept broadcasting and the other mass media dependent on this source of revenue at home. In the Cold War, however, the drive for greatly expanded military communications to serve the hundreds of bases scattered about the world; the opportunity to obtain revenue from advertising the products of U.S. firms that were rapidly expanding their exports and, even more, their production facilities in foreign countries; and the efforts to win the support of foreigners in the Cold War and to spread "the American way of life"—all these forces led to a vast expansion of the American communications industry and to its closer integration with the state.

For our present purpose it will suffice to give an account of the most recent and most sensational development in the communications industry—space communications.[24] In every respect the communications satellite is a product of the Cold War. It was primarily a by-product of the enormous research expenditures on missiles and rockets. The first operational system utilizing communications satellites was established by the Department of Defense to provide mobile communications in any part of the world in conjunction with its counter-insurgency program. The first non-military communications satellite system was organized in such a manner as to assure American corporate control and preclude participation by Soviet Russia or other socialist countries despite the system's global reach and its vulnerability to competitive activity. Furthermore, it was initiated explicitly to prevent British maintenance and extension of control over international cable communications.

Although President Kennedy emphasized the use of communications satellites for commercial, educational, and economic development purposes,[25] priority was given to the military possibilities. Lt. Gen. Arthur D. Starbird, Director of the Defense Communications Agency and Manager of the National Communications System, stressed the importance of the communications satellite in providing the "means of establishing, on the shortest time-scale, reliable communications to out-of-the-way areas where tension develops—that is to say, flexibility to extend rapidly into new areas. . . . Any system which will give a rapid, instantaneous, reliable communication to a new, troublesome, out-of-the-way area will have a tremendous advantage in the future."[26]

Use of the communications satellite for global military purposes required an international agreement allocating a part of the radio spectrum to this end. The Extraordinary Administrative Radio Conference to Allocate Frequency Bands for Space Radio Communications of the International Telecommunications Union, held in Geneva in 1963, provided the opportunity for the U.S. government to achieve this goal. The U.S. proposals, originally formulated in the Department of Defense and revised over a period of several years in interdepartmental committees, called for the reservation of a narrow band of frequencies for satellite communications. The agreement reached at Geneva allocated 2,800 megacycles of frequency space, but only 50 megacycles were reserved exclusively for transmission in the earth-to-satellite mode; the other 2,750 megacycles were to be used also by various ground communications networks, in particular microwave relay systems. Dr. Charyk, the president of the Communciations Satellite Corporation (Comsat) and a member of the U.S. negotiating team at the conference, testified that the 50 megacycles of exclusive frequencies were for the use of "mobile stations which could be quickly transported to any part of the world, set up and be in operation with high quality communications in a very short period of time." If these stations had to use non-exclusive frequencies, extensive coordination would be required to prevent interference with and from other communications facilities in the region. Dr. Charyk and other authorities made clear that these exclusive frequencies are of military value only.[27] These mobile communications stations are viewed by the Pentagon as the alarm system which will facilitate intervention in any part of the underdeveloped world where people attempt to pursue a course contrary to that considered appropriate by Washington.

By 1966, the Department of Defense had the first truly global system of space communications in operation.[28] Two of the eight initial ground stations were in Vietnam, and most of the others were located in the southern hemisphere, the poorest half of the world.

The dominance of the giant corporation in the American economy and its close integration with government is epitomized in the creation of the Communications Satellite Corporation, the chosen instrument for the exploitation of this new medium in commercial and other non-military fields. Despite the peculiarly public nature of the origin and function of this device—which made it a particularly appropriate object of ownership and operation by a public agency, even an international one—President Eisenhower proposed, at the end of his second term, that "the government should aggressively encourage private enterprise in the establishment and operation of satellite relays for revenue-producing purposes."[29] President Kennedy adopted essentially the same position within six months after he took office. A state-ment of Presidential policy on communications satellites, issued July 24, 1961, reaffirmed the desirability of private ownership and operation, although it included an invitation to all nations to participate in the ownership of an international communica-tions satellite system.

Despite the fears of a number of senators that the choice of a private entity for the development of space communications would be the source of future conflicts, the Communications Satellite Act was approved in August 1962, and the Corporation was organized as a private enterprise in February 1963. Half of the shares were sold to individual investors and half were pur-chased by 163 authorized communications carriers. AT & T, the largest stockholder, acquired 29 percent of the total stock issue (57.9 percent of the industry allocation), and the four largest industry stockholders—AT & T, IT & T, General Telephone, and RCA—came out with 45.5 percent of the total (90.9 percent of the carrier allocation). Under the terms of the act, three members of the board of directors were named by the President, six were elected by the carriers, and six by the public shareholders.

The hurried organization of Comsat reflected the determina-tion of industry and government to obtain maximum advantage from the technological lead that the U.S. held: it "was established for the purpose of taking and holding a position of leadership for the United States in the field of international global com-mercial satellite services."[30] Two things were necessary to achieve this: interference-free channels on an international scale and sufficient numbers of foreign message-receivers. The pursuit of these two goals required close cooperation between government and industry. The U.S. move to secure an international agree-ment on the allocation of radio frequencies for space communica-tions at the 1963 conference in Geneva has already been described. Some of the seventy countries participating in the conference wanted the allocation to be temporary, but the U.S. delegation insisted that it be definitive and in an informal vote in committee its position was upheld 18 to 4, the minority consisting of the U.S.S.R. and three Soviet bloc countries. The members of the American delegation, which was led by Joseph H. McConnell, president of Reynolds Metal Company, and which included the president of Comsat, Joseph Charyk, and board member Leonard Marks, as well as a number of government representatives, were very pleased with the results of the conference. Their attitude was expressed by Dr. Charyk: "Who is there first has a priority, so to speak."

The assurance that there would be customers for Comsat's services was provided by the organization of a consortium to establish an international communications system. The agreement to organize Intelsat, signed in August 1964, was preceded by a series of meetings with representatives of twenty-two Western European states organized as the European Conference on Satellite Communications, as well as bilateral meetings with representatives of Canada, Australia, and Japan. The U.S. delegation at these meetings was nominally chaired by Ambassador Bruce, but the principal American negotiator was the vice-chairman of the delegation, Dr. Charyk. As James McCormack, chairman and chief executive officer of Comsat, said several years later, the company must be viewed "as a unique concept in corporate structure and purpose. It is a privately owned corporation, but it also serves as a representative of the United States Government."[31]

Of the nineteen original signers of the agreement to organize Intelsat, all but the United States, Canada, Australia, and Japan were Western European countries (including the Vatican). Ownership was distributed on a share basis to communications agencies designated by the signatory countries in proportion to their capital contributions. Subsequently, thirty-nine other countries affiliated with the consortium, making necessary a redistribution of ownership shares. Comsat, the designated U.S. agency, had originally held 61 percent of the shares in Intelsat but with the increase in the number of participating countries, the share dropped to 54 percent. The agreement specified, however, that no matter had many countries eventually affiliate the U.S. share cannot be reduced below 50.6 percent. Thus the president of Comsat could assure the Congress that "the corporation in any event has a veto on all actions."[32]

In the background of the negotiations that led up to the formation of Intelsat was a typical imperialist struggle. The American industry-government team, taking advantage of their lead in satellite technology, rushed "a program for Early Bird which would supply this North Atlantic capability in 1965" in order to forestall the efforts of British and other European interests to "get in with . . . another generation of cables" that would maintain their dominant position in international communications. The effort was successful; it "broke the resistance of these certain European countries and resulted in . . . a highly favorable climate for cooperative participation in an early system . . . as the Europeans have seen the determination and speed with which we have been moving, their interest in climbing aboard has intensified. And that is exactly what we wanted."[33] Comsat did need European and other foreign customers, so it was necessary to give them a share in the enterprise to secure their participation. The European countries, refusing to bargain individually with the Americans, had joined together in the European Conference on Satellite Communications to enhance their bargaining position. However, Comsat was determined to maintain control of Intelsat: "The fact is the Europeans are anxious to put up a greater share of the money than we think they are entitled to." This remark by the State Department's legal adviser led Representative Randall of Missouri to conclude that "they are trying to get their nose under the tent."[34]

Obviously, the Soviet Union and the other socialist countries were not likely to participate in a system that gave them such a small voice compared to that of the United States. Furthermore, there is little reason to think that Comsat wanted them to participate. As the State Department's Mr. Chayes put it: "Their international communications are not very great when you take them as a share of world international telecommunications."[35] This was to be a private enterprise for profit and paying traffic was what counted. However, the Soviet Union has announced its intention of establishing an international satellite communications system "open to all countries,"[36] and other nations have initiated or are considering national or regional systems. These plans point up the vulnerability of the American attempt to dominate international communications.

Conclusions

This review of the way the Cold War has come to dominate the economy of the capitalist world has been devoted primarily to its impact on the structure and performance of the U.S. economy. The logic of this emphasis lies in the leading role of the United States in the initiation and prosecution of the Cold War and in the dominant position of U.S. capitalism in the capitalist world. United States arms expenditures dwarf those of the rest of the so-called free world, both in absolute terms and in relation to Gross National Product. Similarly, the U.S. aid program, first in the form of the Marshall Plan and later as assistance for the underdeveloped countries, has greatly outweighed the aid programs of Western Europe and Japan. Furthermore, the United States has been the principal source of armaments for the "West" in the limited "hot" wars of this period, as well as the leading participant on the "Western" side in several of them.

All of this has been of direct consequence in the maintenance of effective demand in the United States. Indirectly, the contribution of these expenditures to the high level of economic activity in the United States has been crucial to the economies of the other capitalist countries, for the United States is the major market for their exports. No one believes that Europe and Japan could have enjoyed boom conditions if the United States had experienced a prolonged depression. Directly, Marshall Plan aid, the aggressive investment activities of American corporations in Europe, and the troop pay and military procurement expenditures of the United States in Europe and Japan have contributed greatly to their postwar prosperity.

The United States has been a leading advocate of the Common Market as an essential step toward political unity in Western Europe. It has offset the danger to its exports from the Market's common tariff by pressing for general tariff reductions in the Kennedy Round and in earlier negotiations, while American corporations have established production facilities inside the Market. The restrictions on trade with the socialist countries were imposed at U.S. insistence, and it has been primarily U.S.

trade that has been affected. The United States at times encouraged and at times resisted movements for national independence in the former European and Japanese imperial domains. Where these movements have succeeded in winning political independence, they have in many cases remained economically dependent, subject to more subtle forms of exploitation. American corporations have been the principal direct beneficiaries of these neocolonialist relationships.

Finally, the multi-national corporations are primarily American institutions. Their export of capital and the return flow of their profits are important influences on the level of economic activity in the United States and on its balance of payments. Their integration with the U.S. government, and that of the more nationally oriented giant enterprises, is more directly related to the Cold War than is the integration of business with government in most other advanced capitalist countries. In the U.S., business is integrated with the government to obtain contracts and to advance its interests abroad, whereas in Europe the integration of business with government is more a response to pressures for social reform and to foreign competition.

What contradictions have these developments produced? First, there is the problem inherent in armament expenditure of how to maintain a level of spending sufficient to keep the economy from stagnating or going into a depression in an era of thermonuclear weapons. Overkill gets to seem redundant even in the Pentagon. The Vietnam War has provided a sink into which sharply increased expenditures could be poured, but this war has proved more divisive of American society than any preceding one. It has made most Americans aware of how difficult it is to order the affairs of a distant people who are determined to control their own country. And it has made them conscious of how easily a small war can become a big one. This or another Administration would probably want a better organized consensus before taking on another Vietnam, and that might be hard to get with the Bomb in the background.

Having raised the rate of military spending by 50 percent in pursuit of victory in Vietnam, how, once the war is over, do we keep it at the higher level or raise it further if the economy needs an additional infusion? Is there a substitute? The advantages of armaments as an outlet for government spending (or as an absorber of surplus) are widely recognized. But some have suggested that expenditures for "the moon race" have some of the same advantages. Others have listed whole catalogues of deficiencies that would require large public expenditures for their correction. Many are convinced that reductions in tax rates, particularly on personal incomes, will do the trick. It is not our purpose to evaluate these alternatives; others have questioned their effectiveness or their acceptance by those who determine policy.[37] It is sufficient to point out that even with military spending running at a $74 billion annual rate and the federal government deficit at a $15 billion annual rate, capacity utilization by manufacturers dropped from 87 percent in the first quarter of 1967 to 83.8 percent in the third quarter.[38]

Another problem-area is evident in the balance-of-payments crises of the United States and of certain other capitalist countries. In the case of the United States, it is a crisis of liquidity that is a direct product of the Cold War. Military spending abroad and aid payments for off-share procurement are significant factors in U.S. payments to foreigners. In a broad sense the large current outflow of capital for direct investment is an aspect of the Cold War. The federal government has attempted to secure the voluntary curtailment of this outflow, but is hard-pressed to meet the argument of the capital-exporting firms that the profits returned from their accumulated investments abroad exceed the current outflow of capital. Meanwhile, some foreigners choose to use the dollars they receive to buy gold from the United States or to acquire bank balances that can quickly be converted to demand for gold.

In the case of Great Britain, also, military spending abroad is a big factor in its recurrent balance-of-payments crises. A recent study reports that in 1966 British government spending abroad amounted to $1.32 billion; this plus a deficit of $386 million on merchandise trade more than offset net invisible earnings of $1.53 billion, leaving a current deficit of about $171 million after corrections for rounding figures.[39] Britain has responded in part by trying to persuade the West German government to carry a larger share of the cost of maintaining British troops in that country and by reducing overseas bases, most recently in Aden. Britain's greater dependence on foreign trade makes its balance-of-payments more vulnerable than that of the United States. When its usual trade deficit expands, British governments, reluctant to reduce significantly their role in the Cold War, are faced with a choice between deflationary policies and devaluation. Both policies tend to shift the burden to the working class and thus threaten the social harmony so essential to the pursuit of the Cold War.

In general, international competition among the capitalist powers threatens to disrupt the post-World War II agreements that have provided the basis for the Cold War. The existence of national sovereignties casts a shadow over many of the institutions developed in this period. Businessmen and others have never been reluctant to use the power of the sovereign state when it seemed to their advantage. France's attitude toward Britain's application to join the Common Market is a case in point. So, too, is the recent outburst of protectionist demands in the United States following the completion of the Kennedy Round of tariff negotiations. The rumblings against the invasion of Europe by the American multi-national corporations point up the latter's vulnerability to national sovereignty. The pattern of social harmony in the leading capitalist countries, based on the concession of apparently significant wage increases which are partly offset by creeping inflation, is under pressure from the competition of the low-wage countries.

Even the growing integration of business and government may prove to have generated its own contradiction. Certainly there is little basis for complacency among those accustomed to rule.

Notes

1. Paul A. Baran and Paul M. Sweezy, *Monopoly Capital* (New York: Monthly Review Press, 1966), p. 176.

2. Richard P. Oliver, "The Employment Effect of Defense Expenditures," *Monthly Labor Review*, September 1967, pp. 9-16.

3. *Ibid.,* p. 9n.

4. William L. Baldwin, *The Structure of the Defense Market, 1955-1964* (Durham, N.C.: Duke University Press, 1967), p. 21.

5. *Ibid.,* p. 28.

6. *Ibid.,* p. 40.

7. Merton J. Peck and Frederic M. Scherer, *The Weapons Acquisition Process: An Economic Analysis* (Boston: Division of Research, Graduate School of Business Administration, Harvard University, 1962), pp. 150-152; cited in Baldwin, *The Structure of the Defense Market,* p. 40.

8. Many examples are summarized by Victor Perlo, *Militarism and Industry: Arms Profiteering in the Missile Age* (New York: International Publishers, 1963), Chap. II.

9. Baldwin, *The Structure of the Defense Market,* p. 182n.

10. Perlo, *Militarism and Industry,* Chap. III.

11. *Ibid.,* p. 193.

12. National Science Foundation, *Federal Funds for Research, Development and Other Scientific Activities,* Fiscal Years 1965, 1966, and 1967, Vol. XV, NSF66-25 (Washington, D.C.: U.S. Government Printing Office, 1966), p. vi.

13. National Science Foundation, *Reviews of Data on Science Resources,* No. 10, December 1966.

14. Baldwin, *The Structure of the Defense Market,* p. 15.

15. *Our Depleted Society* (New York: Holt, Rinehart and Winston, 1965).

16. *New York Times,* October 15, 1967.

17. *New York Times,* September 11, 1967.

18. U.S. Congress, Subcommittee on Foreign Economic Policy of the Joint Economic Committee, *The Future of U.S. Foreign Trade Policy, Hearings,* 90th Cong., 1st sess., July 11-13, 18-20, 1967, vol. I, p. 273.

19. "Multinational Enterprise and National Sovereignty," *Harvard Business Review,* March 1967, p. 156.

20. U.S. Department of Commerce, *U.S. Business Investments in Foreign Countries* (Washington, D.C.: U.S. Government Printing Office, 1960), p. 144.

21. Walther Lederer and Frederick Cutler, "International Investments of the United States in 1966," *Survey of Current Business,* September 1967, p. 40.

22. C. Wright Mills, *The Power Elite* (New York: Oxford University Press, 1956); Fred J. Cook, *The Warfare State* (New York: Macmillan, 1962).

23. See Dallas W. Smythe, *The Structure and Policy of Electronic Communications,* University of Illinois Bulletin No. 82 (Urbana, Illinois: Bureau of Economic and Business Research, 1957).

24. I have drawn heavily on Herbert I. Schiller, *Mass Communication and American Empire* (New York: Augustus A. Kelley, 1969), for this section.

25. Statement of the President of the United States on Communications Satellite Policy, July 24, 1961, reprinted in *Satellite Communications-1964* (Part 1), Hearings before a Subcommittee of the Committee on Government Operations, House of Representatives, 88th Cong., 2nd sess., p. 590.

26. U.S. Congress, House, Subcommittee of the Committee on Government Operations, *Military Communication Satellite Program, Hearings,* 88th Cong., 1st sess., April 23, 1963, p. 8.

27. *Satellite Communications-1964* (Part 1), pp. 109-110, 193.

28. *Telecommunications Reports,* June 20, 1966.

29. *New York Times,* December 31, 1960.

30. U.S. Congress, Senate, Subcommittee on Communications, Testimony of McGeorge Bundy, *Progress Report on Space Communications, Hearings,* 89th Cong., 2nd sess., August 10, 17, 18, and 23, 1966, p. 81.

31. "Comsat's Role in Communications," *Signal,* May 1967 p. 52.

32. *Space Communications-1964* (Part 2), p. 741.

33. Testimony of Abraham Chayes, U.S. State Department legal adviser, *Satellite Communications-1964* (Part 1), p. 364.

34. *Ibid.,* p. 363.

35. *Space Communications-1964* (Part), p. 267.

36. *Aviation Week and Space Technology,* August 28, 1967, p. 31.

37. See, for example, Baran and Sweezy, pp. 161-175, 176-77n.

38. *New York Times,* October 19, 1967.

39. *New York Times,* October 19, 1967; report of the British National Export Council publication, *Britain's Invisible Earnings.*

The Militarization
of the American Economy
by Charles E. Nathanson

It must be apparent to any somewhat detached observer that the enormous sums spent in the Cold War on the development and production of weapons of war have been quite beneficial to the functioning of the present-day corporate economy. Yet there are important questions about the degree to which military interests have penetrated the American business community, questions about the exact extent to which business as a whole has become dependent on the military budget and thus on a continuation of the Cold War. The present essay is an attempt to reveal, as if it were an anatomical X-ray, the direct economic bonds between the military and the major sectors and corporate structures of American manufacturing. Since I am interested primarily in the influence of long-term Cold War military production on business interests, I have tried to avoid the biasing effect of Vietnam War expenditures by using data primarily from the years prior to the large expansion of our effort in that war.

An indication of the enormity of the amount spent on military production and research and development is that in fiscal 1964, funds paid out for these two items came to almost $31 billion.*

---

* This figure breaks down as follows: Defense Department weapons procurement: $15.8 billion; Defense Department Research and Development: $7.1 billion; Defense Department Military Assistance: $1.5 billion; National Aeronautics and Space Administration: $4 billion; Atomic Energy Commission: $2.4 billion. The AEC budget is distributed primarily among weapons, research, special new materials, raw materials, and nuclear reactor production. The NASA budget has been included in this total because it is virtually impossible to dissociate our interests in space from our military interests. The Air Force, which itself spends about $1.5 billion on space, uses NASA's greater resources in this area for its own purposes. For example, Air Force pilots receive training for space bombers and interceptors in NASA's Gemini

If this 1964 "peace" rate had been extended for six years, it would have equalled the amount that we spent in the five years and two months of our participation in World War II.[1] In only two years of that war did the expenditures for munitions significantly exceed $30 billion: in 1943, they were $51.7 billion and in 1944, $57.5 billion. War output as a percentage of total output was, of course, far greater in those years than it is now.

The "Encystment" Theory

As a first step in dealing with the question of how much of an interest the business community has in military production, we must analyze the currently dominant theory of military production, the "encystment" theory, because it forms the basis of much liberal optimism about the viability of a non-militarized American capitalism and thus of the prospects for changing the direction of foreign policy by means of political pressure.[2] Developed primarily by liberal economists, many of them under contract to the U.S. Arms Control and Disarmament Agency, the theory holds that modern weapons production is a highly specialized and distinct process, located primarily in the electronics and aerospace industries and having little connection with the traditional manufacturing centers of the economy. Proponents of the theory often contrast production for old-style conventional warfare, when the heavy industrial goods sector of the economy was obviously deeply involved in the manufacture of tanks, artillery, ships, and aircrafts, with modern production for push-button missile warfare, where the demand is for sophisticated electronic equipment, and for hundreds of missiles instead of thousands of aircraft. Production runs tend to be lower than they used to be, and investment is more in scientists and engineers and less in heavy production machinery. Components have been

---

program. In general, the Air Force makes use of space hardware after letting NASA fund the initial cost of research and development. "The space program of NASA is completely tied in with the space program of the military. They are identical," Senator Anderson, chairman of the Senate Space Committee, told the Senate in 1963. On this militarization of the space effort see Amitai Etzioni, *Moondoggle* (Garden City: Doubleday and Co., 1964).

miniaturized, and metals are special lightweight alloys. All these factors, it is argued, diminish the traditional manufacturing industries' stake in armaments.

The fatal shortcoming of the "encystment" theory is that it focuses on the military product rather than on the military producers. The theory correctly identifies the specialized nature of military goods and components—although this too may be exaggerated in view of the current trend toward semi-conventional, counter-revolutionary warfare—but it fails to ask who the military producers are, where they come from, and what the circumstances were under which they entered the military market or failed to leave it. A number of critical features of the business community's stake in military production are therefore lost from sight. Two of the most important are the large-scale effort and failure of specialized aircraft, missile, and military electronics firms to diversify into the civilian economy, and the large-scale diversification into aircraft, missiles, and military electronics by firms that are, or were previously, primarily engaged in the production of commercial electronics, fabricated metals, non-electrical machinery, and various other key civilian goods. When the evidence is viewed from this perspective, it becomes evident that manufacturing as a whole, and especially the key metalworking, producer goods industries, have a far greater stake in militarization than the "encystment" theory allows. It also becomes apparent that the liberals' program of civilian diversification for military producers is highly questionable since many of these firms have only recently diversified *out* of the traditional manufacturing centers because of strong structural obstacles to their expansion or survival there. In short it would seem that the relation of military production to the body of American capitalism should be pictured not as a concentrated cyst but as an extensive network of veins vital to the performance of the whole.

The Input-Output Analysis

The empirical basis for the "encystment" theory is an input-output analysis of military production that shows the proportion of an industry's output that goes directly or indirectly into military products. (See table, p. 211.) Using this approach, we find that the production of military goods consumes 93.7 percent of the output of the aircraft industry, 60.7 percent of the output of the shipping and boating industry, 20.9 percent of the output of the electrical machinery industry, and 20.1 percent of the output of the instruments industry. In the traditional producer goods industries, however, military production consumes only about 8 percent of the output of the fabricated metals industry, 5 percent of the output of the non-electrical machinery industry, and 13 percent of the output of the primary metals industry.

It should be pointed out that, even according to these figures, the involvement of the heavy goods industries in military production is not insubstantial. When one considers, for example, the slow growth and excess capacity of the iron and steel industry in recent years, the military factor in its output (10 percent) cannot be dismissed lightly. In general, the demand for durable producer goods tends to be highly erratic, tied closely to the boom and recession of the business cycle, and the stabilization of output by military demand is no doubt of considerable importance to firms in these industries. Furthermore, figures on the percentage output of an industry going to the military often understate the contribution of military profits to total profits. Military goods and components are highly specialized and tend to be in relatively scarce supply; they are rarely sold in the civilian market and therefore have no standard market price. All these factors lead to higher profits on military items than on civilian items.[3]

A second objection to the input-output statistics is that they fail to reveal the contribution of military production to civilian production. The specialized new products that go into military goods will in some cases become the standard commercial and industrial products of the future. For example, the special refractory metals used in missiles will become standard material in the construction of civilian nuclear power reactors. Firms that are engaged in developing and producing these metals for the military are at the same time developing their future civilian products cost free.

Finally, the input-output statistics grossly understate the extent to which the electronics industry has been militarized. The 20 percent figure given above was based on inter-industry relationships as of 1948. Since that time the percentage of electronic material goods and instruments has increased enormously. Because of its importance to the ensuing argument, it is necessary to analyze the current situation in electronics in some detail.

The best recent estimate—and even this tends toward understatement—was compiled in 1962 by *Electronic News* in conjunction with the Department of Commerce, the Department of Defense, the National Credit Office, and several industry trade associations.[4] The study concluded that 56.2 percent of the total sales of the electronics industry in 1962 went to the military or the closely allied space market. The electronics content of missiles alone accounted for 22.5 percent of the value of all electronics shipments. Consumer electronics products, on the other hand, accounted for only 18.5 percent of the electronics market, and industrial-commercial electronics products accounted for only 19.5 percent of the market. (The remaining 5.8 percent was for replacement parts.)* To some extent, these figures are already outdated: Since 1962, annual missile procurement alone has increased by \$1 billion and space procurement is up by almost \$3 billion. Thus the military share of the electronics market is probably well over 60 percent today.

There is a major source of understatement even in this estimate: The industrial-commercial electronics market is itself

---

* The *Electronic News'* figures on the consumer electronics market are also substantially inflated by the inclusion of phonograph records, which are not really an electronics product. The removal of phonograph records would reduce the consumer sales figure by 10 percent. Another relevant consideration is the fact that television sales, the major commercial market for large firms, have fallen off drastically since the early 1950's. In absolute terms, TV sales have failed to increase since 1955, and their share of the total electronics market as of 1962 was only 7.5 percent. This is only the equivalent of one-third the value of electronics equipment in missiles alone; on the other hand, the development of the transistor, on which the military spent \$35 million,[5] has helped radio sales retain a relatively constant share of the market.

heavily dependent on military demand. It includes many standard industrial products, such as computers and communication equipment, sold directly to military agencies or to industrial concerns which are working on military contracts.[6] Computers have been the fastest growing sector of the industrial-commercial electronics market, and by 1962 accounted for 45 percent of its total sales.[7] But 40 percent of all computers installed up to 1959 were purchased directly by the military or by the weapons industry with government funds.[8] In terms of dollar sales, military purchases were even more significant than the 40 percent figure indicates, since they mainly involved large computers.[9] And in one sense, the entire computer market can be traced to the military, since military requirements financed and directed most of the research and development.[10]

What is true for computers applies equally to other large segments of the industrial-commercial electronics market, such as test and measurement equipment and industrial control instruments. Together with computers, these items make up 65 percent of the industrial market. They are most commonly used in the design and testing of military electronics equipment, which has exceptionally high performance requirements compared to civilian electronics products.[11] Probably as much as 50 percent of the sales of this equipment goes directly or indirectly to the military, and a substantial part of the equipment owes its origin or refinement to military research and development.

Altogether then, indirect and direct military demand may account for close to 70 percent of the total output of the $14-billion-a-year electronics industry. This is just the reverse of the market situation in 1950, when consumer products possessed over 60 percent of the market and military products about 20 percent.[12] Since then consumer sales have increased only about $500 million while military sales have increased more than $7 billion.

Given these figures, it is not surprising to find that practically all major electronics firms are heavily dependent on military markets, although most of the really big military electronics companies once produced primarily consumer products.

Present Output of Major Industry Groups Used by the Military in 1958

Industry	Percent of output to military*
Chemicals	5.3
Fuel & power	7.3
Petroleum	10.4
Primary metals	13.5
Iron & steel	9.8
Fabricated metals	7.9
Non-electrical machinery	5.2
Electrical machinery	20.9
Radio, communications	38.0
Transportation equipment	38.5
Aircraft & parts	93.7
Ships & boats	60.7
Ordnance	100.0
Instruments	20.1
Transportation	5.9
RR & trucking	5.4
Trade	1.4
Services, etc.	1.3
Business services	3.8
Prof. & service industries	1.9
Construction	2.1
Other industries†	2.4
Total industry	5.6

* Refers to output used directly in military end-products and indirectly used by manufacturers of military end-products.

† Food and kindred products, apparel and textile mill products, leather products, paper and allied products, rubber and rubber products, lumber and wood products, non-metallic minerals and products and miscellaneous manufacturing industries.

Source: Leontief-Hoffenberg 1958 matrix. Printed in Seymour Melman, *Disarmament, Its Politics and Economics* (Boston: The American Academy of Arts and Sciences, 1962), p. 138.

RCA, Magnavox, Philco, Sylvania, Motorola, Collins Radio, Emerson, Westinghouse, and General Electric are just a handful of the companies that have diversified out of the more slowly growing consumer field and today at least 20-30 percent of their annual sales are in the military-space field.[13] Other major electronics firms that never had large commercial markets, such as Raytheon, Lear, and General Precision Equipment, sell over 80 percent of their output to the military. The situation is just as serious among small electronics companies: a survey of successful small firms found that three-quarters depend "directly and significantly" on military contracts for their success,[14] while a number of other companies produce components or other products used indirectly in the military effort. In general, the survey found that some small firms managed to be quite successful with no military production, but that "in order to continue their growth after they have passed the small business stage, they must resort to military production also."[15] Thus both in terms of markets and producers it appears that the electronics industry, the fastest growing industry in the economy, is thoroughly militarized.

The Ability to Diversify

Now we are ready to turn our attention more directly to the two key aspects of the military production picture which the "encystment" theory fails to reveal. We shall first discuss the extent to which specialized aircraft, missile, and military electronics firms appear to be locked into military production because of the large barriers preventing entry into civilian markets, and then we will turn our attention to the widespread diversification into the defense sector by firms located in other industries.

The large specialized defense companies—Boeing, Lockheed, North American Aviation, Raytheon—correspond most closely to the "encystment" theory's picture of military production because they produce almost entirely for the military market and have in the past had very little relation to any civilian market. But in most cases this seems to be a situation of necessity rather than choice, for the evidence strongly suggests that, despite their huge size, financial resources, and the powerful security incentives to diversify into civilian markets, they have had no alternative.

The aircraft companies made their first effort at civilian diversification after World War II. Civilian aircraft demand had turned out to be much lower than expected, sales were down to one-tenth of their former peak, and net losses totaled over $50 million.[16] Nevertheless, according to one corporate insider—Murray Weidenbaum, formerly an economist for Boeing—the effort at civilian diversification flopped. "Most of the activities were abandoned as unsuccessful or marginal or sold to firms traditionally oriented to industrial or consumer markets."[17] The same failure marked post-Korean and more recent efforts at civilian diversification. From a detailed analysis of the non-aircraft, non-military sales of the major aircraft companies, Weidenbaum concluded that these sales "represented less than 0.5 percent of sales in 1955 and less than 3 percent in 1960."[18]*

To be sure, in recent years there have been some notable exceptions. General Dynamics has made a number of large purchases of primarily civilian companies, and the Glen Martin Co. merged with American Marietta, one of the largest domestic producers of concrete. (This, of course, might just as well be considered diversification by Marietta into the military field.)† It should also be noted that the successful entrances into the civilian market have been through the acquisition of firms already possessing a market rather than through conversion of the defense company's plant and equipment. This means entrance

---

* In 1966, the U.S. Arms Control and Disarmament Agency published a paper whose main aim was to encourage diversification into civilian markets. Yet even this study could find little ground for optimism in past experience: "Practically every major firm in the [defense] industry has had one or more . . . failures. . . . Successful experiences in non-defense diversification are not lacking, but the significance of these efforts, in terms of their contribution to sales and profits, was small compared to defense sales." See John S. Gilmore and Dean C. Coddington, *Defense Industry Diversification*, U.S. Arms Control and Disarmament Agency Publication 30 (Washington, D.C., January 1966).

† Other companies have had a more difficult time. Aerojet went so far as to send scientists to Colombia to look into cattle raising.[19]

into the civilian markets was possible only because of the large funds generated by defense contracts. As *Business Week* noted: "Without big defense contracts to act as a buffer, the results [of commercial diversification] could be disastrous."[20] Consequently, in recent years the aircraft companies seem to have turned to military rather than civilian diversification in order to protect themselves against the cancellation or abandonment of particular weapons systems. They have especially turned to military electronics, and have been far more successful here than in the civilian field.[21]

The diversification story is much the same for the large military electronics firms. Many companies have attempted to diversify from military into industrial electronics, but there do not seem to have been any outstanding examples of success.[22] After the war there was a concerted effort to product many different types of non-military, non-electronics products, including cooking utensils, boats, caskets, prosthetic devices, home appliances, and auto parts, but most of these were abortive and soon abandoned.[23] One of the main problems encountered was "the problem of building a marketing organization and gaining acceptance as a reputable supplier."[24] Like the aircraft companies, the electronics firms have also turned to military diversification, especially into the field of missiles and space.[25]

What is the explanation for this failure at civilian diversification? The evidence is not great enough to support any conclusion with certainty, but this much is clear: such widespread failure cannot be attributed simply to bad management or, in the case of large firms, to a lack of financial resources or influence. (All of the companies are among the two and three hundred largest manufacturing corporations in the economy, and five of them are among the top fifty.) Therefore it is most likely that the explanation lies in the nature of the civilian market and here oligopoly and the slow growth in consumer demand may be among the most important factors. Whatever the explanation, one conclusion is inescapable: major firms with huge aggregations of corporate capital and productive capacity owe their survival after World War II to the Cold War, and today they are almost totally trapped in the military sector.

To turn to the second aspect of the military production picture, what is the situation outside of the defense sector, especially in the critically important metalworking and producer goods industries, the industries that the "encystment" theory claims have relatively little stake in armaments? A suggestive approach to this problem is offered by a Department of Commerce study of corporate acquisitions by manufacturing firms in the three year period 1959-1962.* The report shows that in these three years alone, manufacturing firms outside of the defense sector purchased 137 companies in the defense sector (i.e., aircraft, aircraft engines and parts, ships and boats, ordnance, electrical machinery, scientific instruments, and computers). Sixty-two out of the 137 acquisitions were made by firms located primarily in either the fabricated metals industry or in non-electrical machinery, and the total becomes sixty-nine if we include acquisitions by firms in the closely allied industry of motor vehicles and equipment. Every major industry group except tobacco and leather products is registered as having made an acquisition in the defense industries. The groups most active in acquiring defense firms, besides fabricated metals and non-electrical machinery, were chemicals (10), rubber and plastic products (7), stone, clay, and glass products (7), furniture and parts (6), primary metals (6), and wood products (3). There were even three defense acquisitions by firms primarily engaged in the food and food products industry. The extent of this buying can also be seen from the fact that 12.1 percent of the total employment of the instruments industry (16,774 employees) and 8.3 percent of the total employment in communication equipment and electronic components (38,571 employees) was acquired by firms outside of these industries.

The *Fortune Plant and Product Directory* (1966) provides a

---

* Part I of the report is reprinted in the appendix to vol. 2 of the Senate Antitrust Committee's hearings on economic concentration, pps. 1019ff. My figures have been taken from this reprint. The study was published as a special addition to the 1962 *Annual Survey of Manufacturing* and covers about 90 percent of the total manufacturing acquisitions during this period. The report fails to cover acquisitions where the acquired firm was immediately integrated into the acquiring one.

second approach to diversification into the defense sector by firms primarily engaged in other manufacturing areas. The directory lists each of the 1,000 largest manufacturing corporations and their products. The list for each company is compiled by the company itself in accordance with a *Fortune* questionnaire, and is updated every three years. I carefully checked the products manufactured by each of the 500 largest corporations on this list in order to identify the traditional manufacturing base of the company and the extent to which it may have diversified into aircrafts, missiles, military electronics, and instruments. It should be made perfectly clear that my results do not measure the total involvement of the top 500 in military production. For instance, a primary metals company producing aluminum for aircrafts will not be registered here because its military products are located in the same industry as the firm itself. (The importance of this kind of military output is reflected in the input-output statistics discussed earlier.) We are interested only in the primary metals firm producing military products that are classified in what we have referred to as the defense sector (missiles, aircraft, military electronics, instruments).

The scope of the movement toward military diversification can be seen from the fact that 93 major firms whose traditional manufacturing base is outside the defense sector are now producing within it. These firms come from almost every segment of industry, but the overwhelming majority of them (60) are primarily located in either fabricated metals, non-electrical machinery, or primary metals.* The chart on the following pages lists these 60 companies, their rank among the 500 largest firms, their traditional field of manufacturing (as best as could be estimated from the product list), and the nature of their production within the defense sector. All the major rubber companies (Goodyear, Firestone, U.S. Rubber, General Tire and Rubber, and B. F. Goodrich) have gone into missiles and military electronics. Elgin Watch, Bulova, American Optical, Bell and Howell, and Fair-

---

* The 33 other firms that have entered the defense sector represent a broad cross section of manufacturing. It should be noted that a rough check of the remaining 500 companies in the directory showed a similar pattern of military diversification and, if anything, a somewhat heavier involvement.

child Camera, all makers of precision equipment like watches and movie cameras, have gone heavily into defense. Other major military diversifications include Corning Glass, Phillips Petroleum, Signal Oil and Gas, National Distillers, Armour Meatpacking, Celanese (a textile firm), Philadelphia and Reading (an apparel firm), and Brunswick (a sporting goods firm). The three major automobile makers have also increasingly diversified into the defense area, presumably in order to replace declining demand for conventional military items such as jeeps, tanks, aircraft, and other ordnance. Ford bought Philco in 1959 and GM formed a special Defense Systems Division in the same year in order "to help increase GM's contribution to the nation's defense effort."[26] To some extent, this constitutes a change in policy for the auto-makers. After World War II and the Korean War, they withdrew rather rapidly from military production in order to concentrate on the expanding automobile market. Their active entry into the guided missile field has been attributed, at least in part, to the leveling off of automobile demand.[27] As a final comment, it should be noted that the 1966 *Fortune Directory* fails to capture companies that entered the defense sector and then left it. Maytag Washer, Hoover Vacuum, and General Mills are among the companies that I have identified from other sources.

The Importance of Military Diversification and Production

Up to this point, we have shown only that in a brief period a substantial number of firms located in industries outside the defense sector, and especially in the heavy producer goods industries, have entered specialized military production. It is also clear that these firms are among the largest in the economy and in their respective industries. A number of important pieces to the puzzle are still missing, however, and one of these involves the question of how important this military diversification is to the diversifying firms. A suggestive but indirect measure is provided by the National Science Foundation's figures on research and development expenditures. These figures are usually given only in aggregate industry-by-industry amounts, but buried away in the appendix to the NSF's annual survey of industrial re-

Producer Goods Firms Diversifying
into the Defense Sector

Firm and Rank	Major Traditional Products	Sample of Defense Products
International Harvester (19)	farm equipment	systems for rocket engines
Continental Can Co. (45)	tin cans and other containers	aircraft, guided missiles, components, sub-assemblies
FMC Corp. (69)	farm and industrial equipment	remote control systems for missiles, launching systems
Textron (80)	conglomerate	all major military categories
Borg-Warner (81)	auto parts, machinery	milit. electronics, sub-assemblies
Litton Industries (85)*	conglomerate	all milit. electronics products
National Cash Register (90)	cash registers	guided missile frames, sub-assemblies, electronic components
Allis Chalmers (97)	farm and industrial equipment	nuclear fuels, AEC power plants, milit. electronics
Eaton Manuf. (111)	auto supplier	aircraft, parts
Auto Radiator (112)	fabricated metals	milit. electronics, instruments
Ogden (128)	construction equipment	milit. instruments, ships
American Metal Climax (137)	primary metals	precision parts for aerospace, missiles, aircraft
Avco (139)*	farm machinery, commercial appliances	17 defense product classes in all areas
Babcock & Wilcox (140)	metalworking, boilers	nuclear plants, fuel elements, ships, milit. instruments
American Machine & Foundry (150)	industrial machinery	guided missile systems, major milit. electronic components

Firm and Rank	Major Traditional Products	Sample of Defense Products
Kaiser Indus. (155)	primary metals	milit. electronics, aircraft, missile parts
Budd (164)	auto supplier, railroad equipment	milit. electronics, instruments
Rockwell Standard (167)	auto supplier	aircraft
Crane (171)	heating equipment	milit. electronics components, aircraft parts
Carrier (185)	refrigeration, heating equipment	milit. electronics components
ACF Indus. (221)	railroad equipment	milit. electronics
Studebaker (233)	automobiles, appliances	nose cones, jet engine components, wide variety of items
Dresser Indus. (235)	industrial machinery	milit. instruments, electronics
General Cable (242)	all kinds wire and cable	guided missiles, parts
Eltra (246)	auto parts	electrical instruments for aircraft
Norton (247)	construction gear, abrasives	instruments, space simulation equipment
Westinghouse Air Brake (255)	mining and drilling equipment, air brakes	milit. electronics, computers, aircraft, missile parts
American Brake Shoe (256)	fabricated metals and machinery	aircraft parts, electronic components
Kelsey-Hayes (273)	auto supplier	aircraft, missiles, milit. electronics
Midland Ross (282)	air conditioning, auto supplier	aircraft, missile parts
Colorado Fuel & Iron (285)	machine work, steel products	aircraft parts
Scovill Manuf. (295)	metalworking, hoses, and valves	aircraft parts

Firm and Rank	Major Traditional Products	Sample of Defense Products
Sunbeam (296)	industrial furnaces, water sprinklers, appliances	milit. instruments, electronics, specialty devices for missiles
Federal Mogul (301)	roller bearings, auto valves	aircraft and missile assemblies, parts
Continental Motors (318)	engines	aircraft and missile systems
Ex-Cell-O (324)	machine tools, machinery	guided missile components, large variety of milit. electronics
American Enka (325)	household furnishings	components for missiles
Blaw-Knox (327)	machinery for chemicals industry, food industry and others	radar, deep space-tracking, milit. electronics, control systems
Cincinatti Milling (331)	metalworking, precision grinding	plasticizers, insulators, high frequency heating for space and missiles
Rockwell Manuf. (332)	metalworking	milit. industrial controls, instruments
Hupp Corp. (335)	heating equipment, home appliances	rocket and missile engine parts, aircraft parts
Colt Indus. (337)	machine metalworking, generators	jet engine and missile engine parts, standard ordnance
Kern County Land Co. (362)	industrial furnaces	milit. electronics, guidance systems
Chicago Bridge & Iron (366)	furnaces, oil tanks	space simulation systems, nuclear reactor vessels
American Chain & Cable (388)	cranes, hoists, machine metalworking	milit. instruments, computers, gyros
Universal American (389)	machine tools, auto equipment	aircraft bearings, standard munitions
Stewart Warner (393)	air conditioning, heaters	missiles, instrument controls, milit. electronics

Firm and Rank	Major Traditional Products	Sample of Defense Products
Eagle Picher (399)	iron and steel castings	test equipment, electronic gear
Joy Manuf. (406)	oil field tools	aerospace heaters, plastic parts
Maremont (408)	auto parts, brakes	Ordinance, aircraft, microwave antenna systems, rocket motors and systems, milit. electronics
SCM (416)	construction equipment	milit. electronics, computers
Houdaille Indus. (427)	machine work	radar antenna systems
E.W. Bliss (428)	metal-forming and machine equipment	rocket and missile engine components, other missile parts
Calumet & Hecla (431)	copper working	rocket engine piping systems
Arvin Industries (451)	exhaust systems, auto parts	milit. communication equipment
Chicago Pneumatic Tool (452)	construction, diesel brakes, hand tools	aircraft transmission gear, special motors
Clevite (453)	auto and railroad supplier	milit. electronics, instruments, under-water weapons
Bell Intercontinental (470)	industrial heating and cooling, crude oil machinery	missile assemblies and sub-assemblies, milit. electronics
Universal Match (471)	fabricated sheet metal products, refrigeration equipment	components and assemblies for missile launching systems, milit. electronics
Rex Chainbelt (472)	machinery, fabricated metals	automatic control panels, aircraft parts

* Indicates company should probably be classified primarily in defense and not as a producers goods firm.

search and development is a chart that breaks down industry expenditures by product classes.[28] Here we find, for example, that the non-electrical machinery industry spent a total of $927 million for applied research and development in 1960,* but only $477 million of this, or 51 percent, was spent on products in the non-electrical machinery field. Most of the rest, about $357 million or nearly 40 percent, was spent on products in the defense area: $127 million on guided missiles; $161 million on communication equipment and electronic components; $23 million on aircraft and parts; $16 million on atomic energy devices; and an unspecified sum on scientific instruments and other electrical machinery. The same is true for research and development in the fabricated metals industry. The industry as a whole spent $111 million on research and development in 1960, but only $36 million of this was spent on fabricated metal products: $24 million was spent on atomic energy devices, $7 million on electronics equipment, $2 million on aircraft, $2 million on instruments, and an unaccounted for amount on guided missiles. Altogether the industry seems to have spent at least as much in the defense areas as it did on its own industrial products. The primary metals industry spent $153 million on research and development, but again only $90 million was for primary metals products: $6 million went for atomic energy devices, $3 million for guided missiles, and an unaccounted-for portion of the remaining $42 million on aircraft, electronics, instruments, and other products.†

The product breakdown for the motor vehicle and parts industry is also interesting. The industry spent a total of $844 million on R & D, but $226 million of this was spent on defense-area products: $56 million on guided missiles, $77 million on aircraft, $87 million on electronics, and $6 million on atomic energy devices. In general, it would seem that the producer goods

---

* The 1960 survey was the latest one available to me, although the 1961 and 1962 surveys have been published. Since considerable military diversification has taken place since 1960 and defense spending has increased as well, the later figures should show even more striking results.

† Aside from the major iron and steel firms, which seem not to have done any military diversification, I counted some 35 non-electrical machinery firms and fabricated metals firms among the top 50 that did not diversify.

industries are spending almost as much on defense-area R & D as they are on products in their own field; and some of this latter category also probably includes defense products.

The R & D criterion, however, is a rather crude measure of the importance of military diversification to the producers goods industries. *Steel* magazine approached the problem more directly in a 1964 survey of 5,000 metalworking plants covering the following industries: primary metals, fabricated metals, non-electrical machinery, instruments, electrical machinery, and transportation equipment.[29]

It is hardly an overstatement to say that the metalworking industries are the critical center of American manufacturing and, to a large extent, the key to whatever prosperity this economy generates. As of 1962, they accounted for more than 47 percent of all manufacturing employment, 41 percent of total expenditures for plant and equipment, and 49 percent of the total value added in manufacturing. As consumers, they bought almost 40 percent of all purchased electrical energy and spent 42 percent of all money paid out by manufacturing for materials.[30] Unfortunately for our purposes, the *Steel* magazine survey was taken on a plant rather than a company basis. Companies in primary metals, fabricated metals, and non-electrical machinery that have diversified into the defense area through acquisitions probably conduct their defense production in separate electronics plants or aircraft and missile plants, and the survey thus probably understates the involvement of the producer goods industries in military production in the same way that input-output statistics do. Also, the survey seems only to have asked for information about "defense procurement" and so probably does not include indirect military sales, such as the sale of instruments and equipment for the production of military goods. Nevertheless, the survey results provide an interesting picture of the dependence of the entire metalworking complex on armaments production.

The survey found that four out of ten metalworking plants produce for defense, and of these, 71 percent said that *at least* 31 percent of their output was military products. Broken down industry-by-industry, the results are as follows: primary metals—

48.7 percent of the plants produce for defense and at least 14.5 percent of total plant output goes for defense; fabricated metals —27 percent of the plants produce for defense and at least 16.4 percent of total plant output goes for defense; non-electrical machinery—31.4 percent of the plants produce for defense and at least 22.3 percent of total plant output goes for defense; instruments—70.9 percent of the plants produce for defense and at least 38.9 percent of total plant output goes for defense; electrical machinery—54.5 percent of the plants produce for defense and at least 54.9 percent of total plant output goes for defense; transportation equipment—42.5 percent of the plants produce for defense and at least 50.3 percent of total plant output goes for defense.

One of the most interesting of the survey's findings was that a majority of all plants in every industry group except electrical machinery and instruments said they were looking for more military business. The most eager industry was fabricated metals plants, 69.4 percent of which said they were looking for more business. The figure for the primary metals industry was 62.2 percent and for non-electrical machinery, 55.9 percent.

Research and Development

Another measure of the importance of military production and diversification to American industry is the extent to which industry as a whole relies on the military for its new products and processes of production. One approximate yardstick of this dependence is the amount of money spent on industrial research and development independent of the military effort, but here the offiical figures are grossly misleading. They show that the federal government finances about 60 percent of industrial research and development and "virtually all" of this is funded by the Department of Defense, the Atomic Energy Commission, and NASA.[31] Using this percentage, the military spent $6.1 billion on research and development in 1960 and private industry spent another $4.4 billion.

This $4.4 billion figure is inflated in two important respects. First, a very large portion of privately financed R & D is indirectly generated by military R & D. This happens in three ways: (1) Private firms wanting a military research and development contract often have to undertake an initial research and development program at their own expense in order to come up with the promising material which will then get them the military contract. (2) Private industry spends a large amount of its own funds trying to refine and develop for commercial use products that were initially funded and developed by and for the military. (3) When a military prime contractor orders a special new product from a subcontractor, the funds spent for the development of this product frequently go down in the National Science Foundation's books as privately financed R & D even though the subcontractor is eventually reimbursed for the cost of development.[32] Since aircraft, missile, electronics, and instrument firms account for $1.4 billion of this $4.4 billion of privately financed R & D, it is a good bet that all of this $1.4 billion is indirectly related to and dependent upon the military effort. All the other major research and development industries receive large amounts of military money, and it is therefore likely that a fair share of the remaining $3 billion is also indirectly tied to the military.

The second source of overstatement in the $4.4 billion figure comes from the fact that private industry often labels as research and development activities which should not be considered as such. In testimony before the Senate Antitrust Subcommittee in 1965, Dr. David Novick, head of the cost analysis department at Rand Corporation, explained that "in many companies the terms 'research and development' include (and in some cases are entirely for) marketing and advertising, packaging and routing and similar other activities. . . ."[33] Westinghouse, for example, according to one of its own vice-presidents, spent 80 percent of its $185 million research and development budget for 1959 on "development to customers' orders for customer-tailored equipment."[34] Novick cited two economic incentives for this inflation of privately financed R & D figures: it looks good to corporate stockholders, and research and development expenditures have received exceptionally favored tax treatment since 1954.[35]

The above suggests that private industry probably undertakes and finances no more than $1.5 billion of serious research and development independent of the military effort. As a percentage of GNP, this is about equivalent to research and development expenditures during the depression.[36] What is missing, however, is some notion of how much private industry would spend for research and development if the military were not doing its R & D for it. Since the answer depends in part on the theory of innovation under monopoly capitalism, about which there is now considerable debate among economists,[37] we shall have to rest with the conclusion that under present circumstances monopoly capitalism is generating very little of its own basis for innovation.

Another question, harder to answer than it might appear, arises as to how the benefits of military R & D are distributed among the major industry groups. Figures on the distribution of funds are misleading, for although two-thirds of the money is concentrated in aircraft, missiles, and electronics, the recipient firms in these industries often subcontract the work to firms in other industries. Furthermore, the research and development work in the defense sector often turns up products and processes of benefit to other industries, especially chemicals, primary metals, and fabricated metals. *Chemical Week,* for example, ran a story in 1959 entitled "Pairing Chemicals with Plane Production,"[38] which told how thousands of representatives of various industries, especially chemicals, visit aircraft plants to obtain marketing and production licenses for new products that the aircraft companies developed with military funds. Douglas Aircraft reported that it received twenty to twenty-five such visits every month. (One of its big products was non-flammable, high temperature brake fluid.) North American Aviation even established a special subsidiary, Navan Products, which licenses and markets products of relevance to other industries. It licensed twenty such inventions in its first year of operation and had $1.5 million in additional sales of its own. Among its products were new coatings for metals and a chemical milling process. Convair, according to *Chemical Week,* was engaged in a similar enterprise.

It is also interesting that industries which do not seem to be heavily involved in military production nevertheless receive substantial funds for military research and development. According to input-output statistics, for example, only 5.3 percent of the output of the chemical industry goes to the military, but in 1950 20 percent of the industry's total expenditures for R & D were financed directly by the Defense Department and the "other chemicals" subgroup of the chemicals industry received almost 30 percent of its total R & D funds from the military.[39] As we have already seen, one explanation for this is simply that the input-output statistics are not an accurate reflection of military production by firms primarily located in the non-defense sector. But many companies which have not diversified into aircraft, missiles, instruments, or military electronics still receive substantial military R & D money. For example, chemical companies such as Charles Pfizer, American Cyanamid, and DuPont—all among the major chemical companies—are large military contractors for research and development, yet have not diversified into the defense sector.* One tantalizing explanation may be that the Defense Department uses R & D funds as a political device to buy business support for its enormous military budget.

Probably the best way to see the distribution of military R & D benefits among industries is to examine the range and value of the civilian products it has produced. Needless to say, we are not repeating here the frequent official and semi-official tactic of justifiying the cost of military research and development because of its civilian by-products. The results of research may be unpredictable and may have broad and unexpected application, but it remains fairly obvious that money spent on missiles will result in far fewer benefits to the civilian economy than the same amount spent directly on civilian products.[40] Compared to any rational allocation of resources, the current situation makes little sense, but it nevertheless has produced significant benefits to industry and it is these which we wish to examine here. It should be remembered that whatever industry gets from military R & D, it gets not only cost free but at a substantial profit,[41] and a seventeen-year patent monopoly is almost always permitted the company developing a new product, even though the product has been financed solely with government funds. This results

---

* It should be clear by now that there is probably no such industry as a "non-defense industry."

in monopoly prices for the consumer and monopoly profits for business.*

The following is a compilation of just a few of the hundreds of civilian by-products of military R & D, selected from a 437-page appendix to a Johns Hopkins' 1958 study, *Defense Spending and the American Economy,* and from a 145-page appendix to the Denver Research Institute's book, *Commercial Application of Missile/Space Technology.* Both list a fantastic number of products and processes of production, although the Denver Research Institute's book unfortunately does not include the results of military R & D on non-missile space products. The material has been reorganized into an industry-by-industry list, giving the approximate amount of money spent on the products wherever possible. As a point of comparison for the dollar figures, it should be remembered that a product as revolutionary as the jet engine required only $25,000 for its initial development.[42]

Food Products and Processing: The Defense Department spent over $300,000 between 1955 and 1960 on the development of pre-cooked, dehydrated food products and ready-to-eat items. There is now a large consumer market for these products. Another $7,800 went into the development of aluminum packaging for food and other products to protect them against small amounts of moisture. (Lipton Soup, Dry Milk, and Kodak are some of the companies which benefited.) General Mills, through work on a $3 million biological warfare contract for the army, developed a new food processing system, new materials for handling plastics, and new ingredients for protective coatings. A $90,000 contract for inspection of ammunition by means of radiography resulted in a new high-speed process for checking packaged foods.

The Packaging Industry: The U.S. Army Chemical Corps spent $80,000 a year for about five years on the development of reinforced plastics for packaging. Among the major results are plastic suitcases, plastic bags, and polyethylene carboys. Bemis Bag Co., Continental Can, and Minnesota Mining and Manufac-

---

* Senator Long of Louisiana, Chairman of the Senate Small Business Committee, has been fighting a losing battle for almost ten years now to get the Defense Department and other federal agencies to place new products developed with government funds in the public domain.

turing are among the major beneficiaries. The aerosol can owes its initial design and development to the armed forces; it now brings in $190 million of civilian business a year and is used for everything from shaving lather to paint remover. In recent years, there have been several important developments in the packaging and shipping of fragile products.

The Rubber Industry: In the 1950's, $200,000 went into the development of chemical additives to protect rubber from degradation and degeneration.

The Leather Industry: The Defense Department spent $75,000 for the refinement of durable leather insoles and an additional $100,000 for the development of cold weather boots.

The Petroleum Industry: Lubricating oils and fuel oil filters were developed at a cost of $150,000. The oil and construction industries now use a collapsible tank for handling liquid fuels which was developed by the military for $125,000. The oil industry also uses light-weight, corrosion-resistant aluminum alloy tubing for transporting oil (cost of development—$100,000) and bolted steel tanks for crude oil gathering and storage (cost of development—$100,000).

The Chemical Industry: The major products here run from chemical defoliants in agriculture—developed by the military for anti-crop warfare at a cost of $750,000—to low-cost, high-energy fuel cells, solar cells, epoxy resins, and gases for conducting electricity. The latter will probably be used in power generators to convert heat directly into electrical energy. The military has also contributed to the development of emulsion paints for use on concrete, stucco, and masonry surfaces ($20,000), odorless paints for use in hospitals and office buildings ($5,000), paint primer for automobile and construction use ($20,000), fire retardant paints ($55,000), and high temperature paints ($25,000). Two of the major new growth areas for chemicals—boron compounds used in fuels, and special metal alloys of titanium, beryllium, and zirconium—owe their development to missile work. The metal alloys will be in great demand in the construction of civilian nuclear reactors.

Primary Metals, Fabricated Metals, and Machinery: These industries have also benefited from the development of special alloy metals and from military experimentation with ultra-pure metals in the field of solid-state physics. The military has spent $200,000 on welding techniques for high-strength steel, important in construction and in the production of heavy machinery, trucks, and earth-moving equipment. An additional $120,000 was spent on other welding techniques, and missile work has resulted in a new plasma jet torch. A machine developed to plant explosive mines for the army at a cost of $807,000 is now being marketed by International Harvester as a plow that causes minimum disturbance to the soil. A modification of the flame thrower is being used to burn thorns off desert plants to make them edible for cattle. Examples of heavy machine equipment by-products include a snow plow ($500,000), a special crane ($75,000), a mine-digging machine ($30,000), a lift-truck for materials handling ($70,000), a two-cycle diesel engine for construction and oil drilling ($850,000), and a pile driver ($100,000).

The Electronics Industry: Here the commercial benefits have been myriad. Among the most important are the computer and the transistor; the latter was not invented under a military contract but received $35 million in military funds for its development. It has been estimated that this financing brought transistor products to the civilian market 75 percent sooner than would have otherwise been the case. Practically all areas of industrial electronics sales have benefited from military R & D. These include infrared instrumentation, pressure and temperature measuring equipment, microsystems electronics, medical electronics, and thermoelectric energy conversion.

Even a partial list such as this makes it difficult to think of a new product on the market today that is not heavily indebted to military R & D. The evidence clearly suggests that militarization has substantially eliminated the major risk area of capitalism: the development of and experimentation with new processes of production and new products. Many of the products here attributed to military R & D have become the new commercial growth areas of the economy. Many more have resulted in substantial civilian profits to a broad segment of industry by reducing the costs of production. Moreover, military R & D is the kind of gift horse where no one knows who is going to get the next present or how big it's going to be. This generates a state of mind in industry which has led to a reliance on military R & D far beyond its actual ability to produce.

It might be objected that the increasing emphasis on missile-space will result in far fewer benefits to the traditional manufacturing industries. To some extent this is probably true, but as a counter-argument it should be noted that in 1964 alone the Defense Department managed to spend over $300 million just on the research and development of conventional ordnance, combat vehicles, and related machinery and equipment.* This is a sum probably great enough by itself to finance all the new products listed above and a hundred additional ones. The super-large expenditures for missile work serve as a kind of protective umbrella concealing expenditures for conventional warfare that must be termed large by any historical standard.

Corporate Size and Military Production

The material presented in this paper has largely taken the form of an industry-by-industry analysis. As a partial summary, it may be helpful to approach the same material from the standpoint of corporate size. Using *Standard & Poor's, Moody's,* and the *Fortune Plant and Product Directory,* I tried first to get some measure of the total involvement of the 500 largest manufacturing corporations in military production. I found that *at least* 205 of the top 500 corporations are significantly involved in military production, either through their primary industry of production, through diversifiction into the defense sector, or through military research and development contracts. If we exclude from the top 500 the large number of food, apparel, and tobacco firms, then military production involves about 50 percent of the major firms in the economy. Among the top 100, there were 30 to 35 corporations that probably have no direct involvment with the military, while there were 39 for whom military demand consumes 1-10

---

* An additional $275 million was spent for R & D on ships and boats. The large military R & D expenditures for conventional items suggests that the military develops many items for production at a later date. The figures come from the 1966 *U.S. Budget.*

percent of total output, 11 for whom it consumes 10-50 percent of total output, and 14 for whom it consumes over 50 percent. As regards small business, the evidence is scattered but impressive. The deputy administrator of the Small Business Administration noted in 1964 that there were some 50,000 to 100,000 small companies engaged in defense work.[43] (As a point of comparison, there are only about 420,000 manufacturing companies in the whole economy; 1,000 of these control 80 percent of all manufacturing assets, and 500 control 67.6 percent of all assets.[44]) Just one major defense company, Aerojet, bought $167.5 million of merchandise from 15,000 vendors, of whom 83 percent employ fewer than 500 people.[45] *Business Week* has estimated that 500 to 700 companies turn out 150 military items with the aid of 5,000 to 10,000 major subcontractors.[46] No estimate was offered on sub-subcontractors or general suppliers.

In conclusion, it should be pointed out that the argument presented in this essay has been conducted within a necessarily limited framework. I have presented a picture of the situation as it currently exists. I have not usually said why these industries sought out military production, which would have involved theoretical speculation about whether the causes are deep-rooted in the nature of the economy itself, or only peripheral to it.* But, on the basis of the preceding evidence, and contrary to the complacent picture presented by liberal economists, it is clear that every major sector of American manufacturing has become deeply militarized in the course of the Cold War—with all this may imply for the character of American politics and policies —and it is necessary to consider seriously the possibility that

---

* Probably the ablest theoretical discussion of monopoly capitalism's need for military production is Paul Baran's *The Political Economy of Growth* (New York: Monthly Review Press, 1957). The crucial function of military expenditures, according to Baran, is to create profitable investment opportunities for the monopoly sector. These opportunities are necessary, Baran argues, because monopoly production creates large surplus funds whose reinvestment in profitable civilian enterprises is prevented by the monopoly structure itself and the maldistribution of income that results from it.

the prosperity and stability of American society now firmly rest on a totally destructive base.

Notes

1. Bureau of Demobilization, Civilian Production Administration, *Industrial Mobilization for War*, p. 962.

2. See, for example, Emile Benoit, "The Economic Impact of Disarmament in the United States," in Seymour Melman, ed., *Disarmament, Its Politics and Economics* (Boston: American Academy of Arts and Sciences, 1962); Leslie Fishman, "The Expansionary Effects of Shifts from Defense to On-Defense Expenditures," in Emile Benoit and Kenneth Boulding, eds., *Disarmament and the Economy* (New York: Harper and Row, 1963); Horst Brand, "Disarmament and the Prospects of American Capitalism," *Dissent*, Summer 1962.

3. See U.S. Congress, House Committee on Armed Services, *Relation of Cost Data to Military Procurement, Hearings*, 1963. This reveals several cases of 100 percent profits and more on specialized non-civilian items.

4. I rely here on the recounting of the *Electronic News* study in John Ullmann, ed., *Conversion Prospects of the Defense Electronics Industry, Hofstra University Yearbook of Business*, Series 2, Vol. 1, 1965.

5. Johns Hopkins University, Operations Research Office, *Defense Spending and the U.S. Economy*, p. b-169. This is the figure as of 1958; more has been spent since then.

6. Stanford Research Institute, *A Study of Small Business in the Electronics Industry* (Washington, D.C.: Small Business Administration, 1962), p. 21.

7. Ullmann, *Conversion Prospects*, p. 18.

8. Stanford Research Institute, *Study of Small Business*, p. 70.

9. *Ibid.*

10. Denver Research Institute, *Commercial Application of Missile/Space Technology* (Denver, 1963), p. 101.

11. Stanford Research Institute, *Study of Small Business*, p. 74.

12. Ullmann, *Conversion Prospects*, p. 14. This estimate is based on a different set of figures than that of the *Electronics News* survey.

13. *Moody's; Standard & Poor's;* Merton J. Peck and Frederic M.

Scherer, *The Weapons Acquisition Process: An Economic Analysis* (Boston: Division of Research, Graduate School of Business Administration, Harvard University, 1962), p. 622.
University, 1962), p. 622.

14. Stanford Research Institute, *Study of Small Business*, p. 102.

15. *Ibid.*

16. Murray Weidenbaum, "Problems of Adjustment for Defense Industries," in Boulding and Benoit, *Disarmament and the Economy*, p. 81.

17. *Ibid.*

18. *Ibid.*, p. 83.

19. *Forbes*, July 1964.

20. *Business Week*, July 18, 1964, p. 67.

21. Peck and Scherer, *Weapons Acquisition Process*, pp. 22, 137; Weidenbaum, "Problems of Adjustment," p. 83; H. O. Stekler, *The Structure and Performance of the Aerospace Industry* (Berkeley: The University of California Press, 1965), pp. 97-102.

22. Stanford Research Institute, *Study of Small Business*, p. 26.

23. *Ibid.*

24. *Ibid.*, p. 23.

25. Stekler, *Structure and Performance*, pp. 102 ff.

26. Annual Corporation Report, 1959, p. 24.

27. Peck and Scherer, *Weapons Acquisition Process*, p. 192.

28. The exact source is National Science Foundation, *Funds for Research and Development in Industry*, 1960, Table A-19, p. 80.

29. *Steel*, June 29, 1964, pp. 42-47, 83-85.

30. *Iron Age*, "Metalworking Marketguide" (Philadelphia, 1969), pp. 7, 8, 9.

31. National Science Foundation, *Funds for Research and Development*, p. 11. In 1963, for example, DOD financed $7.1 billion out of $7.3 billion federal funds for research and development.

32. Richard Nelson, "The Impact of Disarmament on Research and Development," in Boulding and Benoit, *Disarmament and the Economy*, pp. 114-115.

33. U.S. Senate, Committee on the Judiciary, *Economic Concentration, Hearings*, 1964, Part 3, p. 1244.

34. *Ibid.*

35. *Ibid.*, p. 1252.

36. Nestor E. Terleckyj, *Research and Development: Its Growth and Composition* (New York: National Industrial Conference Board, 1963), p. 21. My figure was calculated from this source.

37. See the articles on this subject in Richard A. Tybout, ed., *Economics of Research Devlopment* (Columbus: Ohio State University Press, 1965). To my mind, the debate is a sterile one since it by and large fails to control for the effects of military R & D.

38. *Chemical Week*, August 22, 1959.

39. National Science Foundation, *Funds for Research and Development*, pp. 9, 12. Military R & D figures for other industries are: rubber, 31 percent; fabricated metals, 34 percent; machinery, 39 percent; and non-ferrous metals, 20 percent.

40. This has been confirmed by Nestor Terleckyji, "Sources of Productivity Growth," (Ph.D. diss., Princeton, 1961); cited in Tybout, *Economics of Research Development*, p. 290.

41. Peck and Scherer note that the profit on military R & D contracts, especially for small firms, sometimes runs over 100 percent on invested capital. See *Weapons Acquisitions Process*, p. 211.

42. Tybout, *Economics of Research Development*, p. 321.

43. Quoted in *Steel*, June 22, 1964.

44. *Economic Concentration, Hearings*, p. 113.

45. *Chemical Week*, June 27, 1964, pp. 41-42.

46. *Business Week*, "Money in Old-Style Munitions," July 25, 1964, p. 144.

Index

237